Reconstructing Prehistorical Dialects

Trends in Linguistics
Studies and Monographs 91

Editor

Werner Winter

Mouton de Gruyter
Berlin · New York

Reconstructing Prehistorical Dialects

Initial Vowels in Slavic and Baltic

by
Henning Andersen

Mouton de Gruyter
Berlin · New York 1996

Mouton de Gruyter (formerly Mouton, The Hague)
is a Division of Walter de Gruyter & Co., Berlin.

Library of Congress Cataloging-in-Publication-Data

Andersen, Henning, 1934−
    Reconstructing prehistorical dialects ; initial vowels in
Slavic and Baltic / by Henning Andersen.
        p.   cm.   − (Trends in linguistics. Studies and
monographs ; 91).
    Includes bibliographical references and index.
    ISBN 3-11-014705-X (cloth ; alk. paper)
    1. Proto-Slavic language − Vowels.   2. Proto-Baltic
language − Vowels.   3. Slavic languages − Vowels −
History.   4. Baltic languages − Vowels − History.   I. Title.
II. Series.
PG46.A83   1996
491.8−dc20   96-12946
                                                        CIP

                    1001234654

Die Deutsche Bibliothek − Cataloging-in-Publication-Data

Andersen, Henning:
Reconstructing prehistorical dialects : initial vowels in Slavic
and Baltic / by Henning Andersen. − Berlin ; New York :
Mouton de Gruyter, 1996
    (Trends in linguistics : Studies and monographs ; 91)
    ISBN 3-11-014705-X
NE: Trends in linguistics / Studies and monographs

Typesetting and Printing: Arthur Collignon GmbH, Berlin.
Binding: Lüderitz & Bauer, Berlin.
Printed in Germany.

Acknowledgements

This study grew out of one of the lectures I prepared for a graduate seminar on "Recent advances in the history of Russian" at Kungälv near Gothenburg, Sweden in the summer of 1992, which was funded by the Nordic Council. I am grateful to the organizers of the seminar, Professors Peter Alberg Jensen and Barbro Nilsson of the University of Stockholm and Professor Sven Gustafsson of the University of Uppsala, who in this way provided me with an incentive to review the old, intractable problem that is the main subject of this study.

The research for this study was supported by a grant from the Academic Senate of the University of California, Los Angeles.

Several colleagues read the typescript version of this work and offered comments which have reduced the number of errors and increased the clarity of the exposition in numerous places. It is a pleasure to acknowledge the debt of gratitude I owe, in this regard, to Henrik Birnbaum, Michael S. Flier, Alan Timberlake, and Viktor Zhivov. I am especially grateful to Werner Winter, the editor of this series, for encouragement, expert advice, and patience — it seems to me — far beyond measure.

Contents

List of tables

List of figures

Abbreviations

Arm.	Armenian	Mod.	modern
Av.	Avestan	Mor.	Moravian
B	Baltic	o.	old, obsolete
Bg.	Bulgarian	OCS	Old Church Slavonic
Br.	Belarusian	OE	Old English
Bret.	Breton	OFi.	Old Finnish
ChS	Church Slavonic	OHG	Old High German
CS	Common Slavic	OIr.	Old Irish
Cur.	Curonian	OLi.	Old Lithuanian
Cz.	Czech	ON	Old Norse
d.	dialect	OPr.	Old Prussian
	(E-d. eastern dialect, etc.	OR	Old Russian
	kaj-d., ča-d. Croatian	OSw.	Old Swedish
	dialects)	P	Polish
E.	Elbing Vocabulary	Pb.	Polabian
Est.	Estonian	PB	Proto-Baltic
Eng.	English	PGmc.	Proto-Germanic
Fi.	Finnish	Pom.	Pomeranian
Fr.	French	Pre-	See section 9.1.2.
Gaul.	Gaulish	Ps.	Psalter
Gk.	Greek	PS	Proto-Slavic
Gm.	German	R	Russian
Go.	Gothic	RChS	Russian Church Slavonic
Hesych.	Hesychius	Rum.	Rumanian
Hitt.	Hittite	Sc.	Slovincian
IPA	International Phonetic	SC	Serbo-Croatian
	Association	Sk.	Slovak
Ir.	Irish	Skt.	Sanskrit
Ka.	Kashubian	Sn.	Slovenian
La.	Latvian	SS	South Slavic
Lat.	Latin	st.	standard
Li.	Lithuanian	Tm.	Tememmatian
LS	Lower Sorbian	top.	toponym
M	Macedonian	U	Ukrainian
Mak.	Ancient Macedonian	US	Upper Sorbian
MHG	Middle High German	W	Welsh
Mlr.	Middle Irish		

Graphic and reference conventions

I. Attested forms

Forms cited from the modern languages follow the spelling of the sources with these exceptions: (1) standard forms in the Cyrillic alphabet are not transliterated, but represented in a phonemic notation; (2) dialect forms in the Cyrillic alphabet are converted to a phonetic transcription in Roman letters. Both these deviations are aimed at a consistent representation of word-initial vowels with and without prothesis, a difference often obscured by the several Cyrillic spelling conventions.

2. Reconstructed forms

Elements from reconstructed stages of the different languages are marked with an asterisk and italized in a basically phonemic notation. Individual phonemes and phoneme sequences will occasionally be written in slants where matters of phonemic interpretation are discussed. Slants are also used for phonemic interpretations of Old Prussian forms.

Reconstructed Proto-Slavic and Proto-Baltic forms are written in small capitals without an asterisk; see further section 9.1.3.

3. Cross references

Cross references are to chapters (e. g., chapter 3), sections (e. g., section 3.1), tables (e. g., table 3.1), and figures (e. g., figure 3.1). In all four types of reference, the initial digit identifies the chapter.

Examples are numbered consecutively within each chapter and referred to by numbers in parentheses, e. g., (3.1).

Numbers in square brackets index the lexemes discussed in this study and refer to the sections of chapter 7 where they are analyzed; e. g., the etymon PS EMELA- 'mistletoe' [18] is analyzed in section 7.18. A full inventory of these lexemes is presented in table 7.1.

Introduction

0.1. Common Slavic and the Slavic Migrations

This study undertakes the difficult task of shedding light on the Slavic dialects that existed before the Slavic Migrations.

The Slavic Migrations, the territorial expansion of the Slavs which peaked in the 500–600s, divide the prehistory of the Slavic languages into two separate periods – a recent period, Common Slavic *post migrationes*, fully accessible and amenable to the historical dialectologist's methods of analysis and interpretation, and an earlier period, Common Slavic *ante migrationes*, seemingly out of reach.

Historical sources record the Slavic conquest of the Balkan Peninsula from north to south in the 500–600s and a practically contemporary expansion of Slavic territory towards the northwest, where the Slavs crossed the river Oder around 400 and reached the lower Elbe around 700. In Eastern Europe, archaeological evidence attests to the Slavic infiltration of the cultural areas associated with Baltic peoples in what is now Belarus and contiguous parts of Russia from the 400s on and to the establishment of Slavic colonies around Pskov and Novgorod, in the West Finnic cultural areas north of these Baltic territories, already in the 500s, but with especial vigor during the subsequent two or three centuries.

It is the period after about 500 that sees the differentiation of post-Migration Common Slavic into the groupings of languages and dialects that are known from modern times. The historical dialectologist who examines this diversity easily recognizes isoglosses that cut across the Slavic territory, delimiting one segment from another, or which circumscribe a central portion of the territory, delimiting it from outlying, peripheral areas. The phonological changes that gave rise to these isoglosses, which criss-cross the Slavic lands, interacted in intricate ways and differently in different parts of this vast territory. This permits us to establish their relative chronology. But they are reflected as well in Slavic lexemes and, especially, names which are recorded in dated medieval texts – first and foremost Byzantine Greek and Latin sources – long before the Slavic textual attestation begins to flow after the Christianization of the Slavs. The sound changes that we can infer from the isoglosses have left their imprint in thousands of place names, some of them adopted by the Slavs from other peoples, others coined by the Slavs and subsequently taken over by the successor populations in the regions where Slavic speech was later superseded by other languages (e. g., Greek, Albanian, Rumanian, Hungarian, German). These rich data allow the historical linguist to date the phonological differentiation of post-Migration Common Slavic in absolute terms (see, for instance, the useful sections on chronology in Shevelov [1965]; or Lamprecht [1987: 161, English summary, 192]).

By contrast, the period before the Migrations is largely a black box. True, there is plenty of evidence that there were dialect differences in the Common Slavic speech area in this period. To mention just one clear example, there are several dozen pairs of synonymous Common Slavic lexemes, of different provenience, which must owe their origin to prehistoric loan contacts between Slavs and other language communities (Italic, Iranian, Celtic, Germanic; cf. Martynov [1985]). In such contact situations, one can imagine, borrowings spread across the ante-Migration Common Slavic speech area from diverse points of entry, in various directions, reaching different extents. But the modern distribution of the reflexes of these lexemes has not yielded any coherent conclusions about areal divisions in the ante-Migration Slavic territory. Nor is it likely to, for − as Gaston Paris taught − each word has its own history, and so it is almost certain that this lexical variation did not divide the Slavic speech area into neatly distinct dialects.

For clear-cut dialect boundaries one would rather look to areal differences in morphology, or preferably phonology, for the systematic character of these parts of a grammar typically allows any difference between dialects to be manifested with great regularity in numerous tokens.

In this study I investigate a phonological peculiarity of the modern Slavic languages which probably goes back to a clear-cut dialect difference in the ante-Migration Common Slavic speech area. I think one can make a strong case in favor of this thesis. But I recognize it is a genuine problem how to go about defining isoglosses in a speech area that has long since ceased to exist, and whose existence came to an end by a major displacement of its people. Consequently, in addition to marshaling whatever evidence I think may be relevant to the substantive issues I will discuss, I will pay more attention than is usually done in studies of historical dialectology to questions of method, both concerning such general problems as the relation between assumptions, data and (hypothetical) conclusions and the more particular issues that arise out of the lack of temporal continuity between the modern dialects and the dialect divisions that may be discerned in the ante-Migration Common Slavic speech area.

0.2. LCS *jezero ‖ *ozero, La. ezars, Li. ẽžeras ‖ ãžeras, OPr. Assaran 'lake'

The topic of this study is the lack of regularity in both Slavic and Baltic of the reflexes of Proto-Indo-European (PIE) initial *e-, *a-, and *o-. While word-internal reflexes of PIE *-e-, *-a-, and *-o- are quite regular (cf. table 0.1), each of the Proto-Indo-European initial vowels *e-, *a-, and *o- is represented by both of the short low vowels in both Slavic and Baltic, with lexical distributions of the reflexes varying widely from language to language and from dialect to dialect.

Table 0.1. Slavic and Baltic reflexes of PIE *e, *a, *o

	Word-initial			Word-internal		
PIE	*e-	*a-	*o-	*-e-	*-a-	*-o-
LCS	*je- ‖ *o-	*je- ‖ *o-	*je- ‖ *o-	*-e-	*-o-	*-o-
CB	*e- ‖ *a-	*e- ‖ *a-	*e- ‖ *a-	*-e-	*-a-	*-a-

This irregularity is a striking common characteristic of Slavic and Baltic, which was noted in the nineteenth century (cf. Bezzenberger [1897]; see Endzelin [1923] for additional references), but which has not played any role in discussions of the common inheritance or shared innovations of Slavic and Baltic. And yet − as I intend to show in this study − it is a feature which it is fruitful to examine in precisely such a genetic perspective.

The reason, or at least the main reason why this feature has not been viewed as a significant similarity between Slavic and Baltic, is probably the fact that it is not a simple, clear-cut similarity, but a fuzzy one that apparently results from more than one layer of innovation. One of these layers has been the subject of a long tradition of scholarship in comparative Slavic phonology, which predominantly has regarded such correspondences as Late Common Slavic (LCS) *jezero* ‖ *ozero* 'lake' as the results of an internal Slavic development, an East Slavic (some have thought Old Russian) change of LCS *je-* > *o-*; for some examples, see

Table 0.2. Sample correspondence sets for PS ε-: LCS *jedinŭ* ‖ *odinŭ* 'one', *jedva* ‖ *odva* 'hardly', *jeleně* ‖ *oleně* 'deer', *jeseně* ‖ *oseně* 'autumn', *jesetrŭ* ‖ *osetrŭ* 'sturgeon', *jezero* ‖ *ozero* 'lake'

LCS	US	LS	Sk.	Cz.	P	Pm.	Pb.	Sn.	SC	B	M	OCS	R	Br.	U
jedinŭ	S	S	S	S	S	S	S	S	S	S	S	S	S	S	S
odinŭ								D		D		D	S	S	S
jedva	(S)	(S)	(S)	S	O			S	S	S	S	S	S	D	O
odva								D		D	D	D	D		
jeleně	S	S	S	S	S			S	S	S	S	S	D	D	D
oleně								D					S	S	S
jeseně		S	S	S	S	S	S	S	S	S	S	S	D		D
oseně			O	O									S	S	S
jesetrŭ	S	S		S	S	S	S	S	S	S	S		D		D
osetrŭ													S	S	S
jezero	S	S	S	S	S	S	T	S	S	S	S	S	D		D
ozero		D	D				T		(T)		(T)	S	S	S	

s marks exclusive or standard forms, D marks dialect forms, O marks old attestations or obsolete forms, and T marks toponyms. The toponyms indicated under Bulgarian and Old Church Slavonic are actually in Romania and Greece, respectively.

table 0.2. Adherence to this approach has created the impression that the similar irregular correspondences which can be observed in Latvian, Lithuanian, and Old Prussian (e. g., La. *ezars*, Li. *ẽžeras* ‖ *ãžeras*, OPr. *Assaran* 'lake') have an independent, Baltic origin. At the same time, it has been apparent − to some scholars, at least − that the correspondences between Slavic and Baltic initial **e-* and **a-* and PIE **e-*, **a-*, and **o-* present deeper irregularities, which are distinct from those that may have produced the correspondences of the LCS *jezero* ‖ *ozero*, La. *ezars*, Li. *ẽžeras* ‖ *ãžeras*, OPr. *Assaran* type. But without a coherent understanding of the later layer or layers of innovation it has been difficult even to define this putative earlier layer.

Meanwhile, the explanations that have been proposed to account for the supposedly narrowly Slavic innovation exemplified in table 0.2 have all been quite unconvincing. They have been based on antiquated methods of analysis and antiquated assumptions about linguistic change, and, in addition, most of them have viewed the hypothetical East Slavic sound change in an erroneous chronological perspective. Fortunately − one might say − as more and more detailed information about the dialects of the Slavic languages has accumulated over the years, it has become possible to maintan these old-fashioned explanations only at the cost of disregarding or explaining away more and more of the relevant data. This is very much apparent in the most recent major publication on the issue, Popowska-Taborska (1984), which provides a meticulous and conscientious compilation and scrutiny of the available data, but shows a remarkable reluctance to acknowledge their relevance (see chapter 8).

In this study I will make a fresh start and examine first of all the Slavic side of this Slavic and Baltic feature from a new point of view.

I will first consider the chronological perspective in which the Slavic data need to be understood (chapter 1).

Then I will try to clarify the phonological nature of the relevant Slavic sound changes by drawing a typological parallel between the presumable prehistoric Slavic developments and similar actual developments in the prehistory of Lithuanian (chapter 2).

Against this background it becomes possible to interpret the geographical distribution of the Slavic *jezero ‖ *ozero reflexes and eventually to see these isoglosses as connected, spatially and temporally, with the Lithuanian ẽžeras ‖ ãžeras reflexes (chapter 3).

The following chapter (chapter 4) considers the wider Baltic context of the La. ezars, Li. ẽžeras ‖ ãžeras, OPr. Assaran isoglosses and concludes that these may be part and parcel of the same relatively recent layer of innovation that has had Slavists puzzled for so long.

Only when this has been done can one draw up a complete list of the layers of innovation that have produced the modern reflexes of initial PIE *e-, *a-, and *o- in Slavic and Baltic and define the earliest of these layers, which accounts for the diachronic correspondences between Proto-Slavic and Proto-Baltic word-initial *e- versus *a- and Proto-Indo-European *e- versus *a- versus *o- (chapter 5).

A separate chapter is dedicated to a discussion of the change that resulted in these correspondences (chapter 6).

The lexical material, Slavic and Baltic, on which the investigation is based is surveyed lexeme by lexeme in chapter 7.

Since a new approach is being advocated here, it makes sense to put off discussion of the scholarly tradition dedicated to the individual Slavic and Baltic sound changes to a later point (chapter 8), when the contributions made in this tradition can be reviewed and evaluated in relation both to the alternative methods of analysis and assumptions that are applied here, and to the relevant data.

The perspectives discussed in chapter 9 have the status of brief excursuses on questions of theory, of method, and of terminology that appear relevant at several points in the exposition, and are referred to there, but which are more conveniently collected in one place; see, for instance, the introductory section of chapter 9 and section 9.1.

The conclusion (chapter 10) provides a summary of the exposition and a statement of the main results of this study.

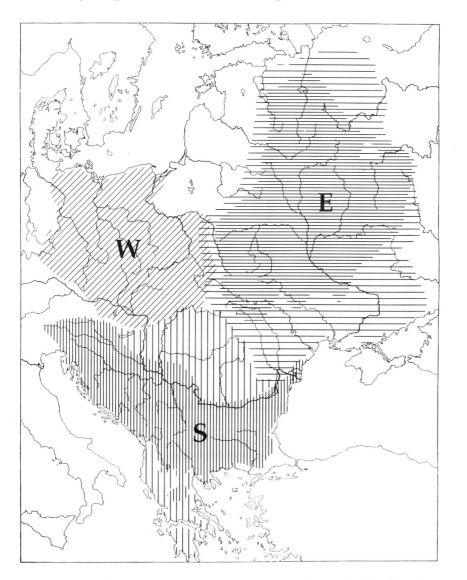

Figure 0.1. Slavic territories ca. AD 900 (based on Diels 1970). W = West Slavic, E = East Slavic, S = South Slavic.

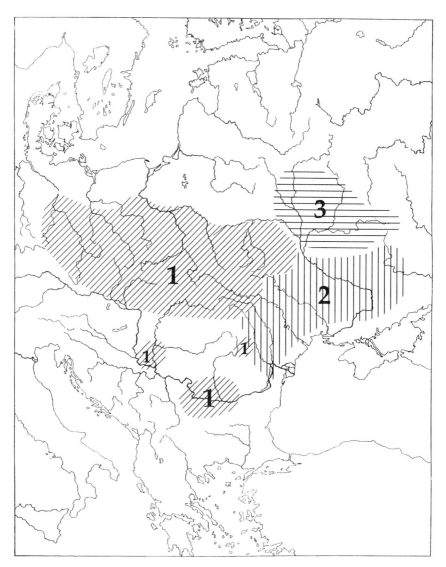

Figure 0.2. Cultural areas associated with the Slavs ca. AD 500–750 (1) Prague culture; (2) Pen'kovo culture; (3) Koločino culture (based on Baran et al. 1991, figure 37).

Chapter 1

Proto-Slavic E- and A-

The Slavic languages present three sets of correspondences for Proto-Slavic (PS) word-initial E- and A-. One set is reducible to LCS *je-; see (1.1). The second set represents LCS *je- ‖ *o-, that is, reflexes of LCS *je- and *o- in different Slavic languages or dialects; see (1.2). The third set of correspondences is reducible to LCS *o-; see (1.3).

Provisionally the two sets of correspondences that involve LCS *je-, sets (1.1) and (1.2), will be taken to represent PS E-, and the set with invariant LCS *o-, set (1.3), will be taken to represent PS A-. In other words, it is assumed initially that the examples in (1.1) and (1.2) reflect a partial split of PS E- into LCS *je- and *o-. At a later point, when we confront the reconstructed Proto-Slavic forms with their congeners in other Indo-European languages, it will be possible to revise this reconstruction on a few points; see section 5.3.3.

(1.1)   LCS *je-: R jél', P jodła (PS EDLI-, EDLĀ-; with the regular Polish *-e- > -o- before plain dental) 'fir' [4], R jel'éc (PS EL-IKA-) 'whitefish' [9], R d. jólkij (PS EL-UKA-; with the regular Russian *-e- > -o- before plain consonant) 'rancid, bitter' [17], R jest' (PS ES-TI) 'is' [32]; for detailed correspondences and discussion, see chapter 7.

(1.2)   LCS *je- ‖ *o-: P jeden 'one', Sn. d. odnok 'once', R od'ín 'one' (PS ED-EINA-, ED-INA-) [1]; P jeszcze, Bg. ószte, R ješčó (PS ED-S-KE?) 'still, also' [2]; P o. jedwa, Bg. d. odvá, R jedvá (PS ED-UĀS) 'hardly' [3]; P ołów, Bg. elav, R ólovo (PS ELAUA-) 'tin, lead' [6]; P jelito, Sn. olito, R d. olitka (PS ELEITA-) 'gut, sausage' [10]; P jeleń 'deer', Bg. ólenica 'thyme', R ol'én' 'deer' (PS EL-ENI-) [11]; P olcha, Sn. jélša, R ol'xá (PS ELIXĀ-) 'alder' [13]; P jemioła, SC d. òmela, R om'éla (PS EMELĀ-) 'mistletoe' [18]; SC jèsika, R os'ína (PS EPSĀ-) 'aspen' [19]; P d. jerzȧbek, SC d. orèbica, Br. d. órabka (PS ER-IM-B-I-) 'grouse, partridge' [20–21]; P orzeł, LS heroł, R or'ól (PS ER-ILA-) 'eagle' [22]; P jesion, SC d. jèsēn, toponym Osenik, R jás'en' (PS ES-ENA-, ĀS-ENA-) 'ash' [27]; P jesień,

R *ós'en'* (PS ES-ENI-) 'autumn' [28]; P d. *jesiora*, d. *osiory* (PS ES-ERĀ-) 'awn, fishbone' [29]; P *jesieć*, R *os'et'* (PS ES-ETI-) '(lattice) sieve' [30]; P *jesiotr*, SC *jèsetra*, R *os'ótr* (PS ES-ETRA-) 'sturgeon' [31]; P *jezioro*, SC *jëzero*, R *óz'oro* (PS EZ-ERA-) 'lake' [35]; P *jeż*, Br. *vóžik*, OR *oží* (PS EZ-IA-) 'hedgehog' [37]; P *jeżyna*, P d. *ożyna*, R *ježev'íka* (CS *ež-, PS EZ-I(A)- 'hedgehog; blackberry' [38]; P d. *jemiesz*, SC d. *jemješ*, R d. *óm'ex* (PS EM-EX-IA-, LEM-EX-IA-) 'coulter' [44]; for detailed correspondences and discussion, see chapter 7.

(1.3)   LCS *o-: R *o-/ob-* (PS AB) 'around', *óba* (PS ABĀ) 'both', *ogón'* (PS AGNI-) 'fire', *óko* (PS AK-AS-) 'eye', LCS *olkŭtĭ, R *lokot'* (PS ALK-UTI-) 'elbow', OR *olŭ* (PS ALU-) 'ale', R *ón* (PS ANA-) 'he', *onúča* (PS AN-AU-T-IĀ-) 'foot-cloth', OR *opakŭ* (PS APĀKA-) 'back', R *orát'* (PS AR-Ā-TĒI) 'plough', *orát'* (PS AR-Ā-TĒI) 'bawl', *or'éx* (PS ARĀIXA-) 'nut', *osá* (PS APSĀ-) 'wasp', *ós'* (PS ASI-) 'axle', *oslá* (PS AS-LĀ-) 'grindstone', *óstr* (PS AS-TRA-) 'pointed', *ot-* (PS AT) 'from', *ot'éc* (PS AT-IKA-) 'father', *ovcá* (PS AUI-KĀ-) 'sheep', *ov'ós* (PS AUISA-) 'oats'.

To illustrate the character of the attestation of these lexemes in the Slavic languages and their dialects, I summarize the geographical distribution of the LCS *je-* and *o-* reflexes of the sets in (1.1) and (1.2) in table 1.1. The entries in table 1.1 indicate, where relevant, which reflexes are dialectal (D) or obsolete (O), and which are the only ones known or standard (S); the signature T marks attestation in toponyms; boldfaced signatures serve to highlight the LCS *o-* reflexes. A fuller account of the lexical correspondences is given in chapter 7.

1.1. PS E- − LCS *je- ‖ *o-

The lexemes listed in (1.1) and (1.2) and displayed in table 1.1 illustrate a predominance of LCS *o-* reflexes of PS E- in the East Slavic languages, Russian, Belarusian, and Ukrainian, a fact which was observed by linguists already in the 1800s in many of these lexemes. In an era dominated by *Stammbaum*-theory thinking, such an observation would naturally be interpreted in just one way − and hence flows the century-long tradition

Table 1.1. Initial LCS *e-* ∥ *o-* variation by language

LCS	US	LS	Sk.	Cz.	P	Pom.	Pb.	Sn.	SC	B	M	OCS	R	Br.	U
[4] *jedlĭ	S	S	S	S	S	S	S	S	S	S	S		S	S	S
[32] *jes-mĭ	S	S	S	S	S	S	S	S	S	S	S	S	S	S	S
[9] *jelĭčĭ	S	S	S	S	S	S			S				S	S	S
[17] *jelŭkŭ				D									D	D	S
[44] *jemešĭ				D				S	S		D		O		
*omešĭ													D		
[31] *jesetrŭ	S	S		S	S	S	S	S	S	S	S		D		D
*osetrŭ													S	S	S
[26] *jese								S	S			S	O		D
*ose													S	S	S
[11] *jelenĭ	S	S	S	S	S			S	S	S	S	S	D	D	D
*olenĭ										D			S	S	S
[10] *jelito	S	S	S	S	S			D	S					S	S
*olito								S	D				D		
[30] *jesetĭ				D											
*osetĭ				D									D	D	D
[29] *jesera					D	D	D								
*osera					D										
[28] *jesenĭ			S	S	S	S	S	S	S	S	S	S	D		D
*osenĭ			O	O									S	S	S
[1] *jedinŭ	S	S	S	S	S	S	S	S	S	S	S	S	S	S	S
*odinŭ								D		D		D	S	S	S
[3] *jedva	(s)	(s)	(s)	S	O			S	S	S	S	S	S	D	O
*odva								D		D	D	D	D		
[20] *jerębĭ	S	S	S	S	D			S	S	S	S		O		
*orębĭ					D				D				D	D	D
[21] *jeręb-	S	S	S	S	D			S					S		
*oręb-					D			D					O		O
[37] *ježĭ	S	S	S	S	S	S	S	S	S	S	S	S	S	S	S
*ožĭ													D	S	D
[38] *jež-			S	S	S			S	S	S			S		D
*ož-			D	D	D								D	S	S

Table 1.1. Continued

		US	LS	Sk.	Cz.	P	Pom.	Pb.	Sn.	SC	B	M	OCS	R	Br.	U
[2]	*ješče	S	S	S	S	S	S	S	S	D	S	D	S	S	S	S
	*ošče					D			D	S	S	S		D	D	
[27]	*jesenŭ			D	D	S		S	S	D	D	T				
	*osenŭ					D			T	T	D					
[18]	*jemelo	S	S	D	D	S	S	S	D		D				D	D
	*omelo			D	D				D	D	D			S	S	S
[35]	*jezero	S	S	S	S	S	S	T	S	S	S	S	S	D		D
	*ozero			D	D				T		(T)		(T)	S	S	S
[19]	*jesika								S	S	S	S				
	*osina	S	S	S	S	S					D			S	S	S
[13]	*jelĭxa			S	D				S	S	S	S		D		D
	*olĭxa	S	S	D	S	S	S	S	D	T				S	S	S
[6]	*jelovo										D					
	*olovo	S	S	S	S	S			S	S	S	S	S	S	S	S
[22]	*jerelŭ		S													
	*orĭlŭ	S	O	S	S	S	S	S	S	S	S	S	S	S	S	S

s marks exclusive or standard forms, ᴅ marks dialect forms, ᴏ marks old attestations, and ᴛ marks toponyms. The toponyms indicated under Bulgarian and Old Church Slavonic are in Rumania and Greece, respectively.

(to which we return in chapter 8), which: (i) posits a conditioned phonetic change, ascribed to "Proto-East-Slavic", traditionally written "*je- > *o-", which splits LCS *je- into *je- and *o-; (ii) explains the exceptional forms with *je- reflexes in East Slavic, which appear to defy the putative sound change, as products of analogical leveling or as borrowings from South Slavic through Church Slavonic; and (iii) explains away the many forms with *o- reflexes outside East Slavic by simply assuming that these are inherited by-forms which reflect Proto-Indo-European apophony, and which therefore have no bearing on the putative, early East Slavic sound change.

Most of the contributions to this tradition have been vitiated by an erroneous conception of the chronology of the hypothetical East Slavic phonetic change. Let us consider the traditional account.

The rich attestation of Old Russian, in which the earliest dated texts are from the mid-1000s, documents both East Slavic forms with *o-* (e. g., *odinŭ, osenĭ, ozero*) and presumably South Slavic (Church Slavonic) forms with *je-* (*jedinŭ, jesenĭ, jezero*, etc.), which differed from the native East Slavic forms, at least at the time of their introduction, it is assumed, by their connotation of high style; cf. Lukina (1968). Hence the supposed "East Slavic change of *je- > *o-" is evidently older than the beginning of our textual attestation.

However, outside its inherited vocabulary, Old Russian documents initial *o-* for original *e-* in borrowings from Old Norse (1.4) and from Greek (1.5), propria as well as appellatives.

(1.4)   OR *Olĭgŭ,* R *Oleg* (ON *Helgi*); OR *Olĭga,* R *Ol'ga* (ON *Helga*).

(1.5)   R *olad'ja* (Gk. *eládion*) 'pancake', *ol'éj* (*élaion*) 'oil', OR ChS *opitimija* 'retribution' (Gk. *epitimía*), *oklisiastŭ* (Gk. *ekklēsi-ástēs*), *Omelĭjanŭ* (Gk. *Aimilianós*), *Oléna* (Gk. *(H)elénē*), *Oli-savéta* (Gk. *Elisabét*), *Ofrosinĭja* (Gk. *Euphrosúnē*), *Ostapŭ* (Gk. *Eustáthios*), *Onfimŭ* (Gk. *Euthúmios*).

The Old Norse borrowings undoubtedly date from the 800–900s, when there were lively contacts between Scandinavia and Ancient Russia. The Greek borrowings (an extensive list is in Popowska-Taborska [1984: 93–100]) are inseparable from the Christianization of Russia, which must have begun prior to the official establishment of Christianity by Prince Valdemar (OR *Volodimirŭ*) in 988, probably already in the 800s. Hence the conclusion is drawn that the supposed "East Slavic change of *je- > *o-" occurred in the 800–900s; thus most recently Popowska-Taborska (1984: 102), Lamprecht (1987: 36).

Several scholars have noted that the occurrence of *o-* for original *e-* in the borrowings from Old Norse and Greek is not subject to the phonological limitations that have been postulated for the "East Slavic change of *je- > *o-" in the native vocabulary; cf. Shevelov (1965: 426). This could be taken as an indication that these borrowings have nothing to do with the supposed change of "*je- > *o-", but few scholars have made this inference (one of the few is Šaur [1986].

If one takes this indication seriously, what these borrowings actually reflect is not a sound change that occurred after their adoption, but a (synchronic) phonological constraint that was in effect during the period of borrowing. This constraint is easy to describe: it excluded all but four vowels from word-initial position and motivated speakers of East Slavic dialects to substitute their native vowel phoneme written *o-* for foreign *e-*

sounds when borrowings were adapted phonologically. The phonological constraint in question resulted from an earlier development of prothetic glides before Common Slavic word-initial vowels, which left eastern dialects of Late Common Slavic (later attested as Old Russian) with only four vowels admitted in word-initial position, *i-, u-, a-,* and *o-.* Compare the following set of word-internal and initial vowel reflexes in Old Russian (1.6) and the examples in (1.7).

(1.6)   OR *-i- -ĭ- -ě- -e- -ä- -y- -ŭ- -u- -o- -a-*
         -i- jĭ- jě- je- jä- vy- vŭ- u- o- jä-, a-

(1.7)   Prothetic glides in Old Russian before *ĭ, ě, e, ä, a, y, ŭ.* E. g., /ĭ/: OR *jĭmu* (PS ɪм-ā-м) 'I take' − *vŭz-ĭmu* (PS ᴜᴢ-ɪм-ā-м) 'I take up'; /ě/: *jěmĭ* (PS ēᴅ-мɪ) 'I eat' − *sŭn-ěmĭ* (PS sᴜɴ-ēᴅ-мɪ) 'I eat up'; /e/: *jeml'ü* (PS ᴇм-ɪā-м) 'I take; ipf.' − *vŭn-eml'ü* (PS ᴜɴ-ᴇм-ɪā-м) 'I note'; /ä/: *jäti* (PS ɪм-ᴛēɪ) 'to take' − *sŭn-äti* (PS sᴜɴ-ɪм-ᴛēɪ) 'to take away'; /a/: *jäviti* (PS āᴜ-ī-ᴛēɪ) 'show' − *ob-aviti* (PS ᴀʙ-āᴜ-ī-ᴛēɪ) 'reveal'; /y/: *vyknuti* (< CS d. **ūk-nūn-tēi ‖ *ūk-nū-tēi,* PS ūᴋ-ɴū-ᴛēɪ; cf. section 9.1) 'to learn' − *ob-yknuti* (PS ᴀʙ-ūᴋ-ɴū-ᴛēɪ) 'to accustom'; /ŭ/: *vŭpiti* (PS ᴜᴘ-ī-ᴛēɪ) 'to cry' − *vŭz-ŭpiti* (PS ᴜᴢ-ᴜᴘ-ī-ᴛēɪ) 'to cry out'. Contrast /i/: *iti* (PS ᴇɪ-ᴛēɪ) 'walk', /u/: *ulĭjĭ* (PS āᴜʟ-ɪ-ɪᴀ-) 'hive', /o/: *ozero* (PS ᴇᴢᴇʀᴀ-) 'lake', *ostrŭ* (PS ᴀsᴛʀᴀ-) 'sharp', and exceptional /a/: *a* (PS ā) 'and, but'.

The substitution of *o-* for *e-* in the Old Russian adaptation of loan words from Old Norse and Greek shows that these borrowings were adopted after this sequential constraint arose − specifically, after initial *e-* changed to *je-.* This gives us a relative date for the prothesis: the Old Norse loans indicate that prothetic glides developed before 800.

At the same time, the very fact of the prothesis suggests that the sound change traditionally talked about as the "East Slavic **je- > *o-* change" occurred not after the development of prothetic glides, but before it − which means that this was not a change affecting initial *je-,* but initial *e-.* This is in fact what is shown by the few native Slavic lexemes with PS ɪᴇ- or ɪᴀ- which are inherited in all the Slavic languages. These lexemes regularly preserve reflexes of LCS **je-* everywhere; cf. PS ɪᴀ- 'which' [39−41] and PS ɪᴇʙ-ᴛēɪ 'to copulate' [43] in chapter 7.

In short, the change traditionally construed as "**je- > *o-*" was not a change of initial *je-* at all, but of *e-.* And it occurred earlier than the prothesis, which was anterior to 800. At this point we need not consider how much earlier it may have been. But it can be mentioned already here that with such a fairly early date for our change, we have to consider the possibility that it occurred during or before the Slavic Migrations. We will return to this question in chapter 3.

To grasp what this change may actually have consisted in, we need to look at the prehistoric development of the Common Slavic vowel system up to and including the development of prothetic glides.

1.2. The Common Slavic prothesis

The development of the Common Slavic vowel system can be summarized as a sequence of vowel shifts, each giving rise to a vowel system of a type markedly different from the previous one; see section 9.5.

The earliest Common Slavic vowel system is homologous to the one that is reconstructed for Proto-Slavic. It comprises the simple syllable

Table 1.2. Three stages in the development of the Common Slavic vocalism

CS-I				CS-II: After monophthongization					CS-III: East Slavic, after qualitative differentiation			
ī	i	u	ū	ī	i	ȳ	u	ū	i	y	u	tense
									------- ĭ ------- ŭ -------			lax
ē	e	a	ā	ē	e		a	ā	ě			tense
									------- e ------- o -------			lax
					ę		ǫ		ä		a	

CS-III exemplifies the dialectally differentiated Late Common Slavic (LCS).

nuclei under CS-I in table 1.2 and allows for complex nuclei composed of any low vowel followed by a short high vowel and of any vowel followed by a nasal or a liquid — what are traditionally known as oral, nasal, and liquid diphthongs.

After the Common Slavic monophthongization of oral diphthongs, the new simple vowels merge with the inherited long vowels (CS-I *ei* > CS-II *ī*; CS-I *ai* > CS-II *ē* or *ī*), except that CS-I *ū* is delabialized to *ȳ* (IPA [ɨː]) and remains distinct from the reflexes of the *eu* and *au* diphthongs, which change to *(j)ū*. The resulting vowel system is displayed as CS-II in table 1.2, which also includes the nasal vowels that in most Slavic dialects arise as a consequence of monophthongization and subsequent mergers of nasal diphthongs (i and $ę$ > $ę$, u and $ǫ$ > $ǫ$).

The long and short vowels of CS-II are subsequently differentiated in quality, yielding a system with several pairs of tense and lax vowels, the latter continuing the earlier short vowels. In several Common Slavic dialects the nasal vowels are denasalized; in East Slavic, which is typical in this regard, CS-II $ę$ becomes $ä$ and CS-II $ǫ$ merges with u. Thus, very briefly, evolves CS-III, which represents the dialectally differentiated Late Common Slavic, comparable in its general appearance to the reconstructed Slavic traditionally labeled Proto-Slavic or Common Slavic in handbooks of comparative linguistics and in etymological dictionaries (see section 9.1.3).

The development of prothetic glides can be understood as (i) a phonetic innovation, the development of down-gliding allophones of all vowels in word-initial position, followed by (ii) phonemic reinterpretations (bi-segmentations) of (most) word initial vowel allophones as glide plus vowel, e. g., /e-/ → [æ-] > [ɛ̯æ-] ⇒ /je-/ (cf. Andersen 1972: 29−30; see section 9.5). The results of the development contain some interesting indications of its chronology. Thus, the fact that CS-I $ū$- yields LCS (CS-III) initial vy- suggests that both the allophonic prothesis and the bi-segmentation preceded the delabialization of CS-I $ū$; in other terms, CS-I initial $ū$- → [u̯ū-] ⇒ $wū$- [u̯ū-] > [u̯ȳ] ⇒ CS-II $wȳ$-). Perhaps the phonemic reinterpretations of initial diphthongal vowel allophones as bi-segmental sequences were favored, at different points in time, precisely by such changes in vowel quality as the delabialization of CS-I $ū$. If this is so, then the phonemic bi-segmentation of CS e- [ɛ̯æ-] as je- can be dated approximately as contemporary with the qualitative differentiations of vowels that led to the vowel shift from CS-II to CS-III (in other words, CS-II e- [ɛ̯æ] versus a- [ʌ̯ɑ-] ⇒ CS-III je- versus o-).

There is evidence that this vowel shift occurred in the western dialects of Common Slavic some time around 800 − it preceded the so-called metathesis of liquid diphthongs (which dates from around 800) in Polish and Sorbian and in the dialects to the north and west of these, but it followed the metathesis of liquid diphthongs in Czech and Slovak and in the South Slavic languages. One might suppose that the vowel shift occurred around the same time in the East Slavic dialects. This guess is in fact corroborated by the date for the prothesis which was inferred from the Old Norse loan words we touched upon above (section 1.1). But whatever the actual date − long before or not so long before 800 − it is clear that prior to this date, from the beginning of CS-I through CS-II

– before the vowel pairs $e : \bar{e}$ and $a : \bar{a}$ were qualitatively differentiated –
the change traditionally discussed as "*je- > *o-" must have consisted in
a merger, apparently partial, of initial CS-I or CS-II *e- with *a-.

1.3 Discussion

This is perhaps a sufficiently unusual change that before we consider its
relation to the attestation summarized in table 1.1, we should look for a
typological parallel. To know precisely what to look for, let us first of all
consider how such a change might come about, and what would constitute a precise typological parallel.

There are two categories of change to consider, internally motivated
(or evolutive) change (section 1.3.1) and externally motivated (or contact)
change (sections 1.3.2–1.3.3).

1.3.1. Evolutive change

The simplest way to understand a (conditioned) change of *e- > *a-* is
as an evolutive change. Mergers, conditioned or not, of low vowels in
"rectangular" vowel systems (such as the one labeled CS-I in table 1.2)
are probably not uncommon.

The modern Polish triangular vowel system (/i e a o u/) is the result of,
among other changes, an unconditioned merger of earlier /a/ and /ɑ/ into
Modern Polish /a/; the earlier /a/ and /ɑ/ were written « à, á » and « a »
respectively until the 1700s and were maintained as distinct phonemes
until recently in many Polish dialects (cf. Klemensiewicz 1974: 287–288;
Dejna 1981: 35, map 52; Polish dialectologists usually write /ɑ/ as « å »).

In the modern Slovak system of short vowels (/i e æ a o u/), the low
vowels /æ/ and /a/ (orthographically « ä » and « a ») are distinct only after
labials (and, marginally, after velars), having merged after other consonants; but in some Slovak dialects /æ/ and /a/ have merged in all environments, so that the distinction is now lost entirely (cf. Krajčovič 1975:
66–67).

With such examples in mind it is not difficult to conceive of the apparent Common Slavic merger of initial *e-* and *a-* as an internally motivated
merger. This possible interpretation has consequences for an unterstand-
ing of the role of the conditioning that may have been involved, as I will

argue further below (see sections 2.3 and 8.3.4). The apparent lexical irregularity in the reflexes of this putative change, which were displayed in table 1.1, would evidently have to be explained by secondary developments, such as (internally motivated) analogical leveling or interference between different dialects in contact.

1.3.2. Contact change A

On the other hand, it seems that contact between distinct dialects (languages) could directly lead to a similar outcome. One way in which such an outcome can arise is when a dialect with an /a/ : /ɑ/ (or an /æ/ : /a/) distinction is exposed to interference from a dialect with only a single low vowel. In the history of Polish, precisely such a situation is traditionally held responsible for the fact that the earlier Polish /a/ : /ɑ/ distinction was lost first of all in the eastern parts of the language area, where Polish was in contact with Belarusian and Ukrainian, which have no similar distinction (cf. Klemensiewicz 1974: 288). In Polish, the /a/ : /ɑ/ distinction has been lost completely, but one can easily imagine a partial loss as the outcome of such a contact situation, that is, the replacement of one of the vowel phonemes by the other (say, /a/ by /ɑ/) in only some of the relevant lexemes.

1.3.3. Contact change B

However, a (partial) phonemic merger can result from interference in a contact situation also when two dialects (languages) in contact (let us call them L_1 and L_2) both have a phonemic distinction of low front and back vowels — let us symbolize it *æ versus *a — but it is realized differently, say as [æ] versus [a] in L_1 and as [a] versus [ɑ] in L_2. In such a situation, speakers of L_1 may identify the low front [a] of L_2 with their own low back [a], and speakers of L_2 may identify the low back [a] in L_1 with their own low front [a].

   If in a contact situation like this the norms of L_1 by and large prevail, that is, if the speakers of L_2 on the whole adopt the norms of L_1, the result of the contact interaction may be a small change in the etymological distribution of *æ and *a — some lexemes having *a reflexes for expected *æ reflexes — which the language historian centuries later would identify as a "weak change" of *æ > *a, that is, an apparent partial merger with no ascertainable phonological conditioning. If, on the other hand, the norms of L_2 prevail, the only trace of the contact might be the appearance of a "weak change" of *a > *æ.

1.3.4. Conclusion

These are the main types of change that could lead to a partial merger of an original *e*- versus *a*- opposition in a vowel system like the one that can be reconstructed for Common Slavic. While recognizing that real-life situations may be infinitely diverse, the internally motivated merger (1.3.1) and the two kinds of contact interference outlined here (1.3.2, 1.3.3) are undoubtedly the categories of change that have to be considered first of all. We will have to come back to these theoretical possibilities repeatedly below.

Chapter 2

A typological parallel

For a parallel to the Common Slavic change of *e- > *a-, the Slavist does not have to look far afield. The closest conceivable specific parallel is available, with a fair amount of documentation, from neighboring Lithuanian. The Lithuanian parallel in fact comprises two competing changes, a merger of initial e- and a- in some areas and the development of prothetic glides before initial vowels – including a change of e- > je- – in contiguous and partly overlapping areas.

Since the similarity between these changes and the reconstructed Common Slavic ones sketched in chapter 1 is so great, it should be mentioned right away that the Lithuanian prothesis occurred several hundred years after the Common Slavic one and has no apparent genetic relationship with it. It can be taken strictly as a typological parallel.

2.1. The Lithuanian e- > je- change

The Lithuanian change of e- > je- is part of a general development of prothetic glides in the Upland (*Aukštaičiai*) dialects, resulting in j- (phonetically [i̯]) before originally initial i-, ī-, ie-, and ė-, but v- (phonetically a frictionless continuant, IPA [ʋ], earlier surely [u̯]), before originally initial u-, ū-, uo-, and o-; e. g., Li. d. *jim̃ti* (for standard *im̃ti*) 'take', *jyrà* or *jỹr* (st. *yrà*; i. e. *īrà*) 'is, are', *jieškóti* (st. *ieškóti*) 'seek', *jĕsti* (st. *ĕsti*) 'eat', *vùpė* (st. *ùpė*) 'river', *vū̃kė* (st. *ū̃kis*) 'farm', *vúoga* (st. *úoga*) 'berry', *volà* (st. *olà*) 'cave'.

It is interesting to note that different vowels seem differently susceptible to prothesis. Prothesis develops more consistently and over wider areas for the non-high, non-low vowels (ie-, ė-, uo-, o-) than for the high vowels (i-, ī-, u-, ū-). The low vowels e- [æ] and a- [a] are least widely subject to prothesis. Before a- only isolated examples of j- are reported, apparently only in loan words, e. g., d. *jadrà* for st. *adrà* 'measles' (from

P *odra*), d. *jaktāras* for st. *hektāras* 'hectare'. In the latter example, the *j-* may in fact be not a prothetic glide, but rather a (local) reinterpretation of the standard (but foreign) initial *h-*. Original *e-*, on the other hand, has consistent prothesis in the Eastern Upland dialects of the Panevėžỹs dialect group and surrounding areas, e. g., d. *jẽžeras* (st. *ẽžeras*) 'lake', *ješerỹs* (st. *ešerỹs*) 'perch', *jẽglė* (st. *ẽglė*) 'fir', etc. See figure 2.1.

The development of prothetic glides is relatively recent. The different susceptibility to prothesis of *ė-* and *e-* and of *o-* and *a-* shows that prothesis is later than the qualitative differentiation of Old Lithuanian *ē : e* (Mod.Li. *ė : e*, IPA [e:] versus [æ], [æ:]) and OLi. *ā : a* (Mod.Li. *o : a*, IPA [o:] versus [a], [a:]), a change which probably did not occur before the 1300s (cf. Zinkevičius 1966: 156−157); see (2.1).

(2.1)   Old Lithuanian   Standard Lithuanian

ī i		*u ū*		*ī̃ i*		*u ū*
ĩe		*ũo*		*ĩe*		*ũo*
ē e		*a ā*		*ė*		*o*
				e		*a*

There are indications in some dialects that prothesis has been productive till quite recently. One such indication is the fact that the prothesis is subject to very simple phonological constraints. In some dialects, for instance, prothesis is found word-initially and word-internally after a proclitic ending in a vowel, but not word-internally after a proclitic-final consonant (e. g., Li. d. *jiñti* 'take', *pri-jiñti* 'accept', but *at-iñti* 'receive'). In some dialects prothetic *v-* has been lexicalized but prothetic *j-* is still phonologically conditioned, hence Li. d. *vúostyti* (st. *úostyti* 'smell'), *iš-vúostyti* 'smell out', *ap-vúostyti* 'sniff at', but *jiñti* (st. *iñti* 'take'), *at-iñti* 'receive', *už-iñti* 'occupy'. For more details, see Zinkevičius (1966: 188−190).

2.2. The Lithuanian e- > a- change

In large parts of the Lithuanian language area, initial *e-* and *a-* have merged. As the map (figure 2.1) shows, this merger affects *e-* in the sequential diphthong *ei-* more widely than *e-* in other environments. Thus dialects in area 1 distinguish the initials of *ẽžeras* 'lake' and *ãšarą* 'tear;

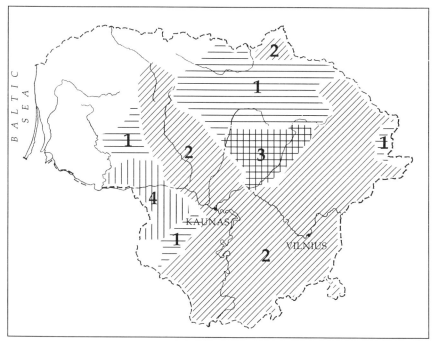

Figure 2.1. The development of initial **e-* and **a-* in the dialects of Lithuanian
(1) *a-* versus *e-*, but only *ai-*; (2) only *a-*, *ai-*; (3) *a-* versus *je-*, but only
ai-; (4) sporadic *e-* for *a-*.

acc.sg.', but have *ai-* in, for instance, *aĩti* (st. *eĩti* 'walk, go') and *áiškus*
(st. *áiškus* 'clear'). The dialects in area 2, on the other hand, have *aĩti,
áiškus, ãžeras, ãšarą*, etc.

Although the map indicates a complete merger of *ei-* and *ai-* in area 1
and of all *e-* and *a-* in area 2, there is evidence for intermediate stages in
this development.

In some area 1 dialects, for instance, a dependency on the nature of
the following segment is attested, with *ei-* merging with *ai-* before plain
(non-palatalized) consonants, but not before sharped (palatalized) consonants, e. g., d. *ainù* (st. *einù* [æɪnù]) 'I walk', but *einì* (st. *einì* [æɪn'ì]) 'you
walk; 2 sg.'; cf. Zinkevičius 1966: 121–124.

In some area 2 dialects, the usage of older speakers suggests that the
change of *e- > a-* occurred earlier in unaccented than in accented syllables; thus some speakers say *ašerỹs* (st. *ešerỹs*) 'perch', but *ẽžeras* (st.
ẽžeras) 'lake'.

In some area 3 dialects, the *e-* > *a-* change is attested before certain consonants, such as *k, g, p, s,* but not before others, for instance, *š, ž, r.* It is difficult to interpret this apparent conditioning in phonological terms. But these dialects are remarkable by the fact that in the latter set of environments, the *e-* > *je-* change has occurred. Even if we make allowance for the possibility that the attested distribution here of *a-* for original *e-* is the result of dialect mixture, it is still clear that in these dialects, as generally in area 3, the merger of initial *e-* with *a-* occurred before the development of prothesis. There is no telling whether the Lithuanian *e-* > *a-* merger occurred shortly before or long before the prothesis. But it is notable that the two changes represent distinct phonological tendencies: once these dialects established allophonic prothesis, any tendency to merge *e-* with *a-* would be effectively eliminated, for the prothesis increased the phonetic difference between initial front and back vowels.

2.3. Discussion

Just as the Old Lithuanian development of prothetic glides is an obvious typological parallel to the Common Slavic prothesis, so the earlier Lithuanian merger of initial *e-* with *a-* provides a striking parallel to the hypothetical Common Slavic change which the analysis in section 1.2 led us to consider.

It is interesting that in Lithuanian, just as apparently in Common Slavic, there were no sequential or suprasegmental constraints on the development of prothetic glides. The only limitations in this change are provided by the phonetic character of the word-initial vowels themselves. These limitations are fairly easy to understand if one makes the traditional distinction between an allophonic innovation and a subsequent phonemic (re)interpretation. We may presume that the establishment of down-gliding initial allophones was a perfectly general phonetic innovation, that is, that it affected all word-initial vowels equally. But in the subsequent phonemic interpretation of these initial diphthongal allophones as segment sequences, there could easily be a more perceptible difference in vowel height between the initial portion and the second, nuclear portion of a down-gliding diphthong if its nuclear portion was a mid vowel than if it was a high vowel − hence mid vowels would be more susceptible to reinterpretation as glide plus vowel than would high vowels. In the case of the maximally low vowels, *e-* [æ] and *a-* [a], the first, raised portion of the word-initial diphthongal allophones would be more easily identified with the palatal glide *j-* in the case of *e-* [ɛæ͡] than the case of *a-* [ʌɑ͡]. In short, the limitations in the development of prothetic glides reflect perceptual conditions that were relevant to the reinterpretation of the word-initial vowel allophones as single segments or as segment sequences. (We will examine the Common Slavic development of prothetic glides in sections 5.1—5.3.)

From a phonological point of view, the merger of initial *e-* and *a-* is a very different story. Both the dependency on the place of accent and the dependency on the tonality of following consonants, which are attested in various Lithuanian dialects, seem equally well motivated in articulatory terms and in perceptual terms. But the essence of this change is not in the elaboration of syntagmatic dependency relations in the phonetic chain, but in the paradigmatic simplification that a merger is. In relation to this central motivation, the phonetically motivated dependency on one or another of several co-present contextual features is a secondary matter, probably originating as an imposition of phonological regularity on the individual or stylistic fluctuation which would naturally arise from the omission of an initial-vowel distinction (cf. Andersen 1989: 21—22; see further section 8.3.4). In any case, these contextual dependencies, which differed from area to area, were evidently on the whole transitory and sooner or later obliterated in most area 1 and 2 dialects by the complete merger of *e-* and *a-*.

The way these two changes interact in the history of Lithuanian is obviously relevant to an understanding of the similar changes in Common Slavic. First, it shows that dialects in which the *e- > a-* merger occurred in one set of environments could later develop prothesis in all the complementary environments. Secondly, it suggests how interference between dialects which merged initial *e-* and *a-* in different environments might later yield a lexical distribution of word-initial *e-* and *a*-reflexes in which phonological conditioning was obscured, and which could then be "frozen" by the subsequent development of prothesis; this is very likely what occurred in the Lithuanian dialects with *a-* before *k, g, p, s,* but *je-* before *š, ž,* and *r*.

There are two more outcomes that have to be noted, which are observable in Lithuanian dialects in which initial *e-* and *a-* have not merged. First, in localities all over the Lithuanian northwest (which lacks any signature in figure 2.1) individual lexemes with etymological PB E- are attested with initial *a*-. Most widely attested with *a*- variants are the lexemes in (2.2).

(2.2)   Commonly attested Lowland Lithuanian dialects forms with initial variation: *ẽglė ‖ ãglė* 'spruce', *ekĕti ‖ akĕti* 'to harrow', *ekĕčios ‖ akĕčios* 'harrow', *eketẽ ‖ aketẽ* 'icehole', *ẽpušė ‖ ãpušė* 'aspen', *erškẽtis ‖ arškẽtis* 'thorn'.

In many localities here, there is a synchronic variation between *e*- and *a*-variants that can be ascribed to influence from the standard language; in such localities, the *a*- forms are characteristic of the older generation, whereas the younger generation follows the norms of the standard language. But in other places, competing variants with *a*- and *e*- appear to be part of the traditional local usage. The source of any given *a*- forms in such dialects is uncertain. But generally speaking three origins can reasonably be hypothesized: (i) interference from the pre-Lithuanian, Curonian substratum dating from the period of Lithuanian colonization (the 400−700s; see further section 4.2); (ii) interference among different Lithuanian settler dialects in the period of colonization; and (iii) more recent borrowing from dialects in areas 2 and 3 (thus Zinkevičius [1966: 123]).

Secondly, in some localities, the majority of them mapped as area 4 in figure 2.1, the original lexical distribution of *e*- and *a*- has been disturbed in a different way. Although the *e*- : *a*- distinction is fully operative here, a few lexemes with etymological **a*- (Proto-Baltic A-) occur with initial *e*-, as in (2.3).

(2.3)   Seemingly hypercorrect forms in area 4: *éiškus* for Li. st. *áiškus* 'clear', *ekmuõ* for *akmuõ* 'stone', *eñtia* for *ántis* 'duck', *ešìs* 'axle', etc.

These forms look like hypercorrections, but it seems doubtful whether there was ever a significant prestige difference between the neighboring varieties of Lithuanian in this area which would motivate hypercorrection. Perhaps these forms are best understood as the result of interference between Baltic dialects with different phonetic realizations of the same phonemic distinction in initial position (cf. section 1.3.3). A few examples like these are known also from the dialects of the northwest; Zinkevičius mentions *ešìs, ešià* for *ašìs* 'axle', *ẽšmenys* for *ãšmenys* 'stones' (1966: 123).

This ends our discussion of the typological parallel to the Common Slavic developments considered in chapter 1. But there is more to be learned from the Lithuanian changes reflected in figure 2.1. This will become apparent in the next chapter.

Chapter 3

The Late Common Slavic *je- ‖ *o- isoglosses

In chapter 1 we were led to form the hypothesis that at some time in prehistory there was a change in some Common Slavic dialects by which word-initial CS *e- merged with *a- under conditions that remain to be clarified. The precise date of this change is not clear, but in any case it was earlier than the development of prothetic glides, and that occurred before 800.

In chapter 2 we examined a fairly detailed example of precisely the kind of change one might hypothesize for prehistoric Slavic. One could hardly wish for a closer typological parallel. But for all the typological similarity, the Lithuanian change differs in a major, albeit external, respect from the Slavic one: it resulted in a number of clearly delimitable geographical areas, each with a well-defined specific development. The Slavic change, by contrast, has yielded a geographical distribution of LCS *je- and *o- reflexes which is too chaotic to be amenable to mapping except on a lexeme by lexeme basis.

If we leave aside the details regarding Lithuanian initial *ei-, ai-,* our typological parallel resulted in outcomes of the following kinds:

(3.1) a. Dialects with the *e-* : *a-* distinction intact, but with sporadic *a-* for *e-* (the Lowland dialects of the northwest)
   b. Dialects with the *e-* : *a-* distinction intact, but with sporadic *e-* for *a-* (the Western Upland dialects, area 4)
   c. Dialects with a *je-* : *a-* distinction resulting from the change of *e-* > *je-* (area 3)
   d. Dialects with a partial merger of *e-* and *a-* and a subsequent change of all remaining initial *e-* to *je-* (localities in area 3)
   e. Dialects with a consistent merger of initial *e-* and *a-* (area 2)

Of these outcomes, only (3.1 a) and (3.1 d) are really similar to the Slavic state of affairs. Outcome (3.1 a) lacks the development of prothesis, to be sure, but otherwise it has a lexically idiosyncratic distribution of *a-* variants of Proto-Baltic (PB) E- words which is quite like the Slavic situation − except for the enormous difference in areal dimensions. Outcome

(3.1 d) is similar too, but also here there is a notable difference, for in the case of Slavic, each lexeme with PS E- has its own isogloss – its own geographical distribution of LCS *je- and *o- reflexes, and it is practically impossible to define any phonological conditioning (see further section 3.8).

Still, the similarities between outcomes (3.1 a) and (3.1 d) and the Slavic distribution of *je- and *o- reflexes are sufficient to suggest the following hypothesis: just as outcomes (3.1 a) and (3.1 d) arose in areas contiguous to area 2, which had a complete *e- > *a- merger (outcome [3.1 e]), so the modern-day distribution of *je- and *o- doublets in Slavic may go back to a state of affairs that obtained in an area, or areas, contiguous to one in which there was a complete, unconditioned merger of CS *e- and *a-. This possibility will be explored in the following.

3.1. Other Late Common Slavic isoglosses

The absence of a single, clear-cut isogloss for the Common Slavic *e- > *a- change is obviously a major explanandum. It is odd that this problem has attracted no serious attention at all in the scholarly tradition devoted to this change. Only a few investigators even mention it as peculiar (see sections 8.3.2.1 and 8.3.3.4). Most of the contributors to the scholarly debate have tried, instead, to explain it away, focusing, for purposes of explanation, on the handful of lexemes which have *o- reflexes only in East Slavic and sweeping the more numerous lexemes with other distributions of *je- and *o- reflexes under the carpet. The meticulous investigation by Popowska-Taborska (1984) is no exception. Throughout her work the author conscientiously cites numerous attestations of *o- forms from places outside the East Slavic language areas, but in the end she reaffirms the traditional account, carefully ‖ avoiding even mentioning the contradictory evidence she has amassed and leaving this contradictory evidence, by implication, an unsolved mystery (see further section 8.1.2).

Yet, the apparently haphazard geographical distribution of *je- and *o- reflexes does not appear particularly mysterious if it is viewed in the right perspective – that of historical dialectology.

It is a well established fact that, of the major isoglosses that criss-cross the Slavic language area today, none is older than, say, from AD 500 or 600 (cf. Shevelov 1965: 607–610; Lamprecht 1987: 162). The reason for this is simple enough: all these major isoglosses arose after the Slavic territorial expansion in the period of the Migrations (the 400−700s), that is, after Slavic speech became established in the vast new areas the Slavs settled during this period.

Prior to the expansion, one may presume, the ancestral dialects of Slavic were spoken in a rather limited area in Eastern Europe, probably north of the Carpathians, south of the Pripet river, stretching in the main between the continental divide (between the Vistula, Pripet, and Dniestr river systems) in the west and the middle course of the river Dniepr in the east. This is where the toponymic evidence places them; cf. Udolph (1979). It is usually assumed that there were some phonological dialect differences in this area, but of these we have no direct, positive knowledge, for − as the Slavs spread out to settle all over continental Europe east of the Elbe and Saale rivers, from the Baltic Sea to the Adriatic and the Black-Sea; all over the Balkan Peninsula, from the Pannonian Plain to the Julian Alps in the west and the Dniestr delta in the east, and south to Thessaly, Epirus, Attica, Euboeia, the Peloponnesos, and beyond; and, in addition, over much of what is now Ukraine, Belarus, and Russia − these earlier dialect differences were to a large extent leveled out. They were leveled out, we may presume, because Slavic speakers came to the diverse regions they settled in several waves, some of these, generations apart, from different points of origin − for changing conditions, in their home localities and in Europe at large, motivated emigrant groups from diverse areas to set out in different directions at different times.

We know that this was so from a number of facts, among them being the dispersion of Slavic ethnonyms. For instance, at one time there were Slavs known as Dulěbi in Volhynia, in northwestern Ukraine, but modern place names document that groups called Dulěbi settled also in the Dniestr basin to the south, in southern Bohemia, in the Pannonian Plain, and in western Carinthia; some Croats settled in the East Slavic area, some in Poland, and some in Bohemia, but others trekked south through the Pannonian Plain to settle along the Adriatic; Serbs settled in what is now western Poland, between the Vistula and the Oder, and they settled farther west, along the middle Elbe River; but other Serbs migrated north from Bohemia to settle between the rivers Saale and Neisse, and still others, south to settle in the Balkan Peninsula, west of the Danube in Serbia, but also farther south, in modern-day Bulgaria, Macedonia, and Greece; and so on (cf. Łowmiański 1963; Xaburgaev 1980; Ivanov and Toporov 1980; Birnbaum 1992, 1993). There may not be any basis for identifying these ethnonyms with particular features of Common Slavic dialects, but their dispersion across the Slavic territories leaves no doubt that the Slavic settlers in the newly settled territories hailed from different parts of the pre-expansion, traditional Slavic lands.

Now, if we assume, with the scholarly tradition, that the merger of initial CS *e- with *a- occurred after the expansion of the Slavic-speaking territories, then the geographical distribution of LCS *je- ‖ *o- doublets displayed in table 1.1 is quite incomprehensible, for the other isoglosses we have from this recent period are all clear-cut. But if we suppose instead that the *e- > *a- change occurred before the Migrations − in some part of the Slavic speech area − then we would not expect a different outcome from the one we actually observe. And furthermore, if we make allowance for this possibility, we would naturally be inclined to inquire how the attested geographical distribution came about.

Let us look at some of the details of the geographical distribution of PS E- reflexes among the Slavic languages.

3.2. Implicational relations

Table 3.1 provides an abbreviated and simplified presentation of the data contained in table 1.1. It reflects, in the horizontal dimension, a division of the Slavic languages into six regional groups. In each group, the languages are listed from left to right according to their proximity to the (virtual) center of the post-Migration Common Slavic territory. In the vertical dimension, table 3.1 shows how the relevant lexemes fall into several subsets according to their attestation with LCS *je- and *o-forms. These subsets are surveyed in (3.2).

(3.2) a. *jedlǐ [4], *jesmǐ [32], *jelǐčǐ [9], *jelŭkŭ [17] are not attested with *o- variants.
   b. *jeměšǐ [44], *jesetrŭ [31], *jese [26] have known *o- variants only in East Slavic.
   c. (i) *jelenǐ [11] occurs with *o- variants in Eastern South Slavic and in East Slavic.
   c. (ii) *jelito [10] is attested with *o- forms in Western South Slavic and in East Slavic.
   c. (iii) *jesetǐ [30] has *o- forms in Lechitic and in East Slavic.

c. (iv) *jeseně* [28] has *o- forms in Slovak−Czech and in East Slavic.

d. (i) *jedinŭ* [1] and its derivatives and *jedva* [3] have *o- forms attested in Western and Eastern South Slavic and in East Slavic.

d. (ii) *jerębĭ* [20−21] and its derivatives are known with *o- forms in Lechitic, Western South Slavic, and East Slavic.

d. (iii) *ježĭ* [37−38] and its derivatives have *o- forms in Slovak−Czech, Lechitic, and East Slavic.

e. (i) *ješče* [2] has *o- forms attested in Lechitic, Western and Eastern South Slavic, and East Slavic.

e. (ii) *jemelo* [18] and *jezero* [35] are attested with *o- forms in Slovak−Czech, Western and Eastern South Slavic, and East Slavic.

f. (i) *jesika* [19] is attested with *o- forms in Sorbian, Slovak−Czech, Lechitic, Eastern South Slavic, and East Slavic.

f. (ii) *jelĭxa* [13] is attested with *o- forms in Sorbian, Slovak−Czech, Lechitic, Western South Slavic, and East Slavic.

g. *jelovo* [6] and *jerelŭ* [20] are attested with *o- forms in all six Slavic regions.

Two of the relevant lexemes are not attested with either *je- or *o- forms in East Slavic: the attestation of *jesera* [29], which is very limited geographically, is otherwise like that of (3.2 c.iii) *jesetĭ* [30]; *jesenŭ* [27], which is represented by a by-form with initial LCS *ja- in East Slavic, has *o- forms in Lechitic, West South Slavic, and East South Slavic like (3.2 e.i) *ješče* [2].

It is a striking fact − which can be seen at a glance in table 3.1 − that not only are there more lexemes with CS *a- reflexes in East Slavic than in West and South Slavic, but any lexeme which is attested with *a- reflexes in West or South Slavic, and which occurs at all in East Slavic, is attested with *a- reflexes there too. This implicational relation suggests that some of the Slavs that settled the West and the South came from the very same area from which the East Slavic territories were mainly colonized, and that these settlers contributed the *a- variants to the regional linguistic traditions in which these variants are attested now.

However, this gross implicational relation is not the only one that can be observed in the data. In fact, if one looks closely at the distribution of *a- forms within each of the six regional groupings of the Slavic languages, one can discern a consistent pattern in four of the regions − Slovak−Czech, Lechitic, Western South Slavic, and Eastern South Slavic:

Table 3.1. Initial LCS *je- ‖ *o- variation by region

		LCS	Sorbian	Sk. & Cz.	Lechitic	Sn. & SC	Bg. & M	East Slavic
a.	[4]	*jedlĭ	e-	e-	e-	e-	e-	e-
	[32]	*jesmĭ	e-	e-	e-	e-	e-	e-
	[9]	*jelĭčĭ	e-	e-	e-	e-		e-
	[17]	*jelŭkŭ			e-			e-
b.	[44]	*jemešĭ			e-	e-	e-	e-/a-
	[31]	*jesetrŭ	e-	e-	e-	e-	e-	e-/a-
	[26]	*jese	e-			e-	e-	e-/a-
c.	[11]	*jelenĭ	e-	e-	e-	e-	e-/a-	e-/a-
	[10]	*jelito	e-	e-	e-	e-/a-		e-/a-
	[30]	*jesetĭ			e-/a-			a-
	[29]	*jesera			e-/a-			—
	[28]	*jesenĭ		e-/a-	e-	e-	e-	e-/a-
d.	[1]	*jedinŭ	e-	e-	e-	e-/a-	e-/a-	e-/a-
	[3]	*jedva	e-	e-	e-	e-/a-	e-/a-	e-/a-
	[20]	*jerębĭ	e-	e-	e-/a-	e-/a-	e-	e-/a-
	[21]	*jeręb-	e-	e-	e-/a-	e-/a-		e-/a-
	[37]	*ježĭ	e-	e-	e-	e-	e-	e-/a-
	[38]	*jež-		e-/a-	e-/a-	e-	e-	e-/a-
e.	[2]	*ješče	e-	e-	e-/a-	e-/a-	e-/a-	e-/a-
	[27]	*jesenŭ		e-	e-/a-	e-/a-	e-/a-	—
	[18]	*jemelo	e-	e-/a-	e-	e-/a-	e-/a-	e-/a-
	[35]	*jezero	e-	e-/a-	e-	e-/a-	e-/a-	e-/a-
f.	[19]	*jesika	a-	a-	a-	e-	e-/a-	a-
	[13]	*jelĭxa	a-	e-/a-	a-	e-/a-	e-	e-/a-
g.	[6]	*jelovo	a-	a-	a-	a-	e-/a-	a-
	[22]	*jerelŭ	e-/a-	a-	a-	a-	a-	a-

whenever an inherited lexeme with PS ᴇ- is attested with CS *a- reflexes in distal parts of a region, it is attested with *a- reflexes in proximal parts of the same region. In other words, an attestation of a given lexeme with CS *a- in West Lechitic implies a similar attestation in proximal East Lechitic, but not vice versa (cf. [3.3 a]); and correspondingly for Czech and proximal Slovak [3.3 b], for Serbo-Croatian and proximal Slovenian [3.3 c], and for Macedonian and proximal Bulgarian [3.3 d]. No clear pattern is discernible between Upper and Lower Sorbian (see section 3.4); but in East Slavic, there is a clear, reverse pattern, with more *a- reflexes in the distal Russian than in proximal Ukrainian, and an intermediate number in Belarusian (see section 3.7); cf. (3.3 e). See table 3.2.

Table 3.2. Implicational relations in the distribution of LCS **o-* forms between distal and proximal areas

West Slavic
(a) Lechitic

Distal		Proximal
Polabian	Pomoranian	Polish
		o. *oščo*
		E-d. *osiory*
		S-d. *ożyna*
vilxă	Ka. *olcha*	*olcha*

(b) Slovak – Czech

Distal		Proximal
Czech	Moravian	Slovak
olše	*olše*	*ol'cha*
omela	*omela*	*omela*
	o. *oseň*	E-d. *ośiń*
	o. *ozero*	o. *ozero*
	d. *ožina*	N-d. *ožina*

(c) Western South Slavic

Proximal	Distal
Slovenian	Serbo-Croatian
d. *još*	d. *još(te)*
olíto	d. *òlito*
d. *olša*	top. *Olešen*
omêla	d. *òmela*
d. *odnok*	
o. *odvaj*	
top. *Asserz*	

(e) East Slavic

Proximal		Distal
Ukrainian	Belarusian	Russian
–	–	d. *odva*
–	–	*ol'ítko*
–	* aščé*	d. *oščé*
–	*vóžik*	d. *ož*
odýn	*aʒ'ín*	*od'ín*
vilxá	*al'xá*	*ol'xá*
oméla	*am'éla*	*om'éla*
osé	*vós'*	*vós'*
ós'in'	*vós'en'*	*ós'en'*
ózero	*vóz'era*	*óz'ora*
ožýna	*ažína*	*ožína*

(d) Eastern South Slavic

Distal	Proximal
Macedonian	Bulgarian
OCS *odĭnače*	d. *adnŭč*, d. *adín*
ošte, još	*óšte*
d. *odva(j)*	d. *ódva*
	top. *Olšani*
	d. *omel*

These repeated transitive, asymmetrical relations in the geographical distribution must either be deemed a coincidence and ignored (cf. section 9.7), or they must be interpreted as meaningful correlations between (i) the relative distance of the attested **e-* and **a-* reflexes from a presumable (central?) area in which initial **e-* and **a-* merged and (ii) particulars of the migration and settlement history of the Slavs.

3.3. The *je- ‖ *o- diversity in time

There is by now a fair understanding of the routes and stages of the Slavic expansion, which are reflected in historical sources and in a growing number of archeological finds from the period (see below). But since there are no pertinent linguistic data in these sources of information, the observed correlation between the distribution of *e- and *a- variants and relative distance from the presumable original *e- > *a- merger area can only be interpreted if we consider it in light of our general understanding of the historical development of language areas. Our experience suggests that there are two simple scenarios by which an original dialect difference, such as the one we are dealing with, could become distributed by processes of centrifugal migration and settlement like those we can ascribe to the Slavs.

Both scenarios, call them A and B, assume that in some part of the ante-Migration Slavic speech area, CS *e- merged with *a-, apparently with certain limitations (see further section 3.7). In this way two dialect areas were formed, one with the inherited lexical distribution of initial *e- and *a- intact − we will call this area the "*e- dialects", the other with the result of the merger (like the Lithuanian outcome [3.1 e] or an earlier version of outcome [3.1 d]; cf. the introduction to chapter 3) − we will call those "*a- dialects"; correspondingly we can speak of "*e- speakers" and "*a- speakers".

3.4. Scenario A

We can suppose that the five West and South Slavic regions − Sorbian, Slovak−Czech, Lechitic, Western South Slavic, and Eastern South Slavic − were primarily settled by bearers of *e- dialects, but that secondary settlement included speakers from *a- dialects. Just as in the primary settlement waves, so in the secondary ones, the number of settlers presumably decreased somewhat with the distance from their place of origin. Consequently there were more *a- settlers close to the original *a- dialect area than farther away. During the centuries after the establishment of Slavic speech in these new regions, local norms everywhere generalized one or the other of any competing doublets with *e-* and *a-* reflexes. Since presumably there was no consistent difference in prestige between *e-* speakers and *a-* speakers, the outcome of this process of norm consolidation would naturally reflect their quantitative relations: the more *a-* settlers there were in a given locality or area, the greater the chances of *a-* forms eventually being generalized – hence the greater incidence in modern times of *a-* forms in the proximal than in the distal languages.

Scenario A can easily be reconciled with the exceptional status of the Sorbian region, in which there is no distinction between proximal and distal areas with respect to the attestation of initial *e-* and *a-*. Apparently the Sorbian region received settlers both from the south (Bohemia, distal in relation to Slovak) and the east (Poland, proximal within Lechitic); cf. Schuster-Šewc (1987); we return to Sorbian in sections 5.1.1 and 6.1; for a map, see figure 5.1).

3.4.1. Pro scenario A

It is perfectly realistic to suppose that the modern distribution of *e-* and *a-* forms does not simply directly reflect the original (post-Migration) distribution of these forms, and that in any locality or area the modern occurrence of *e-* and *a-* forms is the historical outcome of a consolidation of norms, a uniformization of usage, which in previous centuries was much more diverse and variable. True, we have very little documentation for a historical process of competing norms with respect to *e-* and *a-* forms in most Slavic regions. But this is surely due to the accidental fact that as a rule we do not have continuous records from individual localities which could document such a process. But when we consider the development of lexical variants of other origins which in the ante-Migration period presumably had different areal distributions, there is no doubt that in the post-Migration period they have been subject to precisely such a process of gradual selection and generalization, so that now they have quite diverse geographical distributions. Good examples of such other lexical variants are the sets of synonyms investigated by Martynov (see Martynov [1983]) or, to stay within the bounds of the material discussed here, the lexemes with PS E- which have by-forms with other initials. See the discussion of PS EMELA- ‖ IMELA- 'mistletoe' [18], ERIMB-I- ‖ ĒRB-, etc. 'grouse, rowan berry' [20–21], ESENA- ‖ ĀSENA- 'ash' [27], LEM-ĒX-IA- ‖ EM-ĒX-IA- 'coulter, plowshare' [44] in chapter 7.

In the history of Russian, there has been a stylistic variation for centuries between indigenous *o-* forms and Church Slavonic *je-* forms. But scholars agree that this variation, in which *je-* forms of some lexemes have served as high-style co-variants of neutral *o-* forms, has coexisted with a vernacular variation involving *je-* and *o-* forms with unclear sociolinguistic values (other than, presumably, that of indicating the speaker's place of origin). Such Old Russian doublets as *jedva ‖ odva* 'hardly' [3], *jesetrŭ ‖ osetrŭ* 'sturgeon' [31], *ješče ‖ ošče* 'still' [2], or *ježĭ ‖ ožĭ* 'hedgehog' [36–37] have traditionally been accepted by Slavists as vernacular variants, even though their episodic attestation does not enable us to correlate them with local or regional dialects. Certainly, Russian dialect variants recorded in modern times such as *jed'in ‖ od'in* 'one' [1], *jólxa ‖ ol'xá* 'alder' [13], *jes'en'ás' ‖ ós'en'es'* 'last fall' [28] (see chapter 7, s. vv.) can only be understood in one way: these are the last surviving examples, in the localities where they have been recorded, of the vernacular *je- ‖ *o-* diversity which must have existed everywhere in the Slavic world since the time it arose, with differences from place to place and down through the centuries in the number of lexemes and with regard to the specific lexemes involved.

Against the background of the generally fragmentary and haphazard historical record, the attested diachronic variation in a few place names recorded at different dates acquires especial interest. Popowska-Taborska mentions the Slovak toponyms derived from PS ELIXĀ- 'alder' [13] in (3.3), which she cites from Kropilak (1977–1978: s. v.) and Majtán (1972).

(3.3)   *Olšovany*: 1290 *Elswa*; 1773 *Olssovjany*
         Ol'šov: 1224 *Elsa*; 1309 *Olsowa*
         Ol'šavica: 1300 *Olsowycha*; 1308 *Elsawycha*
         Jelšava: 1773 *Jolsva, Elesch*, 1808 *Jelssava*

Admittedly there is no obvious, unique interpretation of the variation in their form. The attested spellings may reflect changes in the pronunciation norms of the local population in each locality, or differences in the norms of the authors of the records. And the variation, whether of one or the other kind, may have originated in a number of ways – though a relation to geographical differences within Slovakia seems obvious (*je-* forms now predominate in Central Slovak, *o-* forms in West and East Slovak; cf. Stanislav [1958: 387]). But in any case, this handful of recorded toponyms does attest to the former existence of competing norms

and an eventual consolidation of stable norms, in part as quite a pro-
tracted process. Thus they give the lie to the unreasonable assumption −
never stated explicitly, but tacitly made in all previous discussions of the
"*je- > *o- change" − that the modern geographical distribution of *je-
and *o- forms directly reflects the original Common Slavic state of affairs
(give or take some analogical changes).

3.4.2. Contra scenario A

However, scenario A has certain shortcomings.

First, it is difficult to apply to the East Slavic region. Within the Russian language area, the density of *a- reflexes is greater in northwestern
and south central dialects than in the north and the southeast (see, for
instance, the attestation of PS EDEINA- 'one' [1], ELIXĀ- 'alder' [13], and
ESENI- 'autumn' [28], in chapter 7). This can perhaps be interpreted as
correlating with the proximal location of the former dialects and the distal location of the latter. But there is another density cline in East Slavic:
there is generally a greater incidence of *a- reflexes in Russian than in
Belarusian and Ukrainian (cf. table 3.2). Applying the proximal−distal
distinction here would run counter to what we know about the direction
of settlement, which went more nearly from south to north.

Secondly, even though scenario A, schematic though it is, may have
some affinity with the truth as far as the West and South Slavic regions
are concerned, it implies a prediction that is wrong. If *a- speakers had
simply mixed with *e- speakers all over these new Slavic regions, the
outcome would surely have been a random distribution of *a- forms of
all the relevant lexemes in all the West and South Slavic languages −
with a greater density of *a- forms in proximal than in distal dialects −
and not the much more orderly geographical distribution that is actually
found (see again table 3.2). To account for this, we need a different hypothetical account.

3.5. Scenario A'

Note that scenario A assumes that immediately before the Slavic territorial expansion there was a simple dichotomy between dialects with and

dialects without the effects of the CS *e- > *a- merger. If we assume instead that after this merger, speakers on both sides of the resulting isogloss interacted for some time (say, a few generations), then the originally clear-cut boundary, defined by a tight bundle of isoglosses separating the two dialects, could have eroded into a broad transitional zone defined by widely divergent individual lexical isoglosses. If this was the situation that obtained when the Slavic expansion began, it would be easier to understand why some *a- forms are widespread in West Slavic and others in South Slavic, as tables 1.1 and 3.1 show. In fact, it is a rather simple matter to project back from the modern geographical distribution of *e- and *a- forms and reconstruct a schematic isogloss configuration roughly corresponding to the modern state of affairs such as the

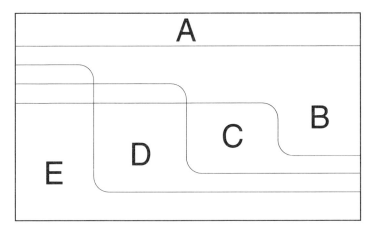

Figure 3.1. Schematic isogloss configuration suggesting a transitional zone separating Common Slavic *a- dialects and *e- dialects before the territorial expansion.
The isoglosses define the following areas: A−*adli-, *adeina-, *adske, *amela-; B−*edli, *adeina-, *adske, *amela-; C−*edli-, *edeina-, *adske, *amela-; D−*edli-, *edeina-, *edske, *amela-; E−*edli- [4], *edeina- [1], *edske [2], *emela- [18].

partial one in figure 3.1. Successive waves of centrifugal migration, the earliest bringing "pure *e- speakers" and "mainly-*e- speakers" west and south, later ones bringing also "mainly-*a- speakers", would naturally lead to an outcome very much like the attested distribution.

This seems a useful second approximation, but it needs to be adjusted in certain regards.

3.6. Scenario B

First, even though most of the distribution of *a-* forms can be viewed as orderly projections from a hypothetical isogloss configuration such as that in figure 3.1, there are isolated occurrences of *a-* forms far from the presumable *e-* > *a-* merger area that perhaps cannot be accounted for by scenario A (or A') alone. They suggest that to some extent the expansion of the Slavic territory involved migrations that did not simply follow radial routes; see section 9.6.

Consider the isolated dialectal *odnok* 'once (upon a time)', attested in dialects in Prekmurje, the easternmost part of the Slovenian language area. There is no apparent continuity between this lone form and the East Slavic heartland of the LCS *odĭnŭ* 'one' [1] forms, nor with the Old Church Slavonic (hapax) *odĭnače* 'however', or with the modern Bulgarian attestations *adnŭč* 'once', *adín* 'one' in the deep south.

Or take the Greek placename *Ozerós* 'lake' [35], which is attested in several localities in Epirus, in Acarnania, and in Aeolia, while several other Greek localities are named *Ezerós* − in part, Slavic translations of Greek *hélos* (n.) 'marsh-meadow'. Apparently troubled by the "East Slavic" initial of *Ozerós*, Vasmer hypothesized that this *o-* might be due to a fusion of the Greek masculine definite article *(h)o* with a Slavic word-initial *e-*. Examples of such fusions are known, and who is to say that this explanation does not account for some instances of *Ozerós*. But it cannot explain *Ho Megás Ozerós* 'big lake' in Epirus (which Vasmer cites), for the definite article would never come between an attributive adjective and its head noun. And Vasmer's explanation is clearly incompatible with the names of the pair of lakes in Acarnania called *Megálē Ozerós* 'big lake' and *Mikrá Ozerós* 'little lake', which are feminine and hence combine with a different form of the definite article (see Vasmer [1941], s. v. *Ezerós*).

Since all the Slavs who settled Greece came from localities in the north, it does not seem far-fetched to suppose simply that some of them came from (more northerly) areas with *a-* in the word for 'lake'. To understand how the settlers maintained their dialect differences in "the new country", we do not have to suppose that *a-* speakers settled only in the places named *Ozerós*, and *e-* speakers everywhere else. It is reasonable to hypothesize that the final forms of all such place names, whether in the end they were *Ozerós* or *Ezerós*, would be established such as we find them only after generations of local variation (as attested in

Russia and Slovakia; cf. section 3.4.1). And there is every reason to suppose that such local variation could be renewed from time to time down through the centuries as a consequence of major or minor population movements. Recall that Slavic speech was current, for instance, in the Peloponnesos throughout the Middle Ages (cf. Vasmer 1941; Malingoudis 1981) and has been in continuous use in other parts of Greece until the present day.

In any case, examples such as these show that even though the "orderly" aspects of the modern distribution of *a- forms point to a centrifugal expansion from a prehistoric distribution like that in figure 3.1 in accordance with scenario A', the Slavic expansion did include cross-migrations, what we can call scenario B, and some of the modern data are best understood in such terms.

The distinction that has been made here between radial expansion (scenario A') and cross-migrations (scenario B) is reminiscent of the distinction drawn by Łowmiański between the two chief types of migration he considers responsible for the Slavic expansion, what he calls mass migrations and group migrations. While the former occurred principally along radial routes (cf. section 9.6), the latter brought bands of settlers, headed and organized by warrior troupes, along a variety of trajectories to different parts of the already expanded Slavic territories (1963: 213). According to Łowmiański, it was the group migrations that left such well-known ethnonyms as those mentioned in section 3.1 as names of villages scattered along their migration routes. As I said in section 3.1, there may not be any direct correlation between the geographical distributions of CS *a- forms and that of the various ethnonyms. But the assumption that there were these two distinct patterns of migration evidently is reasonable from several points of view.

3.7. The East Slavic gradations

Secondly, there is the remarkable fact (mentioned in sections 3.2 and 3.4.2) that a greater concentration of *a- forms is found in northwestern and central parts of the Russian language area than in northern and eastern Russian dialects, on one hand, and in Belarusian and Ukrainian, on the other. The proximal versus distal distinction can evidently be applied to the differences among the Russian dialects. But it is equally evident that the gradation in the incidence of *a-* forms from Russian to Belarusian to Ukrainian, which runs counter to the direction of settlement, poses a problem.

An important clue to a resolution of this problem is found in the Lithuanian dialect map in figure 2.1, which contains a very telling configuration of isoglosses. If we abstract, for the moment, from the vermiform northwestern extension of area 2 (see section 9.6), we observe that the northwestern limits of area 1 and of area 2 run parallel, some 80 kilometers apart, from southwest to northwest. Their parallel courses suggest that the two steps in the merger of Lithuanian initial **e-* with **a-*, which they reflect, originally spread from the southeast towards the northwest. Furthermore, since the two isoglosses run perpendicular to the modern boundaries of the Lithuanian language area and are practically rectilinear, they imply a center of innovation, located beyond the borders of Lithuania, somewhere − perhaps a fair distance − to the southeast, in present-day Belarus. This is territory which was formerly Baltic speaking, but in which Baltic yielded to Slavic in the period from the 400s to the 1000s − in part through a displacement of Lithuanian speakers towards the northwest (see section 4.2), in part through a gradual adoption of Slavic speech by the remaining Baltic population; see figure 3.2.

At this point it should be recalled that the exposition in chapter 1 (and again in chapter 2) led to the conclusion that the CS **e-* > **a-* merger took place before 800. This date places the Common Slavic change in or, possibly, before the period in which East Slavic settlers, moving northward, infiltrated the Baltic-speaking lands in what is now Belarus, a period for which the archaeological record documents extensive Slavic−Baltic biculturalism here, and in which the eventually definitive Slavicization of the Southwestern and Southeastern Balts was proceeding apace (cf. Sedov 1982: 29−41; Volkaitė-Kulikauskienė 1987: 143−145).

This gradual process of language replacement is documented by the more than 2000 Baltic place names (mostly hydronyms) taken over from the Balts by the Slavs in Belarus, for not only does a continuity in toponyms in general attest to a gradual process of ethno-cultural reorientation, but these place names themselves actually reflect distinct chronological stages in the prehistoric Slavic phonological development and thereby prove that they were Slavicized over a long period. For instance, the name of the river *Seližarovka* shows the effects of the Slavic so-called First Velar Palatalization (CS **g* > *ž*) and the change of CS **ē* > *ā* after palatal (*ž*), whereas that of the near-by lake OR *Seligĕrŭ* (at the headwaters of the Volga) shows neither of these changes − evidence of an early

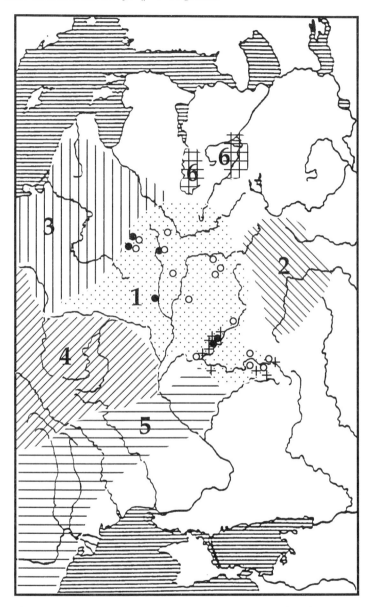

Figure 3.2. Slavs and Balts in Eastern Europe ca. 500−750. Cultural areas associ-
ated with (1) Southeastern Balts; (2) East Galindians (R *Goljad'*); (3)
West and East Baltic; (4) Slaveni; (5) Antes; (6) Kriviči and Lake
Il'men Slovenes. (•) Baltic settlements with Slavic house sites. (○)
Baltic settlements with finds of Slavic and southern provenience. (+)
Settlements with Slavic pottery finds (Sedov 1991: 47).

adaptation of the river name and a later Slavicization of the lake name. Similarly, the river name *Cideľ* near Kaluga shows the effect of the Second Velar Palatalization (*$k > c$; cf. Lowland Li. *Kiduli*), whereas the etymologically identical *Kidel'* in the Dniepr basin was evidently adopted after this constraint lost its productivity (cf. Toporov and Trubačev 1962, s. vv.).

There is unmistakable evidence that the East Slavic settlers who colonized the northwest Russian areas around Pskov and Novgorod in the 500–700s brought with them features of pronunciation characteristic of the now extinct Southeast Baltic dialects formerly spoken in Belarus – that is to say, these settlers did not come straight from the supposed Slavic *Urheimat*, but were in fact – or included – Slavicized Balts (cf. Volkaitė-Kulikauskienė 1987: 146–150; Sedov 1982: 169, 174). One telltale trait of their dialect is the sequential constraint replacing dental stops by velars before *l* (the change "*$Tl > $*$Kl$"), e. g., R d. *klešč*, st. *lešč*, Cz. *dlešt'* < PS TLESK-IA-) 'bream', R d. *žagló* (st. *žálo,* P *žądło* < PS GIN-DLA-) 'sting'. This phonological constraint is a Balticism, known from both West and East Baltic languages, which was transferred to Slavic dialects both in the West and in the East. It was apparently imposed on Pre-Polish dialects by speakers representing a West Baltic (or Southwest Baltic) substratum, and on the East Slavic dialects of the Pskov-Novgorod lands by the Slavicized Southeastern Balts who participated in the colonization of this formerly West-Finnic territory (for Polish, see Taszycki [1961]; for Russian and Belarusian, most recently Nikolaev [1989: 190–198]; cf. also Sedov [1982: 65]).

Just like the "*$Tl > $*$Kl$" change, the prehistoric Southeast Baltic *e- > *a- merger which can be inferred from the isogloss configuration in figure 2.1 produced a phonological constraint which Baltic speakers acquiring Slavic would naturally transfer into their Slavic speech, thereby giving rise to a fluctuation in the occurrence of initial *e- and *a-. Assuming that there was already an existing (phonologically, lexically, stylistically and/or socio-geographically conditioned) variation of *e- and *a- doublets in the Slavic settler dialects brought into this context of bilingualism (cf. section 3.3), such an additional fluctuation would have blurred the original conditioning, increased the frequency of forms with *a-, and hence very plausibly have slanted this variation in favor of *a- variants. As a consequence, a gradation between proximal and distal dialects would arise in the western parts of East Slavic which is directly opposite to the one found elsewhere in Slavic (cf. tables 3.1 and 3.2), but has its own logic: the longer the route of colonization through the Southeast Baltic areas (from the Pripet river watershed, north to those of the Western Dvina and the Velikaja rivers – in modern terms, from Ukraine through Belarus to Northwest Russia), the more generations of speakers of any given Slavic settler dialect would be exposed to interference from the local bilinguals having this sequential constraint, and, as a result, the greater the number of lexemes with *a- for PS E- that would become established in the given settler dialect.

By contrast, in the East Russian and Northeast Russian areas which were not settled through the Southeast Baltic linguistic filter, but by way of the Desna and Oka river basins, more numerous *e- forms survived. It is these dialects that are properly speaking distal in relation to the area occupied by the Ukrainian–Belarusian–Northwest-Russian gradient. And within this latter area, is is the southern, Ukrainian part that should be understood as representing the proximal state of affairs.

3.8. Invariant *je-

Finally there is the fact that although most of the lexemes with PS E-show some variation in the initial vowel reflexes (cf. table 1.1), there are a few lexemes which are known exclusively with *e- reflexes: LCS *jedlĭ, *jedla (PS EDLI- or EDLĀ-) 'spruce, fir' [4], *jelĭčĭ (ELIKA-) 'whitefish' [9], *jelŭkŭ (ELUKA-) 'rancid, bitter' [17], *jesmĭ, *jesi, *jestĭ, etc. (ES-MI, ES-SEI, ES-TI, etc.) 'am, are, is, etc.' [32].

Let us acknowledge first of all that once the modern Slavic distribution of *e- and *a- forms is understood as the product of over a thousand years of linguistic variation and change, we must allow for the possibility that also these etyma had *a- forms in the past, here and there in the Slavic lands, which went out of use before they could be recorded. Perhaps this is not a strong possibility. It is certainly notable, in light of the remarks in section 3.7, that the two of these lexemes which have counterparts in Baltic are both attested with a- forms there; cf. Li. d. ãglė (for ẽglė), OPr. Addle – Tanne (E. 596) 'fir, spruce', Li. d. astì (South Upland for estì; Zinkevičius [1966: 345]) 'is', OPr. asmai 'am'. But neither of these is known with *a- forms in East Slavic. One of them, PS EDL-Ā- 'fir', is represented in Northwest Russian dialects with the characteristic Baltic -gl- (d. jógla, likely d. n'égla, n'ógla 'larch' < LCS *n(e) egla, top. Jegl'ino, elsewhere *Jel'ino, Jélov'ica*), but it is not found anywhere, apparently, with initial *a- forms. Let us leave this possibility aside.

The significance of the lexemes that are attested exclusively with *e-forms in Slavic is that they testify that the *e- > *a- change was in fact no real phonological merger in the ancestral dialects of Slavic. The generations of Slavists who hoped to define a phonological conditioning for the supposed "*je- > *o- change" were prisoners of a restrictive methodology that did not encourage them to consider the full range of possible interpretations, but made them look for only one kind of explanation (see further sections 8.3.4 and 8.5). It is not surprising that these efforts, although applied again and again for over one hundred years, have led nowhere, for there is no definable phonological constraint that will account for the actual exemptions from the *e- > *a- merger; these are marked "•" in (table 3.3).

In these pages we have seen how an analysis of the modern *je- ‖ *o-isoglosses takes us back to a pre-expansion Common Slavic state of af-

Table 3.3. Proto-Slavic etyma with E-, arranged according to segmental surroundings and position relative to the accent

	Stable pretonic E-	Stable pre-pretonic E-	Mobile accent
/___d+fV	EDSKE [2]	EDEINA- [1] EDINĀ- [1]	• EDLI- [4]
/___d+bV	• EDLĀ- [4] ED-UĀS [3]		
/___l+fV		• ELIKA- [9]	ELENI- [11] ELEITA- [10]
/___l+bV			ELUKA- [17]
/___m+fV			EMELA- [18]
/___r+fV		ERIMBĪ- [20−21]	ERIMBI- [20−21]
/___s+fV	• ES-MI [32] ESE [26]	ESERĀ- [29] ESETRA- [31]	ESENA- [27] ESENI- [28] ESETI- [30]
/___s+bV	• ES-MAX [32]		
/___z+fV	EZIA- [36−37]		EZERA- [35]

The place of accent may vary in word-forms with polysyllabic endings. Etyma known only with LCS *je- reflexes are marked with "•". The table omits lexemes which probably had Proto-Slavic by-forms with A- (cf. section 5.3.3).

fairs (figure 3.1) which is not the immediate result of a neat dialect divergence, but a mediate one, a result of secondary convergence brought about through interaction between the populations on both sides of an earlier clear-cut dialect boundary. When we inquire what might be the origin of this boundary, our experience tells us there are two possibilities (cf. section 1.3): either the innovating dialects developed their apparent sequential constraint on initial *e-* through an internally motivated sound change; or they adopted this sequential constraint from a substratum, adstratum, or superstratum that had it.

Let us — at least for a time — suspend the century-long effort to account for the Common Slavic **e-* > **a-* merger and its exceptions in terms of an internally motivated, phonologically conditioned innovation and consider instead how the material would be compatible with other possible interpretations.

One possibility is that an internally motivated, unconditioned **e-* > **a-* merger occurred not in the ancestral dialects of Slavic, but in dialects closely related and contiguous to them. These could be the dialects that formed the core area (A) in the isogloss configuration in figure 3.1. These "Quasi-Slavic" dialects might later have been superseded by some part of the dialects from which the known Slavic languages derive. It is not unreasonable to suppose that there were such Quasi-Slavic dialects in the dialect continuum of which the known Slavic and Baltic languages are the surviving fragments. And where parts of an isogloss system can be discerned which imply the former existence of other parts, which may have been overlaid by subsequent developments, it makes sense to reconstruct the "missing links" — in this instance, the core area in figure 3.1. It is perhaps difficult to imagine the precise location of these Quasi-Slavic dialects, but they may be thought of as intermediate between the ancestral dialects of Slavic and the lost Southeast (and Southwest?) Baltic dialects (which, in turn, might be thought of not simply as Baltic, but more realistically as "Quasi-Baltic"; see section 9.4).

But there are other possibilities. Suppose there occurred some early expansion or displacement of the Slavs which brought Slavic speakers into the southern parts of the Baltic dialect continuum, which — assuming that it coincided with the Baltic cultural areas identified by archaeology — extended southward to the headwaters of the Western Bug in the west and reached beyond the Pripet river to the Middle Dniepr in the east. Or suppose there was an opposite, southward expansion or displacement of Baltic speakers into a northern or northeastern portion of the Slavic territories between the Western Bug and the Dniepr.

If the Southern Balts had the phonological constraint resulting from the *e- > *a- merger which we know from Lithuanian (section 2), and which we can ascribe to the extinct Southeast Baltic dialects (cf. section 3.7; and see chapter 4), their absorption into one section of the Slavic population, at a time before any of the characteristic Common Slavic dialectal changes took place, could very well have left no other discernible effects than the slight alteration of a number of lexemes resulting from the transference into Slavic of the Baltic "*e- → a-*" constraint. These effects would not be surprising in such a situation of language contact: a phonemic substitution of *a- for *e- became codified in a number of lexemes, sharply reducing the lexical frequency of initial *e-; but the phonological constraint as such did not survive, for the language to which it belonged ceased to be spoken when Slavic speech carried the day. Hence a small number of lexemes with CS *e- for PS E- remained, which eventually passed into all the modern Slavic languages with *e- reflexes.

There is perhaps no real need to try to ground such a speculative account in fact. But it is reasonable to compare this tentative, hypothetical Slavic−Baltic contact area with the southern part of the Pripet basin. Here, in the southernmost reaches of the forest zone is an area in which archaic Slavic river names and Baltic river names are distributed side by side (Trubačev 1968 a; see figure 3.3). It looks as if the Slavic hydronyms here are evidence of a relatively early Slavic dominion, and the Baltic ones date from a more recent Baltic colonization, but the actual picture may be more complicated than it seems. Subsequently, both layers of hydronyms have been overlaid with a layer of much more numerous, patently younger Slavic hydronyms.

The archaic Slavic and Baltic hydronyms here are possibly older than the contact episode that would be responsible for the spread of the *e- → *a- constraint, and they may reflect not one, but several prehistoric population shifts − perhaps in different directions, north-to-south as well as west-to-east. But that this region witnessed repeated contacts between Baltic and Slavic populations in prehistory seems beyond doubt. It does not seem implausible that this was the core area of the Common Slavic *e- > *a- merger. But of course, this is only a guess.

3.9. Summary

In this chapter I have undertaken an analysis of the lexical material represented in the modern *je- ‖ *o- isoglosses and tried to tease apart different

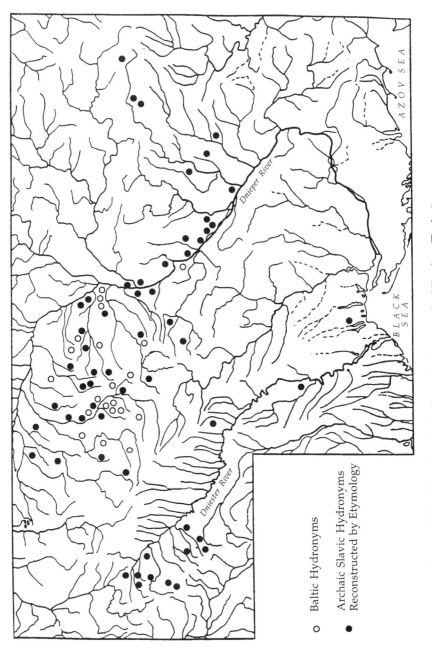

Figure 3.3. Areas with Baltic and archaic Slavic hydronyms in Ukraine (Trubačev 1968 a).

layers of differently motivated changes in the geographical distribution of the reflexes of PS E-.

It is easy to imagine situations in linguistic history where just a few layers of innovation will create such an opaque, apparently chaotic, state of affairs that no amount of analysis will succeed in untangling the different effects of each layer of innovation. Here we have been fortunate in having some information about the relative and absolute chronology of the development of Slavic, about the development of the Baltic languages, about the settlement history of the Slavs, and about their interaction, at various times, with presumable speakers of Baltic dialects – information which can be integrated into a realistic, though naturally quite schematic, chronological account.

Since the exposition in the preceding sections was anachronic, I will end this chapter with a brief chronological synthesis.

3.9.1. Slavic and Baltic

Once upon a time, perhaps several generations before the beginning of the Slavic Migrations, in an area in Eastern Europe, some Slavic and some non-Slavic (Quasi-Slavic or South[east] Baltic) populations came into contact. As the non-Slavic speakers acquired Slavic, they transferred a native sequential constraint (initial e- → a-) to their Slavic speech. The resulting variation of initial *e- and *a- was resolved in favor of *a- in all but a few lexemes with PS E-, which continued to have initial *e-. Thus developed the "*a- dialects"; cf. sections 3.3 and 3.8.

3.9.2. Slavic

Slavic outside this contact area at first maintained the inherited (Proto-Slavic) distribution of *e- and *a- – these are the *e- dialects. But in time, the isogloss bundle defining the boundary between these two dialects of Slavic eroded, certain lexemes with *a- attaining a greater areal distribution than others, some in one direction, others in another; cf. figure 3.1 and section 3.5.

3.9.3. West and South Slavic

The Slavic territorial expansion towards the west and the south, which occurred principally between the 300s and 700s, involved at first pure *e- speakers and secondarily settlers from the transitional zone, mainly-

e- speakers. It proceeded chiefly as a radial expansion, and *a-* forms therefore were more frequently represented in the new Slavic territories closer to the traditional Slavic lands than farther away (cf. section 3.2). Thus arose the orderly distribution of *a-* forms identified in terms of implicational relations in section 3.2. But a certain amount of cross-migration brought a scattering of *a-* forms to probably numerous localities all over the newly settled areas; cf. sections 3.4 and 3.6.

3.9.4. East Slavic

In the East Slavic area, too, there were more *a-* speakers among the settlers that moved north through the western parts of the Dniepr basin than among those that followed the more easterly route north. But in addition, the Southeast Baltic substratum of *a-* speakers in what is now Belarus for a long time exerted an influence on the varieties of Slavic speech that were diffused northward through this area, so that *a-* forms tended to be favored over *e-* forms − with the result that the more northerly dialects in this continuum have more *a-* forms than their neighbors further south (cf. section 3.7).

3.9.5. The consolidation of norms

In the centuries since the period of expansion, much of the *e- ∼ *a-* variation that characterized many early medieval Slavic dialects has been eliminated. But some isolated *a-* forms in predominantly *e-* areas have persisted to this day, and vice versa (see chapter 7).

In the next chapter, this narrowly Slavic account will be complemented with an account of the similar variation in the Baltic languages, which will open up a wider areal and temporal perspective.

Chapter 4

The Baltic change of *e- > *a-

The entire presentation in the preceding chapters was based on the assumption that it is appropriate to reconstruct for Proto-Slavic one set of lexemes with initial PS e- and another with initial a-, and to account for the division of the former of these into subsets with invariant (LCS *je-) and variant (LCS *je- ‖ *o-) correspondences in the modern languages (the lexeme sets in examples [1.2]−[1.3]) as the result of changes in prehistoric Slavic.

This assumption, it should be noted, is merely an instantiation of the general assumption − which is fundamental to the comparative method − that attested diversity among dialects or languages is the result of divergent changes operating on an originally uniform language state. But our assumption marks a significant break with the tradition of scholarship devoted to the „East Slavic *je- > *o-change". In order to account for the occurrence of *o- doublets in West and South Slavic, this tradition assumed that no Proto-Slavic uniformity need be reconstructed, and that Proto-Slavic inherited numerous word-initial ablaut doublets from Proto-Indo-European (cf. section 1.2; see further sections 5.3.2, 8.1.3 and 8.2.1). And it was believed that there was support for this assumed ablaut variation in the fact that also the Baltic languages present a word-initial fluctuation of *e- and *a-, in part in the very same etyma.

Evidently, there is a slight error of logic here. Strictly speaking, even if the word-initial e- ‖ a- diversity in the Baltic languages were indeed inherited from Proto-Indo-European, it would not follow that the Slavic *je- ‖ *o- isoglosses could not all be due to an internal phonological development peculiar to Slavic.

However, as we saw in section 2.2, there was a regular phonological change in prehistoric Lithuanian (originating in the contiguous Southeast Baltic dialects once spoken in what is now Belarus; section 3.7), which gave rise to e- ‖ a- isoglosses in Lithuanian. Hence, the idea that such Slavic lexical doublets as *jelenĭ ‖ *olenĭ 'deer' [11] or *jes-ika ‖ *os-ina 'aspen' [19] are inherited Proto-Indo-European ablaut alternants "just like" the Lithuanian parallels élnis, d. álnis 'deer' or ẽpušė, d. ãpušė 'aspen' is − quite apart from the logical error − simply wrong. There is absolutely no reason to think that this Lithuanian diversity of reflexes is of Proto-Indo-European vintage.

4.1. The Baltic data

But the variation of initial *e-* and *a-* in the Baltic languages is not limited to the effects of the Southeast Baltic *e-* > *a-* merger which were described in section 2.2 (and revisited in section 3.7). It extends to Latvian and Old Prussian, as is acknowledged in discussions of comparative Baltic phonology; cf. Endzelin ([1948] 1971: 31); Stang (1966: 32); Schmalstieg (1976: 98, 133). But this variation appears random. It looks about as intractable as the Slavic *je-* ∥ *o-* variation, and it has never been the subject of systematic investigation. Among the Baltic *e-* and *a-* doublets there are in fact a few reliable examples of word-initial apophony (as we will see below), but on the whole the variation seems very similar to that in Slavic.

The relevant data can be classified into two large correspondence sets. One of the sets includes etyma with initial *e-* in one or more of the three languages; it is displayed in table 4.1. The other shows exclusively initial *a-*; see (4.1). The former set divides into several subsets, which are labeled (a)−(e) in table 4.1. They are presented in abbreviated form in table 4.2. In almost all of these words, Standard Lithuanian, which generally looks to the northwestern (Lowland) dialects for the etymologically correct distribution of initial *e-* and *a-*, has *e-*, while the *a-* variant is dialectal. Only in a few lexemes does the standard language have *a-*, while the corresponding form with *e-* is dialectal, obsolete, or unattested: in Li. *àš* 'I' [34] and *ašvà* 'mare' [33], OLi. and d. *èš* and *ešvà*, other Indo-European languages indicate PIE *eĝʰ-/*eĝ- and *eḱu̯ā-, and hence PB E-; Li. *álvas* 'tin (St.)' [6], which contrasts with OPr. *Elwas* and *Alwis*, possibly has PIE *o- (see further sections 5.2.4 and 6.1 and chapter 7, s. vv.).

(4.1)   Some lexemes with PB A-: OPr. *abbai*, La. *abi*, Li. *abù* 'both' (PB AB-AI, -Ō, PS AB-Ā, OCS *oba*), La. *adata*, Li. *adatà* 'needle' (PB ADAT-Ā-), OPr. *Aglo* 'rain' (PB AGLU-); OPr. *Agins*, La. *acs*, Li. *akìs* 'eye' (PB AK-I-, PS AK-AS-, OCS *oko*), OPr. *Akstins*, Li. *ãksti-*

Table 4.1. Provisional list of lexemes with initial Proto-Baltic E-

		PB	OPr.	La.	Li.	PS
(a)	[31]	EŠ-ETRA- 'sturgeon'	*Esketres* /esketras/		*eršket(r)as*	ES-ETRA-
	[37]	EŽ-IA- 'hedgehog'		*ezis*	*ežỹs*	EZ-IA-
					d. *ažỹs*	
	[25]	ERŽ-ILA- 'stallion'	*Erzelis*		*eřžilas*	(IRZ-Ā-TĒI)
					d. *ařžilas*	
(b)	[18]	EMELA- 'mistletoe'	*Emelno*	*emuols*	d. *ẽmalas*	EMELA-
			top. *Amelung,*	*amuls*	*ãmalas*	
			Ammelink			
(c)	[34]	EŽ 'I'	C: *es* /es/	*es*	o. *eš*	(ĀZ)
			as /as/		*aš*	
	[32]	ES-MI 'to be; pres.'	C: *essei, esti*		*estì*	ES-MI
			asmai, assai, asch,		d. *àsti*	
			asti			
	[32]	ES-TI- 'thing'			*esìmas*	
			astin /astis/			
	[6]	ELUA- 'lead (Pb)'	*Elwas*			EL.AUA-
			Alwis	*alvs, alva*	*al̃vas*	
(d)	[16]	(U)ELU- 'hasp'		*elvete*	*elvėdė, elvýtė*	
			Aloade		*alvýta, alvỹtė*	
	[35]	EŽ-Ī-/-IĀ- 'edge'		*eža*	d. *ežià*	(ĒZA-)
			Asy /azī/		*ažià*	
	[4]	EDL-Ē- 'fir'		*egle*	*ēglė*	EDL-I-
			Addle /adlē/		d. *ãglė*	
	[30]	EK-ET-IĀ- 'harrow'		*ecēsas*	*ekė̃čios*	ES-ETI-
			Aketes /aketēs/		d. *akė̃čios*	
	[35]	EŽ-ERA- 'lake'		*ezers, ezars*	*ẽžaras*	EZ-ERA-
			Assaran /azaran/		d. *ãžaras*	
	[14]	ELK-ŪN-Ē- 'elbow'		*èlkuone*	d. *elkū́nė*	AL-K-UTI-
			Alkūnis /alkūnias/		*alkū́nė*	
			Woaltis	*uolekts*	*uolektis*	
	[22]	ER-EL-IA- 'eagle'		*ereļi, erglis*	*erẽlis*	ER-ILA-
			Arelie /arelis/		d. *arẽlis*	
	[24]	ERŠK-IA- 'thorn'		*ẽršķis*	*erškė́tis*	ERKX-IKA-
					arškė́tis	
	[33]	EŠU-Ā- 'mare'			o. *ešvà*	
			Aswinan		*ašvà*	
	[23]	ER-K-IĀ- 'tick, woodbeetle'		*ẽrce*	*érkė*	
					árkė	
(e)	[15]	ĒL-N-I 'deer'			*élnis*	EL-ENI-
			Alne /alnē/	*alnis*	d. *álnė, -is*	ĀL-N-I-
	[19]	EPS-Ē- 'aspen'			d. *ẽpušė*	EPS-Ā-
			Abse /apsē/	*apse*	*ãpušė*	
	[12]	ELSN-I- 'elder'			*el̃ksnis*	ELIX-Ā-
			Abskande /alisknas/	*àlksnis*	*al̃ksnis*	

Table 4.1. Continued

	PB	OPr.	La.	Li.	PS
[37]	EŽ-(E)GIA- 'bass'			*ežegỹs,*	ĒZG-IA-
		Assegis /azegīs/		*ežgỹs, ežgė*	
				ažagỹs	
[29]	EŠ-ER-IA- 'perch'			*ešerỹs*	ESERĀ-
		Asar(i)s	*asaris*	d. *ašerỹs*	
[5]	EK-ETĒ- 'ice-hole'			*eketẽ*	AK-AS-
			akacis	*aketẽ*	

Old Prussian lexemes marked "C" are attested in the Catechisms; unmarked lexemes are known from the Elbing Vocabulary.

Table 4.2. Old Prussian, Latvian, and Lithuanian correspondences for PB E-

	Old Prussian	Latvian	Lithuanian
(a)	*e-*	*e-*	*e-/a*
(b)	*e-/a-*	*e-/a-*	*e-/a-*
(c)	*e-/a-*	*e-*	*e-/a-*
(d)	*a-*	*e-*	*e-/a-*
(e)	*a-*	*a-*	*e-/a*

nas 'prickle' (PB AKSTI-NA-), OPr. *Ackons* (**akōnis*), La. *akuôte*, Li. *akúotas* 'awn' (PB AK-Ō-NI-/-TA-), OPr. *ālgas*, La. *àlga*, Li. *algà* 'wages' (PB ALGĀ-), OPr. *alkīns*, La. *aîkt*, Li. *álkti* 'be hungry' (PB ĀLK-, PS ĀLK-Ā-TĒI), OPr. *Alu*, La. *alus*, Li. *alùs* 'beer' (PB ALU-, PS ALU-, OR *olŭ*), OPr. *amsis* (**amzias*), Li. *ámžius* 'age' (PB ĀMŽIU-), OPr. *Ane* (**anī*), Li. *anýta* 'mother-in-law' (PB ANĪ-), OPr. *angis* (**angias*), La. *ùodze*, Li. *angìs* 'snake' (PB AN-GI-, PS ANG-IA-, LCS **ǫžĭ*), OPr. *Anglis*, La. *ùogle*, Li. *anglìs* 'coal' (PB ANGLI-, PS ANGLI-, LCS **ǫglĭ*), OPr. *Angurgis* (**angurias*), Li. *ungurỹs* 'eel' (PB A/UNGUR-IA-, PS A/UNGAR-IA-, LCS **ǫgoří*); OPr. *ankstainai*, Li. *ankstì* 'early' (PB ANKST-), OPr. *Anctan* 'butter' (PB ANK-TA-), OPr. *Anxdris* 'adder' (**angzdrias*), La. *anksteri*, Li. *ìnkštiraĩ, ánkštirai* 'maggots' (PB ANKŠTIR-AI), OPr. *Ansis*, La. *ùosa, ùoss*, Li. *ąsà* 'loop' (PB ANSĀ-), OPr. *antars*, La. *ùotrs*, Li. *añtaras* 'other' (PB AN-TARA-, PS UN-TARA-, OCS *vŭtorŭ*), OPr. *Antis*, La. *uots*, Li. *ántis* (d. *eñtis*) 'duck' (PB ĀNT-I-, PS ĀNT-Ū- CS **ǫty*), OPr. *Ape*, La. *upe*, Li. *ùpė, upìs* 'river'

(PB UP-/AP-Ē-), OPr. *Ansalgis* (**anzalias*) 'shoe lining' (PB ĀNŽ-
AL-IA-), OPr. *Ansonis* (**anz-ōn-ias*), Li. *ážuolas* 'oak' (PB ĀNŽ-
ŌLA-, PS ĀNZ-LA-, LCS **ǫzlŭ* 'knot'), OPr. *Artwes* (**ar-tuwēs*)
'boat-trip' (PB ĒR-TUUĒ-), OPr. *Arwaykis* (**ar-w-aikas*) 'foal' (PB
ĀR-, PS AR-I-, OR *orĭ* 'horse'), OPr. *Aclocordo* /arkla-/, La. *ar̃kls*,
Li. *árklas* 'plow' (PB ĀR-TLA-, PS ĀR-DLA-, LCS **radlo*, d. **ralo*),
OPr. *artoys* /artājas/, Li. *artójas* 'plower' (PB ĀR-TĀ-IA-, PS ĀR-
TĀ-IA-, LCS **ratajĭ*), OPr. *arwis* 'true' (PB ARU-I-, PS ARU-I-NA-,
OCS *ravĭnŭ* 'even'), La. *asara*, Li. *ašarà* 'tear' (PB AŠARĀ-), OPr.
asmus 'eighth' (PB AŠ-MA-, PS AS-MA-, OCS *osmŭ*), OPr. *Assanis*
'autumn' (PB ASENI-, PS ESENI-), OPr. *Assis*, La. *ass*, Li. *ašìs* (d.
ešìs) 'axle' (PB AŠI-, PS ASI-, LCS **osĭ*), OPr. *Awis*, Li. *avýnas*
'mother's brother', d. *ava* 'mother's sister' (PB AU-Ī, PS AU-Ā-,
LS *owa* 'grandmother'), OPr. *awins*, Li. *ãvinas* 'ram' (PB AUI-
NA-, PS AUI-NA-, OCS *ovĭnŭ*), Li. *avižà* 'oats' (PB AUIŽĀ-, PS
AUISA-, LCS **ovĭsŭ*).

If we proceed with this corpus in the same way as in the analysis of
the Slavic data, we will provisionally take the set in table 4.1 to represent
PB E- and the set in (4.1) to represent PB A-. It appears that a few adjustments have to be made. For instance, in OPr. *Artwes* − *Schifreise* (E.
413) 'boat-trip' in (4.1), read /artuwēs/, derived from PB ĒR- 'to row' (cf.
Li. *ìrti* 'idem'), the suffix usually implies *e*-grade root vocalism, and we
would therefore be inclined to include this word in table 4.1 (as PB ĒR-
TUU-Ē; cf. Mažiulis [1988], s. v.). On the other hand, a few lexemes, including some prepositions and prefixes, are probably genuine ablaut alternants, in part inherited from Proto-Indo-European, in part perhaps
innovated within Baltic; cf. (4.2).

(4.2)   OPr. *eb-, ab-* 'about; telicity marker' (PB EB, AB, PS AB); OPr.
         et-, at- 'away, back', Li. *at(i)* 'sim.' (PB ET, AT, PS AT 'from');
         OPr. *en* 'in', La. *ie*, Li. *-en* 'locative (postposition)', *in, į-* 'in' (PB
         EN, IN, PS UN, LCS **vŭ* 'in', PS AN-, LCS **ǫ-*); OPr. *er* (particle),
         La. *er, ar*, Li. *ir, ar*. See Toporov (1975) and Mažiulis (1988), s. vv.

These alternants should properly be included separately in table 4.1 and
in (4.1). For simplicity's sake we leave them aside. There are also the
words that are attested with hypercorrect *e-* for *a-* in area 4 on the map
in figure 2.1. These too will be left aside in the discussion here. Finally,
as it turns out, when we confront these reconstructions with PB E- with

their Proto-Indo-European correspondents in chapter 5, some more adjustments must be made. But for the time being we will limit our discussion to the sets of correspondences internal to the Baltic languages which are displayed in table 4.1.

4.2. The geographical distribution

Two interesting observations can be made in table 4.1.

First, there is extensive agreement between PB E- and PS E- in the lexemes shared by Baltic and Slavic. A few discrepancies stand out: PB ELK-ŪN-Ē, PS ALK-UTI- 'elbow' [14], PB ĒLN-Ē-, PS ĀLN-I- 'doe' [15], PB EK-ET-Ē 'ice-hole' [5], PS AK-AS- 'eye'. On the other hand, the list in (4.1) includes PB ASANI- 'autumn', which contrasts with PS ESENI- [28]. These discrepancies will be analysed and interpreted in section 5.3.4; see also the section on the respective etyma in chapter 7.

Secondly, the geographical distribution of initial *e-* and *a-* forms in the Baltic languages is rather similar to that of the *e-* and *a-* forms in the Slavic languages which we analysed in chapter 3. There is no strict implicational relation between *a-* attestations in Old Prussian and in Latvian, but on the whole, any lexeme which is attested solely with *a-* in Latvian is attested solely with *a-* in Old Prussian, but not vice versa. And again, any etymon which is attested with an *a-* form in either of these languages occurs with *a-* forms in Lithuanian. One striking difference is that there are no etyma which are known only with *e-* forms, but this is due to the Lithuanian (and Southeast Baltic) *e-* > *a-* merger. But apart from this, the geographical distribution of *e-* and *a-* forms in Baltic appears to be a sort of counterpart to the one in Slavic.

This is particularly clear if it is seen against the background of the location of the Baltic ethnic groups reconstructed for the 500s; cf. figure 4.1. In fact, viewed in this perspective, the Baltic distribution is nearly a mirror image of the one we reconstructed for Slavic in figure 3.1, and so it complements it and corroborates it: the reconstructed Slavic and Baltic systems of *e-* ‖ *a-* isoglosses can both be interpreted as transitional zones between a central area in which the inherited *e-* versus *a-* distinction was lost (by a merger of *e-* > *a-*) and peripheral areas to the south and to the northwest and north of it in which this distinction remained intact. In the Baltic dialects, as in the reconstructed Slavic configuration, a transitional zone with

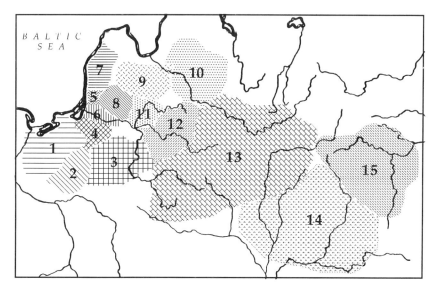

Figure 4.1. Cultural areas associated with Baltic speaking groups ca. 500–800
(1) Prussians; (2) Galindians; (3) Jatvingians; (4) Nadruvians; (5) La-
matitians; (6) Skalvians; (7) Curonians; (8) Žemaitians (Samogitians);
(9) Zemgalians; (10) Latgalians and Selonians; (11) Lithuanianized
Žemaitians; (12) Lithuanians; (13) Southeastern Balts; (14) Koločino
culture, of uncertain linguistic affiliation; (15) East Galindians.

both *e*- and *a*- forms bears witness to a period of interaction between
central *a*- dialects and peripheral *e*- dialects (cf. section 3.5). It is tempting
to round out the picture by interpolating connecting western and eastern
transitional and peripheral dialects, which are missing now, but have been
superseded by Slavic languages — Polish in the west, Belarusian and Russian in the east — in the style of figure 4.2.

In chapter 3 we saw that the Slavic *e- ‖ *a- distribution is best understood in terms of the state of affairs prior to the beginning of the
Migrations. Similarly the geographical distribution of *e*- and *a*- in Baltic
should surely be viewed in terms of the location of the Baltic dialects
before the significant population movements that occurred in the early
Middle Ages, specifically the colonization of the Baltic Northwest — the
territories of the Curonians, Zemgalians, and Selonians in what is now
Latvia and Lithuania — by the Latvians (Latgalians) and Lithuanians.
In their final phase, say from the 800s to the 1000s, these movements of
people are directly related to the consolidation of Slavic political suprem-

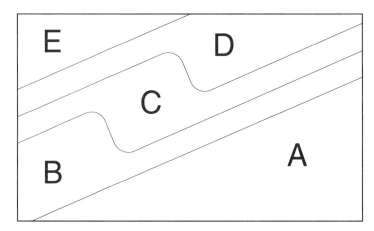

Figure 4.2. Schematic isogloss configuration illustrating the transitional zone separating Baltic *a- dialects and *e- dialects
The isoglosses define the following areas: A−*ašetra-, *adlē-, *amela-,
*ālnia-; B−*ešetra-, *adlē-, *amela-, *ālnia-; C−*ešetra-, *edlē-,
*amela-, *ālnia-; D−*ešetra-, *edlē-, *emela-, *ālnia-; E−*ešetra-,
*edlē-, *emela-, *ēlnia-.
For the attestation, cf. table 4.1.

acy in what is now Belarus and Southern Russia and involved armed
conflict with the Slavs, as is well known from the Russian chronicles
(e. g., Prince Jaroslav's campaign against the Lithuanians in 1040). In the
preceding centuries, these movements were perhaps a less direct response
to the growing infiltration and gradual expansion of the Slavs in the areas
of Belarus. But at their very beginning in the 400−500s, these population
movements have the appearance in the archaeological record of a sponta-
neous territorial expansion, possibly an economically motivated colonization, in which new settlement types, new burial customs, and new varieties of artifacts accompany the northward and northwestward expansion
of a population with the physical characteristics previously documented
in Belarus − by inference, the later Latvians and Lithuanians; cf. figure
4.3 (Volkaitė-Kulikauskienė 1987: 154−156).

The most significant linguistic consequence of this colonization was
the submersion and extinction of the Northwest Baltic dialects. The extent of their territories is amply reflected in the many Curonian, Zemgalian, and Selonian substratum place names taken over by the immigrating
Latvian and Lithuanian settlers, whose dialects came to predominate in
their current areas only in the Middle Ages (800s to 1300s) and eventually

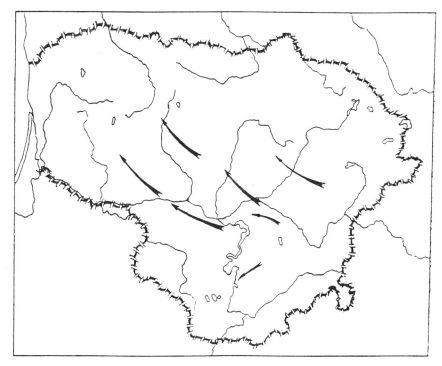

Figure 4.3. Northwestward displacement of Baltic populations, ca. 400−800, as
reflected in the spread of cremation burials
Signatures representing burial sites have been omitted to highlight the
inferred directions of spread (Volkaitė-Kulikauskienė 1987: 154).

definitively superseded the earlier Northwest Baltic forms of speech (cf.
figure 4.1), though modern dialect differences still reflect the earlier linguistic differences. The substratum place names, many of which are
known from Latin, German, and Old Russian sources dating from the
1000s on, are neatly distinct from those of the Latvian−Lithuanian superstratum by virtue of the fact that several of the major, early phonological innovations in the Baltic languages had very different geographical
extensions before the rearrangement of the map that the Latvian and
Lithuanian colonization brought about (cf. Būga 1924: 156−282; Volkaitė-Kulikauskienė 1987: 157−160; Brejdak 1988).

It stands to reason that these population movements affected the geographical distribution of *e*- and *a*- reflexes of PB E- as well. It is not clear
now whether the Northwest Baltic dialects were "pure *e- dialects" or
"mainly-*e- dialects" (these labels were introduced in section 3.5) at the

time when the colonization from the southeast began. Although some of the relevant etyma with PB E- are in fact attested in Northwest Baltic place names recorded since the Middle Ages (these are mentioned in section 6.1 and in chapter 7 s. vv.), this attestation is too sporadic to permit any generalizations. But we may presume that all the pre-Latvian and pre-Lithuanian speaking settlers who moved in came from areas closer to the central *a-* dialects, the ones from the farthest away, who reached southeastern Lithuania last, presumably being "pure **a-* speakers". In this connection it is significant that among the thousands of Baltic hydronyms documented in the Dniepr river basin, there are none with initial *e-*; cf. Toporov and Trubačev 1962.

4.3. Baltic and Slavic

The similarity between the Baltic **e- > *a-* merger and the "East Slavic **je- > *o-* change" was noted a long time ago in Baltic historical linguistics (cf. Endzelin 1923: 36). On the other hand, the similarity between the "East Slavic **je- > *o-* change" and the Baltic **e- ‖ *a-* variation has been mentioned time and again by Slavists (recently, for instance, by Lamprecht [1987: 36]). But it has never been clear in the scholarly literature whether this observed similarity should be understood as a coincidence, as a typological parallel, or as the result of a shared phonological innovation.

In the account that has been put forward here, it seemed reasonable first to secure the chronological context of the Slavic innovation (chapter 1) and then argue for the purely typological identity of the Lithuanian (and Southeast Baltic) **e- > *a-* merger and its less well understood Slavic counterpart (chapter 2). Further, it seemed reasonable to assume first the genetic independence of the **e- > *a-* merger in the Southeast Baltic substratum in Belarus and the posited *e- ~ a-* variation in the Slavic settler dialects that infiltrated and eventually superseded this substratum (section 3.7). But with the interpretation of the Baltic data that has been offered in the present chapter, these diverse prehistoric events can be seen to be pieces of the same puzzle.

A single phonological innovation – the reconstructed **e- > *a-* merger – occurred in an area near the center of the presumed Slavic–Baltic dialect continuum in Eastern Europe and spread from there, radially, in all directions. The spread led to the development of broad transitional zones all around, across which the merger was lexically diffused. The southern segment of this circular transitional isogloss system can be reconstructed by extrapolation for the period before the Slavic expansion towards the south (that is, before AD 400), and the northern segment for the period before the East Baltic northwestward displacement (that is, before 500). The southern segment was strongly deformed and fragmented as a result of the combination of radial expansion of the Slavic-speaking territories and cross-migrations of smaller and larger groups of Slavic colonists which occurred during the 400−700s. During this period the western and the eastern segments of the circular isogloss system were obliterated by the new Slavic settlements in what is now Poland and southern Russia. The northern segment, in turn, was deformed and displaced by the northward and northwestward movements of the Eastern Balts who colonized the Baltic Northwest, the territories of modern-day Latvia and Lithuania, in part in response to the pressure created by the Slavic colonization of what is now Belarus.

Thus, in its relative simplicity, runs the account we have been able to piece together.

4.4. The larger perspective

I claimed in the Introduction (chapter 1) that the Slavic change which we have interpreted as a partial merger of initial CS *e- and *a- needs to be viewed in the perspective of the prehistoric relationship between Slavic and Baltic. This relationship, which for generations has challenged the imagination of Slavists and Baltists, has in recent decades been clarified to such an extent that one can speak of a growing consensus recognizing not only that West Baltic (Old Prussian) and East Baltic (Lithuanian and Latvian) do not provide the basis for reconstructing a single Baltic proto-language (cf. section 9.2), but also that Slavic bears very different relations to West Baltic and to East Baltic. The first of these points was made by Endzelin as early as in 1921 (quoted by Stang [1966: 13]). The second point was definitively demonstrated by Stang (1966: 10−13).

From this understanding it follows that the Slavic and the attested Baltic languages cannot be regarded simply as sister and cousin languages, descended in traditional Stammbaum fashion through a Proto-

Slavic and a Proto-Baltic from a Proto-Balto-Slavic. They should be understood rather as the only surviving, originally not directly contiguous, fragments of a former Slavic—Baltic dialect continuum, which came into being perhaps in the second millennium before our era, when Indo-European speakers first established continuous linguistic traditions in the vast spaces of Eastern Europe. During the subsequent millennia, we may assume, this Indo-European speech area developed a mosaic of internal isoglosses, formed and re-formed in periods of gradual differentiation and undoubtedly shifted and eroded and partially leveled in intermittent periods of convergence and as a consequence of smaller and larger population movements, however motivated − by the relative mobility of these early agriculturalists, by changing economic conditions, in response to waxing and waning pressures from neighboring populations, by the absorption of waves of intruding settlers, and so on.

The net effect of this linguistic differentiation was a polarization of the dialects of the north and the dialects of the south, observable now as the sharp differences between the Baltic and the Slavic languages. But in the period before the Slavic Migrations, this polarization must have been less palpable, not only because Slavic was phonologically much less evolved at that time, but also because the dialects spoken in the central regions of this vast area very likely formed a gradient, lexically and morphosyntactically, between the ancestral dialects of the Slavs in the south and the ancestral dialects of the known Balts in the west, northwest, and north. The current view of these intermediate dialects is that they were Baltic − and in the exposition here they have been named accordingly (Southwest Baltic and Southeast Baltic). But it must be remembered that the linguistic evidence by which we characterize them is their similarities (as reflected in, say, Belarusian toponyms) with the known Baltic languages, and that any features these extinct dialects may have shared with Slavic are naturally indistinguishable from the features of the later Slavic superstratum.

It was in this intermediate area, according to the hypothesis developed here, that the merger of initial *e- and *a- originated some time before the beginning of the Slavic territorial expansion. The phonological innovation − the omission of a vowel distinction in the marked environment of a bare (onset-less) syllable in word-initial position − presumably spread radially towards the northeast, the north, the northwest, and the west. We may guess that it covered the Southeast Baltic dialect areas ahead of the Slavic infiltration of these lands; that it reached the West Baltic lands before the earliest attestation of Old Prussian (though the

Elbing Vocabulary, compiled ca. 1300, documents some forms in *e*-); and that it left most of the Northwest Baltic dialects and parts of the ancestral dialects of the Latvians and the Lithuanians in a transitional zone with a mixture of *e- and *a- reflexes resulting from the lexical diffusion of the results of the merger. As the ancestral dialects of the Latvians and the Lithuanians moved into the northwest from the 500s on, the system of lexical isoglosses forming the northern transitional zone disintegrated and gave way to a state of lexical variation quite similar to the one we have postulated for medieval Slavic (sections 3.4−3.7), which is actually attested until quite recently in some localities in Lithuania (cf. section 2.2). But in the southern parts of eastern Lithuania there was a sufficient flow of settlers from the Belarusian "*a*- area" for the *e*- > *a*- merger to keep its momentum as a developing phonological constraint, and it eventually yielded the basic isoglosses circumscribing areas 1 and 2 in figure 2.1 − presumably some time in the High Middle Ages − the vermiform extension of area 2 along the rivers Dubysa and Venta perhaps arising somewhat later.

The posited *e- > *a- merger was one of the last phonological innovations shared by the Slavic−Baltic dialect continuum. As it has been interpreted here, this was basically a Baltic (or Quasi-Baltic) change, spreading (or diffusing; cf. Andersen [1988]) across the now extinct Baltic dialects of Belarus, reaching parts of the Prussian, Latvian, and Lithuanian dialects to the northwest and north, and perhaps some Quasi-Slavic dialects to the south. But just as its extension in the north was greatly modified by the Latvian and Lithuanian colonization of the Baltic Northwest, so it may have come to be shared by the ancestral dialects of Slavic, already some centuries earlier, owing to an extensive − and intensive − contact situation, such as the one that may be responsible for the layers of Slavic and Baltic hydronyms in northern Ukraine. It is an interesting, open question whether this episode in the prehistory of Slavs and Balts can be linked to interaction with other ethnic groups in the period just preceding the beginning of the Slavic Migrations.

Chapter 5

Layers of innovation: Slavic, Slavic and Baltic, and Indo-European

The cardinal point in the preceding account of the Slavic−Baltic *e- > *a- merger − which actually served as our point of departure in the Introduction − is the chronological separation of this change from the other changes which affected word-initial vowels − especially the development of prothetic glides, which succeeded the *e- > *a- merger both in Slavic and Baltic, and from the substitution in early Old Russian of initial OR o- for Old Norse and Greek e-, which presupposes the prior development of prothetic glides.

In the past, scholars concerned with the problem of the Slavic *je- ‖ *o- variation have paid too little attention to questions of chronology, and as a consequence a variety of anlaut changes − some earlier, some later than the *e- > *a- merger − have tended to be projected onto the same prehistoric language state, the Proto-Slavic (actually Late Common Slavic, cf. section 9.1.3) reconstructed in the nineteenth century. In this way word-initial variation that developed a thousand or fifteen hundred years ago has often been considered on a par with variation resulting from the Indo-European ablaut changes, that is, variation that may easily be more than five thousand years old.

In this chapter I want to make explicit the chronological relations among a number of innovations that have affected word-initial vowels in Slavic and Baltic. I hope to make it clear that some of these changes, which in the past have been considered part and parcel of the Slavic *je- ‖ *o- problem, have nothing to do with it, since they are subsequent to it − though admittedly they have had the effect of obscuring the regular vowel correspondences somewhat, or of confusing the real issue (sections 5.1.1−5.1.4). I want to take a brief look at the Proto-Slavic lexemes with word-initial E- that became word-internal through the Common Slavic metathesis of liquid diphthongs (5.2). And I want to consider in some detail several cases of vowel-initial lexical doublets which reflect alternations in Proto-Indo-European. These have often in the past been set aside as irrelevant to the "*je- > *o- change", but they must − for reasons of methodological consistency — be included in the discussion of this change (sections 5.3.1–5.3.2). The confrontation of Proto-Slavic and Proto-Baltic with Proto-Indo-European which these doublets motivate makes it possible to define the extent to which Indo-European qualitative ablaut might be the source of Slavic and Baltic *e- ‖ *a- doublets. In addition, this confrontation finally leads to the identification of the earliest ascertainable layer of innovation affecting word-initial vowels in Slavic and Baltic, which was alluded to in the Introduction (section 5.3.3).

In this chapter there will be occasion to refer to the following layers of innovation which have determined word-initial vowel reflexes in Slavic:

(5.1) a. Proto-Indo-European apophony,
     b. Pre-Slavic and Pre-Baltic leveling of initial ablaut alternations,
     c. Pre-Slavic and Pre-Baltic vowel changes,
     d. Pre-Slavic and Pre-Baltic stem diversification,
     e. the Slavic and Baltic *e- > *a- merger,
     f. the Common Slavic metathesis of initial liquid diphthongs,
     g. the Common Slavic glide prothesis, and
     h. medieval Slavic changes in word-initial position.

While the last three of these layers are specifically Slavic, the first five layers are observable in both Baltic and Slavic.

5.1. Prothesis in Slavic

We begin with a few particulars concerning the Common Slavic prothesis and changes subsequent to it. Three of these (sections 5.1.1–5.1.3) concern the development of CS *e- and cannot be omitted from a full account of the results of the *e- > *a merger in Slavic: the *he-* reflexes of CS *e- in Lower Sorbian (section 5.1.1), the LCS *je- > e- change in Bulgarian and Macedonian (section 5.1.2), and the (partial) merger of LCS *je- and *ja- in several Slavic language areas (section 5.1.3). Section 5.1.4 examines the putative East Slavic change of *ju- > *u-, which has nothing to do with the topic of this study, but which has traditionally been thought to be part of, or parallel to, the "East Slavic *je- > *o- change" and hence cannot be ignored.

5.1.1. Lower Sorbian je- ‖ he-

Lower Sorbian has two sets of reflexes of CS *e-, the regular correspondences for LCS *je- (LS je-, ja-, jo-) and, in some lexemes, he-. Fortunatov had the impression that Lower Sorbian showed initial he- for LCS *je- in just those lexemes where he thought East Slavic developed o- by the "*je > *o- change"; cf. section 8.1.1. Jakobson, one of the many scholars who accepted this idea, acknowledged that there was at best a somewhat weak correlation: "where Russian has o- corresponding to PS je-, we find, *in some instances* in Lower Sorbian, a dialectal variant with he- beside je-" [emphasis added; my translation; HA] and cited the examples (a)–(c) in table 5.1 (1929 [1962]: 49).

Table 5.1. Lower Sorbian and Russian reflexes of PS E- (Ukrainian where noted)

	a	b	c	d	e	f	g	h	i
LS	jereb	jeleń	ješće	jemioł	jazor	jež	jaden	–	jelito
	hereb	heleń	hešće	hemioł	herjoł	–	–	–	–
R	–	–	ješčó	U jamelýna	–	Jéz'er-	jož	d. jed'in	–
	or'abok	ol'en'	o. oščó	om'elo	or'ól	óz'oro	o. oži	od'in	ol'itka

The additional information about these languages which has become available since that time shows a degree of diversity both in Lower Sorbian and in East Slavic that does not corroborate this putative correlation. It can safely be considered a mirage; see the examples in table 5.1. But the aberrant LS he- reflexes of CS *e- are still interesting for what they do show.

Lower Sorbian forms part of a large North Slavic area — encompassing Sorbian, Polish, Czech and Slovak, Ukrainian and Belarusian dialects — in which, long after the Common Slavic development of prothetic glides, a second wave of prothesis occurred in the High Middle Ages. It is not at all clear when the allophonic phase of this second wave began, but the prothetic consonants it gave rise to are neatly different in type from those of the first. The first (Common Slavic) wave of prothesis originated in an allophonic rule which assigned all word-initial vowels a raised, down-gliding beginning (as described in section 1.2), whence the subsequent susceptibility of initial vowels to be reanalysed with prothetic j- and w- (> v-). The allophonic rule responsible for this Common Slavic prothesis continued to motivate phonemic reinterpretations far into the separate histories of the individual Slavic languages. But in the second wave of prothesis, a different allophonic rule was established, productive until recently in many Slavic dialects, which assigned word-initial vowels a breath'd beginning — that is, phonation initiated from an open glottis position; this is articulatorily the contrary of the stopped beginning of initial vowels in Standard German (called *fester Einsatz*) and Standard Czech (the *ráz*). This new pronunciation rule formed the basis for the reinterpretation of word-initial vowel allophones as *h* + vowel, as seen in such examples as P d. *hapteka* (st. *apteka*) 'apothecary, pharmacy', *hameryka* 'America', *hulica* (st. *ulica*) 'street', *hiść* (st. *iść*) 'walk', LS *huzki* (P *uzki*) 'narrow', *hokno* (P *okno*) 'window', *hiś* (P *iść*) 'walk' — the prothetic *h*- being voiced in dialects in which phonemic /h/ is voiced [ɦ] (dialects of Belarusian, Ukrainian, Slovak, and Czech) and voiceless in dialects where /h/ is voiceless [h] (thus in Polish and Sorbian). The *h*-prothesis and other kinds of prothesis are discussed as sui generis types of diphthongization in Andersen (1972: 28−31).

The fact that Lower Sorbian has by-forms with both *je-* (*ja-*, *jo-*) and *he-* for CS **e-* shows that when the second wave of prothesis developed here, there existed a lexical *je-* ‖ *e-* diversity among Lower Sorbian dialects (and possibly even a lexical variation *je-* ~ *e-* in individual localities). The origin of these doublets is difficult to understand unless one takes them as evidence that this is an area in which at one time Slavic settlers with and without *j*-prothesis mingled — say, early settlers without prothesis before *e-* and newcomers in a later migration wave with prothetic *j-*. It is significant that all varieties of Lower Sorbian have *j-* in lexemes with CS **je-* (e. g., *jabnuś, jébaś* 'copulate with' [43], *jogo, jomu* 'him, it; gen., dat.' [39−41]). The simplest explanation for these data is that in the speech of the early Lower Sorbian settlers the received (CS) **e-* : **je-* distinction was intact, whereas later immigrants had LCS **je-* for both initials.

This interpretation of the origin of the *je-* and *he-* doublets agrees with what is known about the settlement history of the Sorbian areas. The Sorbs appear here around 600, entering from Bohemia through the Elbe River Gorge to settle the watershed of the Ore Mountains (*Erzgebirge*) between the Saale and the Bobr rivers. Lower Sorbian becomes differentiated from Upper Sorbian in part through continued immigration into Upper Lusatia from Bohemia, in part thanks to an admixture or an overlay of Lechitic linguistic features in Lower Lusatia, brought into the lowlands by an entirely different flow of (Lechitic-speaking) settlers coming from the north and northeast, that is, from areas that are now part of Poland; see the map, figure 5.1 (cf. Schuster-Šewc [1987]). If the earliest

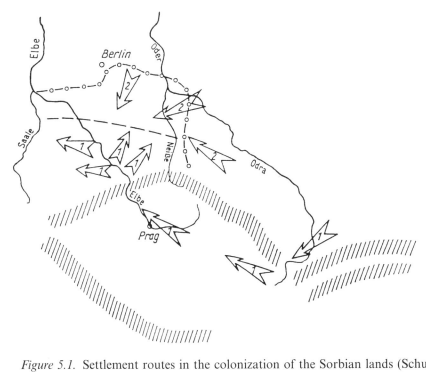

Figure 5.1. Settlement routes in the colonization of the Sorbian lands (Schuster-
Šewc 1987: 158)
  1. —o—o—o Maximal extent of the Upper Sorbian language area
     (LCS *ǫ > *ų > u).
  2. — — — Boundary between Upper and Lower Sorbian dialect
     types.
  3. ⟨⟨1 Settlement routes of Upper Sorbian tribes.
  4. ⟨⟨2 Settlement routes of Lechitic tribes.
  5. ///////// Mountain ranges.

Sorbian settlers had no prothesis before CS *e-, continued immigration
from Bohemia into the Sorbian uplands may have introduced more ad-
vanced varieties of Common Slavic and stimulated the regular development of *j*-prothesis characteristic of Upper Sorbian (together with other
features shared with Czech). By contrast, the original Sorbian dialects
and the Lechitic settler dialects in Lower Lusatia may very well have
presented the clear-cut distinction between the absence of prothesis and
the fully developed, phonemic *j*-prothesis before CS *e-, which the existence of the modern by-forms would lead one to hypothesize.
     The Sorbian data are interesting because, in this interpretation, they
illustrate how innovations that arose in central parts of the Slavic world

may have been in part diffused, in part transported to peripheral areas (cf. section 9.2). Note also that the interpretation the Lower Sorbian *je* ‖ *he-* doublets suggest involves a dialect contact situation identical in type to the one that has been hypothesized in this investigation to account for the **je-* ‖ **o-* doublets.

Most interestingly, perhaps, this interpretation of the Lower Sorbian data implies a dating of the development of prothesis before CS **e* which agrees well with other inferences we can make. In section 1.2 it was surmised that the reinterpretation of allophonic protheses as initial glide phonemes may have been favored by the qualitative differentiation of long and short vowels in the Second Common Slavic Vowel Shift (the transition from CS-II to CS-III). If it is true that dialects with and dialects without prothesis were in contact in the Lower Sorbian area in the 600s or soon thereafter, the attested movements of Slavic populations in this area define a *terminus ante quem* for the development of phonemic prothesis before CS **e-* in at least some (nonperipheral) Slavic dialects. This is quite compatible with the fact that phonetic prothesis must have been established (as a general allophonic rule) before the change of CS-I **ū-* > CS-II **vȳ-*, which can be dated loosely to the period before AD 500 (cf. Shevelov 1965: 246).

In considering this hypothetical confrontation between Common Slavic dialects with and without prothesis before CS **e-* in the period of Slavic expansion, it is well to remember that there is other evidence of diversity in the development of prothesis, which may have been a function of dialect differences in the realization of vowels. For instance, there are stray examples in different Slavic languages of lexemes with prothetic **v-* before PS A- and Ā- (CS-I **a-* and **ā-*), e. g., LCS **voňa* 'smell' beside **ǫxati* 'to smell' (PS AN-IĀ, ĀN-XĀ-TĒI, PIE **h₂enh₁-* 'breathe'), LCS d. **vajĭce* beside **jajĭce* 'egg' (PS ĀIA-, PIE **oh̯uih̯ₓóm*; so Rasmussen [1989: 72]). Such examples are quite plausible evidence that when the general development of prothetic glides occurred, some Common Slavic dialects, probably a minority, pronounced the low back vowels (CS-I **a* and **ā*) with labialization, say [ɒ] and [ɒ:], while the majority dialects, presumably, had nonlabialized realizations until the qualitative differentiation (in CS-II) to the [ɒ] and [æ:] which is presupposed for their development in initial position to LCS **o-* and **ja-*. In a contact situation, speakers of the latter dialects would interpret initial [ǫɒ] and [ǫɒ:] as CS **wa-* and **wā* (> LCS **vo-*, **va-*); cf. Shevelov (1965: 245).

Particulars such as these leave no doubt that the beginnings of prothesis at least in some Slavic areas antedated or, at the latest, were contemporary with the territorial expansion of Slavic. And they support the general view adopted here, that in the formation of the relatively uniform post-Migration Common Slavic, possibly numerous differences among the ante-Migration dialects of Common Slavic were leveled out.

5.1.2. Old Church Slavonic « je- » and « e- »

Fortunatov had the impression that the occurrence in some Old Church Slavonic texts of spelling variants with word-initial (Cyrillic) « je » and « e » formed a parallel to the Late Common Slavic *je- ‖ *o- correspondences. Thus for the usual OCS « jeda, jelenĭ, jese, jeterŭ, jezero » the *Suprasliensis* text has « eda, elenĭ, ese, eterŭ, ezero » 'when, deer, lo, some, lake'; cf. Fortunatov ([1919]: 280−281). Jakobson accepted this putative correlation and integrated it into his account of the hypothetical change of initial LCS *je- > e- (> East Slavic o-), though acknowledging that the attestation actually shows no exact parallelism (1929 [1962]: 48−49). What it shows, rather, is that at the time these texts were written, there was a development in progress in the Bulgaro-Macedonian speech area, in which results of the Common Slavic prothesis were lost, and word-initial *je-* (representing both CS *e- and *je-) changed to e-, as the modern dialects of these languages attest.

Some scholars have tried to explain this loss of prothetic *j-* by claiming that the prothesis was optional when it arose and was not phonemic; thus Bernštejn (1961: 186). But this interpretation overlooks the fact that the development did include a phonemic merger of CS *e- and *je-. It seems better to acknowledge (as Jakobson did [1929 (1962): 48−49]) that the extant ancient and modern attestation is compatible with several distinct interpretations. Here are the basic ones, labeled (i) through (iii).

(i) Optional prothesis develops before CS *e-. The variation [e-] ~ [i̯e-] for e- is then extended to word forms with CS *je- (which is tantamount to a reinterpretation of *je* as *e-). Then the variation is lost in favor of the [e-] allophone, leaving word-initial *e-* [e-] as the reflex of both CS *e- and *je-. This account is a more explicit version of Bernštejn's.

(ii) Prothesis develops before CS *e-. Word-initial *e-* [i̯e] is reinterpreted as *je-* (identical to the reflex of CS *je-). This phonemic distinction gone, word-initial [i̯e] is reinterpreted as a word-initial allophone of *e.* Then the allophonic variation "[i̯e] word-initially, [e] elsewhere" is lost, the allophone [e-] being generalized. This account is close to Jakobson's, which views "the loss of *j-* before *e-* in Bulgarian as a natural process of phoneme unification" (1929 [1962]: 49) [my translation; HA].

(iii) Prothesis develops before CS *e-. Word-initial e- [ie] is reinterpreted as *je-* (identical to the reflex of CS *je-). Subsequently an initial distinction *e-* : *je-* arises through the introduction of neologisms with *e-* (including borrowings from other dialects and languages). This development possibly occurred in some varieties of Eastern Bulgarian that now have *je-* for both CS *e- and *je-, but also instances of *e-* in both native Slavic words and in foreign borrowings.

Development (iii) resembles that in other Slavic languages the most. Russian, for instance, has regular *je-* (*jo-*) for CS *e- and *je-, beside *e-* in native neologisms as well as in borrowings. But very similar outcomes could have eventuated in dialects where either of the two developments (i) and (ii) occurred, for the initial outcomes in these places must have been equally subject to later modification through the creation of neologisms and the codification of borrowings.

In any case, contrary to earlier surmises, there is nothing in the data of either older or more recent stages of Bulgaro-Macedonian that suggests any connection between the Slavic−Baltic *e- > *a- merger and the loss of initial *j-* before *e*, which occurred here centuries after the Slavic settlement of the Balkan Peninsula.

5.1.3. LCS *je- > ja-

Jakobson, who accepted Fortunatov's tenuous correlations between East Slavic *o-*, LS *he-*, and OCS *e-* for LCS *je-, observed that in Slovak and eastern Czech dialects there are examples of *ja-* for LCS *je- in some of the same lexemes where Russian has *o-*. Accordingly Jakobson postulated the diachronic correspondences LCS *je- > Sk. *je-* for the lexemes in

Table 5.2. Slovak and Russian reflexes of PS E-

(a)	Sk.	*jedl'a*	*jest*	*jež*	*jebat'*	*jeho*	*jej*	
	R	*jél'*	*jest'*	*jož*	*jebát'*	*jevó*	*jéj*	

(b)	Sk. d.	*jaseň*	*jazer*	*jarab*	*jarábok*	*jarabý*	*jarabina*	*jalito*	*jaleň*
	R	*ós'en'*	*óz'oro*		*ór'abok*			*ol'ítka*	*ol'én'*

table 5.2 (a), but LCS *je- > Sk. (d.) *ja-* for those in table 5.2 (b), noting that the correspondences between West Slavic and East Slavic might at an earlier time have included Czech, where subsequent vowel fronting (umlaut, Cz. *přehláska* of *ja-* > *je-*) made attested *je-* forms ambiguous.

This supposed correlation is not corroborated by a wider body of data. There are in fact fairly numerous doublets with *je-* and *ja-* not only in

Slovak—Czech, but in West Slavic and Western South Slavic in general, and not only there; cf. (5.2 b). Besides the *ja-* variants corresponding to the East Slavic *o-* variants cited in table 5.2 (b) there are such *ja-* variants as those under (5.2 a) (for further details, see chapter 7).

(5.2) a. LCS **jedlĭ* [4]: U *jalýna*
        LCS **jelĭčĭ* [19]: P d. *jalec*, Ka.-Sc. *jolc*; LS *jalc*, *jalica*; Sk. *jalec*, Cz. d. *jalec*; SC d. *jálac*, *jal*; Br. *jál'ec*, U *jaléc'*
    b. LCS **jedinŭ* [1]: P o., d. *jaden*, Pb. *jadån*, LS *jaden*
        LCS **jelito* [10]: P d. *jalito*; Sk. d. *jalito*; SC *jalito*; U *jalytý*
        LCS **jelĭxa* [13]: Sk. d. *jalcha*, *jalša*, Sn. d. *jálša*, top. *Jalševnica*, SC kaj-d. *jälša*, *jaha*
        LCS **jemelo* [18]: P d. *jamioła*, Ka. *jamèlna*; LS *jamola*; Sk. d. *jamelo*, *jamola*, *jemalo*, Cz. d. *jameł*, *jamela*
        LCS **jerębĭ* [20—21]: P *jarząb*, *jarzębina*, Ka. *jarzbina*; LS d. *jařebina*; Sk. *jarabina*, Cz. d. *jařabina*, *jeřabina*; SC *jarèbica*, *jarebina*; R o. *jaräbĭ*, Br. *jarab'ina*
        LZS **jesenĭ* [28]: P o. *jasień*, Sk. W-d. *jaseň*, Sn. d. *jasen*, Bg. d. *jasen*
        LCS **jesetrŭ* [31]: P o. *jasiotr*, Ka.-Sc. *jasoter*, US *jasotr*; U d. *jasétr*
        LCS **jezero* [35]: LS *jazor*; Sk. *jazero*, U SW-d. *jázer*

It is certain that reflexes of LCS **je-* and **ja-* have merged, by regular or sporadic sound change, at several points in the development of Common Slavic and its successor dialects. Shevelov posits a single, early partial merger of LCS **je-* and **ja-* and subsequent competition among the resulting doublets, "certain languages still not having a fixed form for certain words even today" (1965: 177). But the situation is in fact rather less clear-cut, for there have been changes both of *je-* > *ja-* and of *ja* > *je-* in several Slavic dialect areas since the Common Slavic period; for Polish, cf. Taszycki (1961), for Slovak, cf. Pauliny (1963: 66), for Ukrainian, cf. Shevelov (1979: 159).

The results of these local changes is that in some Slavic dialects both modern *je-* and *ja-* represent CS **e-*, **ē-*, and **ā-* (and **je-*, **jē-*, **jā-*; cf. Shevelov [1965: 176—178]). In practical terms this means that the language historian has a peculiar choice. He can let this irregularity stand in the way of reconstructing unique original forms; for example, taken at face value, (i) P *jezioro*, (ii) Sk. *jazero*, and (iii) R *oz'oro* point to CS (i) **e-* or **ē-*, (ii) **e-* or **ē-* or **ā*, and (iii) **a-*, respectively. Or, alternatively, he can recognize this irregularity as the result of changes occurring at different times, and analyse it so as to reconstruct unique original forms; e. g., P *jezioro*, Sk. *jazero* and R *óz'oro* are all compatible with CS **e-*; cf. figure 5.2.

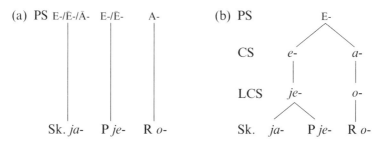

Figure 5.2. Indeterminacies in the correspondences among P *jezioro*, Sk. *jazero*, R *oz'oro*

The latter alternative is the way initial *ja-* is viewed in this study: unless there is comparative evidence that a local or regional initial *ja-* represents PS Ē- or Ā- (or IĒ- or IĀ-), such a *ja-* is assumed to be a secondarily modified reflex of PS E-. An example requiring such consideration is the word for 'ash (Fraxinus)', whose modern reflexes in the Slavic languages point to LCS **jasenŭ*, **jesenŭ*, **osenŭ* [27]. The Baltic correspondences (e. g., Li. *úosis* 'ash') show that it is realistic to posit a LCS **jasenŭ* (and PS ĀSENA- beside ESENA-), and this forces us to grapple with the ambiguity of the modern **ja-* reflexes. The simple derivation in figure 5.3 (a) cannot in principle be ruled out, but the fact that modern *ja-* reflexes occur in Russian (*jás'en'*) and Belarusian (*jás'en'*), where stressed *já-* for LCS **je-* is otherwise unattested, speaks against derivation (a) and for derivation (b) and the even more realistic (c) in figure 5.3; see further chapter 7, s. v.

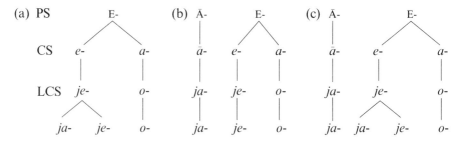

Figure 5.3. Indeterminacies in the correspondences among LCS **jasenŭ*, **jesenŭ*, **osenŭ* 'ash'

5.1.4. Excursus: LCS *ju- > OR u

The East Slavic languages have initial *u-* where the other Slavic languages show reflexes of LCS **ju-* for PS IAU-, IEU-, EU-, e. g., OR *ugŭ* (PS IAUGA-) 'south', *unŭ* (PS IAU-NA-) 'young', *uxa* (PS IEUXĀ-) 'fish soup', as well as in borrowings – appellatives (e. g., OR *upatŭ* 'ruler', *upostasĭ* 'substance', cf. Gk. *hupatós, hupóstasis*) and propria (e. g., OR *Ustinŭ, Uvenalijĭ, Ulĭjanŭ*, via Greek from Lat. *Justinus, Juvenalis, Julianus*). To account for these data, Slavists have proceeded the same way as with the "East Slavic **je- > *o-* change": OR *u-* for foreign *ju-* has been taken as evidence for a **ju- > *u-* change contemporary with and in some way parallel to the "**je- > *o-* change". However, unlike the supposed loss of initial **j-* before *e*, the putative parallel loss of **j-* before *u* appears to be statable without phonological limitations.

But just as the idea of the "East Slavic **je- > *o-* change" was based on a misunderstanding, so was that of the "**ju- > *u-* change": the borrowings with OR *u-* for foreign **ju-* do not necessarily indicate a sound change occurring in the late 800s, after their adoption; they may merely reflect the existence of a phonological constraint, productive at the time of borrowing, which ruled out the word-initial sequence *ju-*.

The question how this sequential constraint came into being has not been seriously addressed. Šaxmatov posited a sequence of phonetic alterations to account for it: CS **ju-* [i̯ü-] > Common Russian [i̯u̇-] > [u̇-] > [u-] – the crucial loss of the initial *j-* [i̯] being explained (that is, classified) as an assimilation ([1915: 142]; his [ü] and [u̇] equal IPA [y] and [ʉ]). But in conformity with the standard Neogrammarian approach, Šaxmatov's concern was limited to the phonetic plausibility of this development and did not include the question of phonological motivation. Jakobson and later specialists in comparative phonology have accepted the diachronic correspondence LCS **ju- > OR *u-* as the phonological gist of this account without explaining, or even wondering, why *j-* would be lost before *u* (cf. Jakobson 1929 [1962]: 45; Vaillant 1950: 184; Shevelov 1965: 241–242, 1979: 162; Lamprecht 1987: 36).

The essential elements in an account of this change are three. First, it must be noted that after the change of CS-I **ū- > vȳ-* (cf. section 1.2), the eastern dialects of Common Slavic did not develop phonemic prothesis before the high tense vowels *i-* and *u-*. There is no explanation for this other than the fact that high vowels are generally less susceptible to phonemic prothesis than non-high vowels, as we noted in sections 2.1 and 2.2. Thus, Old Russian has no trace of prothesis before *u-*, whether from PS IAU-, IEU-,

EU- (where the other Slavic languages have reflexes of LCS *ju-) or from PS AU-. True, there are some modern East Slavic dialects, particularly Belarusian and Ukrainian, that do have prothesis before reflexes of OR *u-* (e. g., U *vúlyc'a* 'street', d. *júlyc'a, húlyc'a* < LCS *ulica, PS AUL-Ī-), but this is a result of more recent developments (dated to the 1300—1500s; cf. Shevelov [1979: 458]). Nor is there any trace of prothesis before OR *i-*, whether from PS IAI-, IŪ-, EI-, or Ī-; cf. (5.3).

(5.3)   OR *ixŭ* 'them; gen.-loc.pl.' (PS I-AIXU), *irijĭ* 'the south; where the birds winter' (PS IŪRIIA-; cf. Li. *jūros* 'sea'), *ili* 'or' (PS EI LAI), *inŭ* 'one, other' (PS EIN-A- 'one'), ChSl. *iva* 'willow' (PS ĒIUĀ-) — U *jíx* 'them', *íryj*, d. *ýrij* 'the warm countries', *inšyj*, d. *ýnšyj* 'other', *iva*, d. *ýva* 'willow'

The implied loss of the distinction between LCS *ji-* (for PS IAI-, IŪ-) and *i-* (for PS EI-, Ī-) must have occurred in a manner analogous to either account (i) or (ii) in section 5.2. We return to this after the next paragraph.

Secondly, it must be assumed that at the time of the Common Slavic umlaut, when all back vowels were fronted after palatals (including the reflexes of the so-called Third Velar Palatalization), all instances of CS-III *ū* (< PS IAU, IEU, EU, AU) were realized as [ü] after a palatal — that is, the word-initial distinction CS-III *ju- : *u-* was realized as [jü] : [u], and in word-internal environments [ü] (for PS IAU, IEU, EU) and [u] (for PS AU) were in complementary distribution.

Thirdly, at the same time as initial [ii] and [i] were interpreted as optionally prothesized realizations of *i* — assuming a development like account (i) in section 5.2 — initial [jü-] must have admitted of two interpretations. It could be interpreted as *j-* followed by the fronted allophone of *u* — which appears to be the interpretation assigned in western and southern dialects of Common Slavic, judging by the *ju-* reflexes in the modern West and South Slavic languages. Or it could be interpreted as the word-initial allophone of a rounded front vowel *ü*, distinct from the rounded back vowel *u* only in word-initial position.

(Note that the reinterpretation of [ii] ~ [i] as *i* must have implied the formation of a pronunciation rule deleting underlying *j-* before *i* in forms of the anaphoric (and relative) pronoun: when [ii] was reinterpreted as *i-* in, say OR *irijĭ* 'the sea' (PS IŪRIIA-), it remained phonemically bisegmental in *j-ix* [ix], *j-im* [im], *j-imi* [imi] 'them; gen.loc.pl., dat.pl., inst.pl.' — as it is to the present day in many East Slavic dialects. In some dialects the pronunciation was subsequently adjusted to conform to the underlying representation; thus in the Old Moscow norm and in Standard Ukrainian. Similarly, when initial [i̯ü] was reinterpreted as *u-*, it would remain bisegmental in *j-u* 'her; acc.sg.f.'.)

Now, if we suppose that this monosegmental *ü* was the interpretation assigned to word-initial [i̯ü] in the early East Slavic dialects, it is not difficult to understand why a phonemic distinction *ü : u* limited to word-initial position in a small number of lexemes would fall by the wayside, especially considering the social context of intensive contact with other languages which is known to have existed during the period when Slavic speech was spreading across the modern-day East Slavic language areas. It is harder to come by solid evidence of this reinterpretation of word-initial [i̯ü] as *ü*. The fact that Old Russian responds to Greek *ü* with *u* (e. g., OR *upostasĩ* for Gk. *hupóstasis* 'substance') is of no value as evidence, for even if this response was based directly on Greek pronunciation, which is not certain, there is no way to tell whether it would be due to a native Slavic merger of *ü > u* or to a substitution of *u* for foreign *ü*. Early spellings with Cyrillic «ju-», which occur beside « u-» for both LCS *ju-* and foreign *ju-*, are in principle ambiguous between a hypothetical conservative, vernacular *ü-* and Church Slavonic *ju-*. But whatever the phonological value of these spellings in the earliest Old Russian, there is no doubt that in the long run (in Shevelov's opinion, from the 1170s on; cf. [1979: 163]) such spellings represent phonemic *ju-*, in both Slavonic and foreign borrowings.

What one needs, ideally, in order to demonstrate the existence of an East Slavic word-initial [ü-] in earlier forms of such lexemes as OR *ugŭ* 'south', *unŭ* 'young', *uxa* 'fish soup', *uže* 'already' is East Slavic borrowings — with word-initial *ü* — into a language distinguishing word-initial *ü-* from *i-* and *u-*, and from *jü-* and *ju-*. Finnish is such a language. And so it is relevant to point out, for whatever it is worth, that there is in fact a Finnish borrowing with *ü-* corresponding to OR, ChSl., R «ju-».

The man's name Gk. *Geōrgios* appears in Old Russian sources variously with syllable-initial obstruent letters — « gjurgii» (Hypatian Chronicle, s. a. 1157), «djurdi» Hypatian Chronicle, s. a. 1135 — and without, «jurii» (Hypatian Chronicle, s. a. 1172); it does not seem to be attested anywhere with « u-» (cf. Shevelov 1979: 163). The spelling variant «jurii» eventually prevails in the East Slavic languages, correlated with a phonemic shape with initial *ju-* (just as the Church Slavonic borrowings R *jug* 'south', *junyj* 'young', etc.), e. g., R N-d. *Jur'ej* 'nom.', oblique stem as in *Jur'j-a* 'acc.gen.' (seemingly presupposing OR *Jŭrĭj-ĭ, Jŭrĭj-a*). But according to the hypothesis developed here, the name may have had the shape OR *Ürĭj-ĭ, Ürĭj-a* with initial [ü-].

This popular (saint's) name, which one would expect to have been diffused early along the trade route through Russia between Scandinavia and Greece, is attested in Finnish in a variety of shapes, borrowed from different sources and at different times. Some variants are of Germanic provenience, thus *Jurva* (with -*v*- < -*g*-) from Old Saxon *Jurgen*, and *Jyrki, Jyrin* (with -*k*- ~ Ø) from OSw. *Jörgen*; cf. Nissilä (1975) and Kiviniemi (1982). Other variants are of East Slavic origin, thus the recent *Juri, Jurkka, Jurkko*, which are clearly from Mod. R *Jurij*, also OFi. *Orja*, which may be an old adaptation of an East Slavic form with [u-], and finally the apparently oldest, most widely used, and most firmly established variant, *Yrjö*. Its initial *ü*- cannot be explained within the history of Finnish as having anything but an original initial [ü-]; it cannot go back to **jü*- or **ju*-. It makes perfect sense to suppose that it is an early borrowing from East Slavic and to take it, at least tentatively, as an indication that East Slavic dialects simplified initial [i̯ü-] to [ü-].

Let us now return to Šaxmatov's hypothesis regarding the phonetic development behind the LCS **ju*- > OR *u*- correspondence − Common Russian [i̯ù] > [ù] > [u] (1915: 142), mentioned above. The account I have offered here views the first step in this phonetic development as a loss of prothesis based on a reinterpretation of *ju*- as *ü*-, parallel (in all but phonemic terms) to the East Slavic identification of LCS **ji*- with **i*-, and thus part of a general loss of prothesis before initial vowels. My account views the second step as a separately motivated merger of *ü*- with *u*-. Admittedly there is not much evidence for the intermediate stage *ü*-, but even if there were no evidence for it, it would still make good sense to construe the diachronic correspondence LCS **ju*- > OR *u*- as the result of two separately motivated phonological changes − (i) [i̯ü-] reinterpreted as /ü/ and (ii) the distinction /ü/ : /u/ merged in /u/, rather than as the single unmotivated change (/ju-/ > /u-/) the handbook tradition has contented itself with.

5.2. PS E- in liquid diphthongs

The set of Proto-Baltic lexemes reconstructed with initial PB E- in chapter 4 (table 4.1) includes two items whose Slavic counterparts are missing from the corresponding list of Proto-Slavic lexemes (table 1.1), PB ELKŪNĒ- 'elbow' [14] and ĒLNI- 'deer' [15]. The reason for this is not so much the fact that their Slavic correspondents underwent the regular metathesis of initial liquid diphthongs and hence no longer have initial vowels in Slavic. More importantly, both are reconstructed with initial PS A-. The modern forms all point to PS ALKUTI- 'elbow' and ĀLNI- 'doe' via LCS N-d. *lokŭtĭ, *lanĭ, S-d. *lakŭtĭ, *lanĭ – with the regular reflexes of the Common Slavic distinction in quantity in northern Common Slavic (*lo- versus *la-), which was lost in southern Common Slavic (South Slavic and Central Slovak) prior to the metathesis.

These lexemes raise two questions: first, is the Proto-Slavic initial back vowel we reconstruct in these lexemes perhaps really an earlier *e- which has gone through the Slavic−Baltic *e- > *a- merger? And secondly, are there other Slavic lexemes with PS EL- diphthongs (but lacking Baltic correspondents) which were subject to the merger?

As for the second question, there are two other lexemes which can be considered in this connection, PS ELBEDĀ- 'goosefoot (Atriplex)' [7] and PS ELBEDI- 'swan' [8]. PS ELBEDĀ- has reflexes that might be due to the *e- > *a- merger (e. g., LCS d. *loboda), but PS ELBEDI- (LCS d. *lebedĭ) does not. This might mean merely that PS ELBEDI- is one of the small number of lexemes that were unaffected by the *e- > *a- merger (cf. example [1.1] and section 3.8). However, both these lexemes have variant forms which may have alternative sources. They require rather detailed discussion, which is best left for chapter 7.

The question of the origin of the initial back vowel in PS ALKUTI- and ĀLNI- is a little difficult to answer. Neither lexeme gives evidence of any *e- ‖ *a- diversity within Slavic. Hence it is possible that their solid back-vowel reflexes are results of the *e- > *a- merger. But it is also possible that they had CS *a- at the time of the merger, that is, that there was an inherited difference between Slavic A-, Ā- and Baltic E-, Ē- in these words. A number of lexemes with such older differences in initial vocalism will be discussed in section 5.3.3.

There are two lexemes with PS ER- diphthongs among the lexemes examined in chapter 7, PS ERKXI- 'thistle' [24] and ERIMBI- ‖ ĒRB- 'grouse; rowan berries' [20−21]. Both of them have reflexes showing metathesis to LCS *rě- (e. g., Sn. rešek 'thistle', U riba 'rowan berries'). Neither provides evidence of the *e- > *a- merger.

5.3. Proto-Slavic and Proto-Baltic by-forms

In addition to the doublets arising from the partial merger of CS *e- and *a-, there are a number of lexemes both in the Slavic and in the Baltic languages with vowel-initial by-forms of other origins.

One somewhat extreme example is the word for 'mistletoe', whose modern Slavic variants superficially appear to represent LCS *jĭmelo, *jemelo, *jamelo*, and *omelo* [18]. Previous investigators have simply projected this diversity back into Proto-Slavic and Proto-Indo-European, but surely such a plethora of forms raises the question of how old the individual by-forms are. They can actually reflect both changes subsequent to the *e-* > *a-* merger and prior to it — in Slavic prehistory and in the Pre-Slavic period. Theoretically some of them can go back to the time when Indo-European ablaut developed, but in fact there is no necessity to suppose that any of them do.

At the other end of the spectrum are such apparent examples of the *e-* > *a-* merger as LCS *jesenĭ* ‖ *osenĭ* 'autumn' (and OPr. *Assanis* 'autumn') [28], which may be reconstructed simply as PS, PB ESENI-, as in figure 5.4 (a), but might also be viewed as a pair of inherited ablaut alternants, PS ESENI- (< PIE *$h_1$es-en-*) ‖ PS (?), PB ASENI- (< PIE *$h_1$os-en-*). The former would match the *e*-grade of the ancient Indo-European borrowing in Finnic, Fi. *kesä* 'autumn'; the latter, the *o-grade* of Gk. *opŏra* 'harvest, autumn' (< *op-os-ar-a*); cf. chapter 7, s. v. Now, if LCS *jesenĭ*, *osenĭ* really reflect Indo-European ablaut variants, then this pair may have developed by one of two routes depicted in figure 5.4 as (b) and (c), that is, either all *o-* forms go back to PIE *h_1o-*, or some go back to *h_1e-* and some to *h_1o-*.

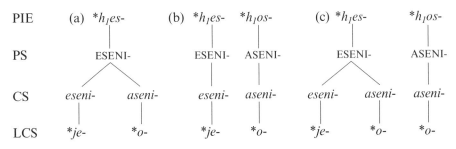

Figure 5.4. Alternative derivations of LCS *jesenĭ*, *osenĭ* 'autumn'

Instances such as this raise the basic question any lexeme with Common Slavic and/or Baltic *e-* ‖ *a-* doublets actually poses: should such doublets be taken as evidence simply of the *e-* > *a-* merger, or do they perhaps antedate the merger? Before we discuss this question in general, we will look at some different examples of word-initial variation.

5.3.1. Kinds of word-initial variation

Several of the lexemes that have CS *e-* ‖ *a-* doublets have one (or more than one) additional variant with a different initial (or different initials).

Previous scholarship has tended to treat these lexemes inconsistently, viewing some of them as examples of the "East Slavic *je- > *o- change", but others as instances of Indo-European ablaut and hence an entirely different story. There are several reasons for this inconsistency, the main one being some traditional ideas about the nature of the supposed "*je- > *o- change", which will be discussed in section 8.1.2.

My view is that any Proto-Slavic or Proto-Baltic word form with initial E-, whether this was an invariant initial, or it was one of several by-forms, was liable to be affected by the Slavic−Baltic *e- > *a- merger; cf. figure 5.4 (a) and (c). This view of the lexemes with a possible "pre-existing" initial variation imposes a chronological hierarchy on any set of multiple by-forms and entails that a clear distinction must be made between those parts of the attestation that are relevant to the Slavic−Baltic *e- > *a- merger and those that are not, though it is not denied that some cases may be indeterminate.

This view is equally applicable to three classes of *e- ‖ *a- doublets, which I will illustrate with Slavic examples in the following: (a) lexemes with initial reflexes of Proto-Indo-European ablaut, (b) lexemes with initial variation innovated within Slavic, and (c) lexemes with initial variation of unknown origin.

(a) In the case of, for instance, LCS *$jesenŭ$ ‖ *$osenŭ$ ‖ *$jasenŭ$ 'ash (Fraxinus)' [27], some previous investigators have treated all the attested by-forms on an equal footing and posited (the equivalents of) Proto-Slavic forms with E-, A-, and Ā- (see Popowska-Taborska 1984: 28−29), thus eliminating the lexeme from the discussion of the "*je- > *o- change". Leaving aside for the moment the non-Slavic cognates of this lexeme, which provide crucial information about its original (Proto-Indo-European) shape (see section 5.3.2), its attestation in the Slavic languages offers us a choice among the following assumptions: (i) that none of the by-forms with LCS *o- originated in the *e- > *a- merger (cf. figure 5.5 [a]) − which is the ingenuous approach just mentioned; or (ii) that just some of them did (figure 5.5 [b]); or (iii) that all of them did (figure 5.5 [c]). In cases such as this I choose the last of these three equally rational assumptions − and posit only PS ESENA- ‖ ĀSENA- − because (i) Occam teaches us not to posit more proto-forms than we need, and (ii) because I have no Slavic or Baltic evidence suggesting that we need more than two, and (iii) because, given the *e- > *a- merger, a reconstructed PS ESENA- can explicate the attested forms with CS *e- and *a-, but a PS ASENA- would not do; see further section 5.3.2. Mutatis mutandis, a similar interpretation is called for by the somewhat more complex LCS

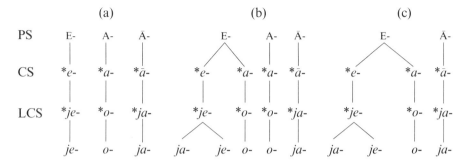

Figure 5.5. Alternative derivations of LCS *jasenŭ, *jesenŭ, *osenŭ 'ash'

*jerębĭ ‖ *orębĭ, etc. 'grouse' [20–21] (cf. chapter 7, s. v.), as well as by the simpler LCS *jesenĭ ‖ *osenĭ [28], which was just discussed in section 5.3.

(b) Whereas neither of the by-forms PS ESENA- and ĀSENA- can be derived from the other within Slavic, and hence both must be posited for the protolexicon, in other instances the relation between Common Slavic by-forms suggests that a single protoform is sufficient. This is the case with LCS *jemĕš- ‖ *omĕš- ‖ *lemĕš- 'coulter, plowshare' [44]. Here it looks as if the initial *l- has been lost from a PS LEMĒXIA-. (There are good reasons for ruling out the alternative, that the *l- was added to a PS EMĒXIA-.) Obviously, this loss is not a regular sound change, but it is a sufficiently plausible ad hoc alteration that there appears to be no need for more than one protoform; see figure 5.6 (a) and chapter 7, s. v.

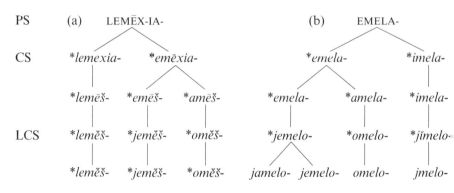

Figure 5.6. PS LEMĒXIA- 'coulter' and EMELA- 'mistletoe'

(c) Some cases are indeterminate and may be interpreted as inherited doublets or as doublets that have developed within Slavic. LCS *jĭmelo ‖

jemelo ‖ *jamelo* ‖ *omelo* 'mistletoe' [18], which was mentioned above, allows of numerous interpretations. If one takes a consistent, purely phonological approach to these variants, one can construct a derivation analogous to figure 5.5 (c), positing PS EMELA- (> LCS *jamelo*, *jemelo*, *omelo*) and PS IMELA- (> LCS *jĭmelo*). However, if LCS *jĭmelo* is the result of a non-phonological innovation (a popular etymology) in the prehistory of Slavic, as I suggest in chapter 7 (s. v.), then all the attested forms can be derived from a PS EMELA-, as in figure 5.6 (b).

There is an obvious similarity between the principle of economy of reconstruction that has been sketched here and the free-ride principle in synchronic phonology. But in linguistic reconstruction, the conformity of this principle to Occam's rule is not simply a matter of simplicity of description. It is an empirical principle, which is motivated by the consideration that the fewer proto-forms we posit to account for a given set of attested forms, the more vulnerable to invalidation our hypothesis will be, and the sooner we will discover it if the hypothesis is wrong.

In historical linguistics this principle corresponds to the generalization that attested diversity among daughter languages is more often due to secondary innovation than to original inheritance. When we reconstruct, therefore, it is reasonable to assume that observed differences among daughter languages are more likely to reflect divergent innovations than inherited diversity. In reality, of course, actual historical developments are of all kinds and take their course without necessarily confirming the generalizations we make from our past experience. But in reconstruction, when there is no evidence to justify the contrary, Occam should rule.

5.3.2. Inherited E- ‖ A- doublets: PIE $*h_1e$- ~ $*h_1o$-

I acknowledged in section 5.3. that every pair of *$*e$-* ‖ *$*a$-* by-forms raises the question whether its *$*a$-* variant is simply a result of the *$*e$-* > *$*a$-* merger, or the origin of the doublets antedates the *$*e$-* > *$*a$-* merger. This question is difficult to answer, for there are in fact several possible sources of "pre-existing" E- ‖ A- doublets in Slavic and Baltic.

The first of these is qualitative ablaut in inherited Indo-European lexemes beginning with PIE *$*e$-* (*$*h_1e$-*), such as the possible PS ESENI- ‖ ASENI- 'autumn' (< PIE *$*h_1es$-*, *$*h_1os$-*) just mentioned in section 5.3.1. Other inherited lexemes which in other Indo-European languages appear to begin with *$*e$-* (*$*h_1e$-*), and which may have had qualitative ablaut, are listed in (5.4); see the individual items in chapter 7. The reason for the uncertainty regarding these lexemes is the possibility that some Pre-Slavic dialects have generalized an *e*-grade alternant, others an *o*-grade alternant of the same lexeme.

(5.4) a. LCS *jedlĭ, Li. ẽglė, PS EDLI-, PB EDLĒ- 'spruce' [4]; PIE *h_1ed^h-*l*- 'fir; elder'; cf. Lat. *ebulus*, Gall. *od-ocos*; cf. Pokorny (1959– 1969, 1: 289–290)

  b. LCS *jelenĭ, OLi. *elenis*, PS ELENI-, PB ELENI- 'deer' [11, 15]; PIE *h_1el-*n*- 'deer'; cf. Gk. *élaphos*, cf. Pokorny (1959–1969, 1: 303– 304)

  c. LCS *jelĭčĭ, PS ELIKA- 'whitefish (Leuciscus)' [9]; PIE *h_1el- 'light-colored'; cf. (5.4 d) LCS *jelenĭ

  d. LCS *jesenĭ, OPr. *Assanis*, PS ESENI- ‖ PB ASANI- (?) 'autumn' [28]; PIE *h_1es- 'to be'; cf. LCS *es-mĭ* 'am' [32], Go. *aran* 'harvest, autumn'; cf. Pokorny (1959–1969, 1: 341–343)

  e. LCS *jezero, Li. ẽžeras, PS EZERA-, PB EŽERA- 'lake' [35]; PIE *h_1eg^h- 'boundary'; Pokorny (1959–1969, 1: 291–292)

  f. LCS *ježĭ, Li. ežỹs, PS EZ-IA- PB EŽ-IA- 'hedgehog' [37–38]; PIE *$h_1eĝ^h$- 'snake'; cf. Gk. *ekhinos*, Arm. *ozni* 'hedgehog'; cf. Pokorny (1959–1969, 1: 292)

A second possible source is borrowings (from non-Indo-European or from other Indo-European languages), some of which are attested in languages other than Slavic and Baltic with both *e*- and *a*- or *o*- variants. Conceivably such lexemes could have been borrowed by some Pre-Slavic or Pre-Baltic dialects with one initial and by others with another (recall the deliberations on vowel systems in contact in sections 1.3.1–1.3.3). Some examples are in (5.5).

(5.5) a. LCS *jelovo, Li. *álvas*, PS ELAUA-, PB ELUA- 'tin (St); lead (Pb)' [6]; <*olǝwo-, source language uncertain; cf. Pokorny (1959– 1969, 1: 31)

  b. LCS *jelito, PS ELEITA- 'gut; sausage' [10]; no convincing cognates outside Slavic

  c. LCS *jelĭxa, Li. el̃ksnis, PS ELIXĀ-, PB ELSNI- 'alder' [12–13]; cf. Pokorny (1959–1969, 1: 302)

  d. LCS *jemelo, Li. ẽmalas, PS, PB EMELA- 'mistletoe' [18]; no convincing cognates outside Slavic and Baltic

Since nothing is known about the actual shape with which the lexemes in (5.4) and (5.5) were established in the precursor dialects of Slavic and

Baltic, and since it is unknown to what extent they were later affected by the *e- > *a- merger, there is really no hard and fast way of separating "pre-existing" E- ‖ A- doublets from the ones that arose through the *e- > *a- merger.

However, if we limit ourselves to Slavic, perhaps we can get a useful hint by comparing the geographical distributions of *e- ‖ *a- doublets in these two sets of lexemes with the apparently native Slavic formations among the PS E- words. If any of the lexemes in the first two sets were established with initial *a- in some Pre-Slavic dialects, one would expect them to have a different distribution of *e- and *a- by-forms than the third set of lexemes. In table 5.3 I display the relevant parts of table 3.1, rearranged to show the geographical distribution of the *e- ‖ *a- doublets of these three sets of lexemes. Observe that the distributions are not very different for the three sets. Specifically, there is no skewing in the distribution of *a- variants in the (a) lexemes which could be attributed to the occurrence of *o*-grade variants in original "*e- dialects". It seems reasonable, therefore, to conclude that there were no marked differences among

Table 5.3. LCS *e- ‖ *a- doublets by origin and region: (a) PIE *h_1e-; (b) presumable borrowings; (c) native Slavic formations

		LCS	Sorbian	Sk. & Cz.	Lechitic	Sn. & SC	Bg. & M	East Slavic
a.	(*h_1e-)							
	[4]	*jedlĭ	e-	e-	e-	e-	e-	e-
	[9]	*jelĭčĭ	e-	e-	e-	e-		e-
	[32]	*jesmĭ	e-	e-	e-	e-	e-	e-
	[11]	*jelenĭ	e-	e-	e-	e-	e-/a-	e-/a-
	[28]	*jesenĭ		e-/a-	e-	e-	e-	e-/a-
	[20−21]	*jereb-	e-	e-	e-/a	e-/a-	e-	e-/a-
	[36−37]	*jež-	e-	e-/a-	e-/a-	e-	e-	e-/a-
	[35]	*jezero	e-	e-/a-	e-	e-/a-	e-/a-	e-/a-
b.	[10]	*jelito	e-	e-	e-	e-/a-		e-/a-
	[18]	*jemelo	e-	e-/a-	e-	e-/a-	e-/a-	e-/a-
	[13]	*jelĭxa	a-	e-/a-	a-	e-/a-	e-	e-/a-
	[6]	*jelovo	a-	a-	a-	a-	e-/a-	a-
c.	[44]	*jemešĭ		e-	e-	e-	e-/a-	e-/a-
	[26]	*jese			e-	e-	e-/a-	e-/a-
	[1]	*jedinu	e-	e-	e-	e-/a-	e-/a-	e-/a-
	[3]	*jedva	e-	e-	e-	e-/a-	e-/a-	e-/a-
	[2]	*ješče	e-	e-	e-/a-	e-/a-	e-/a-	e-/a-

these sets of words before the Slavic – Baltic *e- > *a- merger, that is, as far as one can tell, they all had initial PS E-.

Still, in the first two sets, two lexemes stand out, *jelĭxa and *jelovŭ in set (b). These lexemes are striking in several respects: (i) they are attested with initial *a- in more regions than other lexemes; (ii) they are the only lexemes attested exclusively with *a- reflexes in other regions than East Slavic; and (iii) they are the only lexemes attested with *a- reflexes in the Sorbian languages. We will have more to say about them in section 5.3.3.

5.3.3. Rozwadowski's change: PIE *h₂e-, *h₃e-, *hₓo-

Omitted from table 5.3 are a small number of inherited lexemes which in other Indo-European languages have initials pointing to PIE *a- and *o- (< PIE *h₂e-, *h₃e-, and *hₓo-), but which appear in Proto-Slavic (and Proto-Baltic) with initial E- instead of the expected PS, PB A-. They are evidence of a third source of Proto-Baltic E- ‖ A- doublets, a sound change which occurred, apparently, at an early time in the precursor dialects of Slavic and Baltic, and which disturbed the regular correspondences in word-initial position, yielding PS, PB E- instead of PS, PB A- in a small number of lexemes; see (5.6).

(5.6) a. PIE *a- (*h₂e-):
   (i) LCS *jelŭkŭ, PS ELUKA- 'bitter' [17]; PIE *h₂el-; initial PIE *a- in Lat. *alūmen* 'alum', cf. Pokorny (1959–1969, 1: 33–34)
   (ii) LCS *jesera, PS ESERA- 'fishbones; awn'; PB EŠERIA- 'perch' [29]; PIE *h₂ek̂-er- 'pointed', Gk. *ákros* 'pointed'; cf. Pokorny (1959–1969, 1: 18–20)
   (iii) LCS *jesetĭ, PS ESETI- 'rack', Li. *ekė̃čios*, PB EKETIĀ- 'harrow' [30]; PIE *h₂ek̂-eti-; cf. (5.6 a.ii)
   (iv) LCS *jesetrŭ, Li. *erškė̃tras*, PS ESETRA-, PB EŠETRA- 'sturgeon' [31]; PIE *h₂ek̂-etra-); cf. (5.6 a.ii)
   b. PIE *o- (*h₃e-, *h₃o-):
   (i) LCS *jesenŭ, PS ESENA- 'ash (Fraxinus)' [27]; PIE *hₓh₃-es-; cf. Lat. *ornus*; full grade of the root in LCS *jasenŭ, PS ĀSENA-, Li. *úosis*, PB ŌS-I-; PIE *hₓeh₃-s-; cf. Schrijver (1991: 77)
   (ii) LCS *jerĭlŭ, Li. *erẽlis*, PS ERILA-, PB ERELIA- 'eagle' [22]; PIE *h₃er- 'bird'; Gk. *órnis, -ithos*; cf. Pokorny (1959–1969, 1: 325–326)
   (iii) LCS *jerębĭ, Li. d. *jerumbė̃*, PS ERIMBI-, PB ERUMBĒ- 'grouse' [20–21]; PIE *h₃er- 'bird'; cf. (5.4 d) LCS *jerĭlŭ

(iv) LCS *jesa*, *osa*, PS EPSĀ-, PB EP(U)ŠĀ- 'aspen' [19]; PIE *h₂/₃esp-*.

Although of course there is no guarantee that the initial vowels in all these lexemes underwent the same change at the same time — one cannot exclude the possibility that they changed at different times (see further chapter 6) — some aspects of these deviant correspondences suggest that they are due to a very old innovation. Consider the three Slavic derivatives of PIE *$h_2e\hat{k}$-* 'pointed' (5.6 a.ii–iv), which suggest the character of the change: it has affected PS ESERĀ- 'fishbones; awn', ESETI- 'rack', ESE-TRA- 'sturgeon', but (apparently) not the adjective PS ASTRA- 'pointed' (< PIE *$h_2e\hat{k}$-ro-*). The fact that we find exactly the same distribution of *e-* and *a-* in Li. *ešerỹs* 'perch', *ekẽčios* 'harrow', *erškẽtras* 'sturgeon', but *aštrùs* 'pointed' is hard to dismiss as a coincidence; it points to a single, shared innovation. In addition, there are several morphological differences between the Slavic and Baltic correspondences which also suggest that the shared initial PS, PB E- is due to a very old change. We will examine these in section 6.1.

This change of PIE *a-*, *o-* to PS and PB E-, which I call Rozwadowski's change in memory of the great Polish comparativist Jan Rozwadowski, who was the first scholar to describe the change (see further chapter 6), defines one more layer of innovation — and adds one more source of opacity — to the attestation of PIE *e-*, *a-*, *o-* in the modern

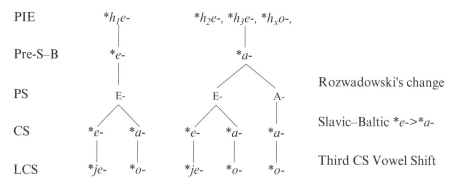

Figure 5.7. Slavic reflexes of PIE *h_1e-*, *h_2e-*, *h_3e-*, *h_xo-*

Slavic and Baltic languages; see figure 5.7. Now, if this change affected Slavic and Baltic uniformly, its only effect would have been to increase the number of etyma with initial PS, PB E-. But it is not certain *a priori* that this is what happened. Rozwadowski's change may have been geographically limited and so have affected different Pre-Slavic and Pre-Baltic dialects to different extents, just as in the case of some of the other changes we have discussed.

It is useful to contrast the set of lexemes listed in (5.6) and displayed in table 5.4 with those in table 5.3. Since their roots have PIE *a- (*h_2e-)

Table 5.4. Slavic lexemes with PS E- for PIE *a-, *o-

	LCS	Sorbian	Sk. & Cz.	Lechitic	Sn. & SC	Bg. & M	East Slavic
[17]	*jelŭkŭ			e-			e-
[31]	*jesetrŭ	e-	e-	e-	e-	e-	e-/a-
[30]	*jesetĭ			e-la-			a-
[29]	*jesera			e-la-			—
[27]	*jesenŭ		e-	e-la-	e-la-	e-la-	—
[19]	*jesika	a-	a-	a-	e-	e-la-	a-
[22]	*jerelŭ	e-la-	a-	a-	a-	a-	a-

or *o- (*h_3e-, *h_xo-), the words in (5.6) and table 5.4 would not reflect qualitative ablaut in Slavic or Baltic. Hence such by-forms as LCS *jesetrŭ ‖ *osetrŭ (< PS ESETRA- < PIE *$h_2ek̂$-) and *jesenŭ ‖ *osenŭ (< PS ESENA- < PIE *h_xh_3-es-) (‖ *jasenŭ < PS ĀSENA- *h_xeh_3-s-) provide a standard of comparison for the issue of word-initial qualitative ablaut, which was discussed in section 5.3.2. As it turns out, these lexemes have entirely similar *e- ‖ *a- distributions to those of the three sets in table 5.3. This is a further indication that none of the lexemes with PIE *h_1e- in table 5.3 (a) reflect word-initial qualitative ablaut; they show only the consequences of the *e- > *a- merger.

At the same time, however, the set in table 5.4 includes two items, LCS *jes-ika, PS EPSĀ- 'aspen' [19] and *jerĭlŭ, PS ERILA- 'eagle' [22], with a geographical *e- ‖ *a- distribution similar to the ones of *jelovŭ, PS ELAUA- 'tin (St); lead (Pb)' [6], *jelĭxa, PS ELIXĀ- 'alder' [13] in set (b) of table 5.3. The distributional similarity of these four lexemes does not reflect any original similarity, for their initials have different origins. Their similar distribution may in theory be a chance outcome of the dispersion of reflexes of the Slavic−Baltic *e- > *a- merger, but in fact the many areas with solid *a- reflexes in these lexemes contrast sharply with the patterns of *e- and *e- ‖ *a- distribution of the other twenty lexemes in table 3.1. Their similar distribution, however, may very well be related to Rozwadowski's change − supposing that at the time of this change these lexemes had initial Pre-Slavic (and Pre-Baltic) *a- and underwent the change in only part of the precursor dialects of Slavic. If this is the case,

then the PS EL(A)UA, ELIXĀ-, EPSĀ-, ERILA- that were reconstructed in section 1.1 are reflexes of Rozwadowski's change, whereas the solid attestations of these lexemes with *a- in several Slavic regions may reflect
doublet forms PS ALAUA- (IE *olǝwo-?), ALIXĀ- (? *alisā-), APSĀ- (PIE
*h₂esp-), ARILA- (PIE *h₃er-), forms which preserved the Pre-Slavic initial
and for this reason match the attestation in the other Indo-European
languages (cf. chapter 7, s. vv.).

Notice that in recognizing these Proto-Slavic doublets we are revising
the provisional reconstructions that were first presented in chapter 1: for
PS EL(A)UA- we substitute PS EL(A)UA- ‖ AL(A)UA- [6], and similarly for
the others, ELIXĀ- ‖ ALIXĀ- [13], EPSĀ- ‖ APSĀ- [19], ERILA- ‖ ARILA- [22].
This revision was actually tacitly anticipated in the discussion of the ante-
Migration isogloss configuration that was reconstructed in sections 3.4–
3.6; it was deliberately based solely on the "normal" CS *e- and *e- ‖ *a-
reflexes, that is, those that reflect the effects of the *e- > *a- merger.

5.3.4. Rozwadowski doublets

But if Rozwadowski isoglosses cut through the ante-Migration Slavic
speech area, the change may have given rise to dialect variants also elsewhere in the Slavic–Baltic dialect continuum.

Consider the pair PS ALKUTI- ‖ PB ELKŪNĒ- 'elbow' [14] (< PIE
*hₓh₃-el-k-), which was discussed in section 5.2. Their initials illustrate a
clear dichotomy between Slavic and Baltic, which cannot be due to qualitative ablaut, since both doublets represent non-apophonic PIE *o-. It
would make sense to interpret the solid CS *a- attestation of PS ALKUTI-
as the regular reflex of Pre-Slavic *a- and to ascribe the initial PB E- to
Rozwadowski's change. Thus the Baltic by-form PB ELKŪNE- alone would
be able to show the variation that normally results from the *e- > *a-
merger, as it does in Lithuanian (and possibly Old Prussian; cf. table 4.1).

In this instance, as in the preceding ones, Slavic–Baltic lexemes appear to have escaped Rozwadowski's change in part of or all of the later
Common Slavic dialect area. Now consider the Baltic reflexes of PB E-
displayed in table 5.5, which presents the data of table 4.1 in an abbreviated form analogous to tables 5.3 and 5.4. Observe first that *a-* attestations in Old Prussian seem equally uninformative for all three sets
of lexemes; we ascribe this to the Slavic–Baltic *e- > *a- merger. But
note that in set (2), solid *a-* reflexes occur in East Baltic in two lexemes
for which we have just reconstructed Proto-Slavic doublets, La. *alva*, Li.
al(a)vas 'tin (St)' (PB ELUA- 'tin') and La. *alksnis* 'alder' (PB ELSNI-).

Table 5.5. Baltic reflexes of initial PIE *e-, *a-, *o- by origin and language

		PB	OPr.	La.	Li.
(1) PIE *h_1e-					
a.	[37]	EŽIA- 'hedgehog'	–	e-	e-/a-
c.	[34]	EŽ 'I'	e-/a-	e-	e-/a-
	[32]	ES-MI 'to be; 1sg.pres.'	e-/a-	e-	e-/a-
d.	[36]	EŽ-Ī-/-IĀ- 'edge'	a-	e-	e-/a-
	[4]	EDLĒ- 'fir'	a-	e-	e-/a-
	[35]	EŽERA- 'lake'	a-	e-	e-/a-
	[33]	EŠUĀ- 'mare'	a-	–	e-/a-
(2) Initial PB E- of uncertain origin					
b.	[18]	EMELA- 'mistletoe'	e-/a-	e-/a-	e-/a-
c.	[6]	ELUA- 'tin (St)'	e-/a-	a-	a-
d.	[16]	(U)ELU- 'hasp'	a-	e-	e-/a-
	[24]	ERŠKĒTI- 'thorn'	–	e-	e-/a-
	[23]	ERKIĀ- 'tick, woodbeetle'	–	e-	e-/a-
e.	[12–13]	ELSNI- 'elder'	a-	a-	e-/a-
	[36]	EŽ(E)GIA- 'bass'	a-	–	e-/a-
(3) PIE *h_2e-, *h_3e-, *h_1o-					
a.	[31]	EŠETRA- 'sturgeon'	e-	–	e-/a-
	[25]	ERŽEL(I)A- 'stallion'	–	e-	e-/a-
c.	[30]	EKETIĀ- 'harrow'	a-	e-	e-/a-
	[14]	ELKŪNĒ- 'elbow'	a-	e-	e-/a-
	[22]	ERELIA- 'eagle'	a-	e-	e-/a-
e.	[15]	ĒLNI 'deer'	a-	a-	e-/a-
	[15]	EPSĒ- 'aspen'	a-	a-	e-/a-
	[29]	EŠERIA- 'perch'	–	a-	e-/a-
	[5]	EKETĒ- 'ice-hole'	–	a-	e-/a-

The letters (a)–(e) index the correspondence categories of table 4.1.

Perhaps these lexemes can be taken as evidence that Rozwadowski's change was areally limited also among the ancestral dialects of Baltic. And in set (3), observe the limited attestation of initial *e-* in Old Prussian (one lexeme) relative to Latvian (four lexemes) and relative to Lithuanian (nine lexemes), which looks like a spatial gradation; and note the initial of La. *apse* 'aspen' (PB EPSĒ-), which also has Proto-Slavic doublets, and in addition La. *asars* 'perch' (PB EŠERIA-), and *akacis* 'pool' (PB EKETĒ-). These may of course have their *a-* from the *e- > *a- merger, but they may also be taken as indications of areal differences in the effects of Rozwadowski's change.

Thus we are led to posit four sets of Rozwadowski doublets. One set that is shared by Slavic and Baltic (table 5.6 [a]), one that is relevant only to Slavic (table 5.6 [b]), one that contrasts Slavic with Baltic (table 5.6 [c]),

Table 5.6. Rozwadowski doublets in Slavic and Baltic

		PS	PB
a.	(i)	ELAUA- ‖ ALAUA-	ELUA- ‖ ALUA-
	(ii)	ELIXĀ- ‖ ALIXĀ-	ELSNI- ‖ ALSNI-
	(iii)	EPSĀ- ‖ APSĀ-	EPUŠĒ- ‖ APSĒ-
b.		ERILA- ‖ ARILA-	ERELIA-
c.		ALKUTI-	ELKŪNĒ-
d.	(i)	EŠERIA-	EŠERIA- ‖ AŠERIA-
	(ii)		EKETĒ- ‖ AKETĒ-

and one that is relevant only to Baltic (table 5.6 [d]); see further section 6.1.

If the *a*- reflexes in Latvian in table 5.5 (3) suggest this revision of the reconstruction made in chapter 4, one cannot help wondering whether the extensive *a*- attestation in Old Prussian should not be interpreted along the same lines and simply be taken at face value, that is, as an indication that Rozwadowski's change did not affect OPr. /aketēs/, /alkūnis/, /arelis/, where the Latvian correspondents have *e*-. This has sometimes been done in the past. For example, it has been argued that Li. *erēlis* results from an assimilation from an older *arēlis*, whose relative antiquity supposedly would be confirmed by OPr. *Arelie*; thus Cowgill (1965: 146).

No doubt the most reliable guidance in answering this question is provided by the lexemes with PIE *h_1e- and OPr. *a*- in table 5.5 (1). They demonstrate the extent to which Old Prussian was subject to the Slavic–Baltic **e-* > **a-* merger and highlight the irremediable ambiguity of OPr. *a*-. Far from OPr. *Arelie* confirming the antiquity of Li. *arēlis*, it is the initial of Li. *erēlis* that must be old (Pre-Slavic–Baltic, an effect of Rozwadowski's change), whereas the OPr., Li. *a*- in principle can be even older, but much more likely is of recent, Slavic–Baltic date.

To return for a moment to the apparent spatial gradation in table 5.5, set (3): it may reflect simultaneously the greater effect of Rozwadowski's change in Lithuanian than in Latvian and the greater effect of the Slavic–Baltic **e-* > **a-* merger in Old Prussian than in Latvian. In a discussion of the Baltic Rozwadowski doublets, therefore, the Old Prussian attestation is of no use and should be left aside. We return to this subject again in chapter 6.

5.4. Summary and results

5.4.1. Summary

In this chapter we have passed in review a series of innovations affecting word-initial vowels in Slavic and Baltic other than the *e- > *a- merger. The aim in discussing the more recent innovations was mainly to clarify their chronological relation to the merger.

In section 5.1.1 it turned out to be possible to provide the Lower Sorbian *he-* ‖ *je-* doublets with an interpretation that ties this detail in with the differentiation of Common Slavic in the period of the Migrations.

The Bulgarian−Macedonian change of LCS *je- > Bg., M *e-*, examined in section 5.1.2, is interesting mostly by the way it encourages us to consider the phonological perspectives in the development and subsequent loss of Common Slavic prothesis.

The regional, partial mergers of LCS *je- and *ja- are all later than the *e- > *a- merger. This makes them irrelevant to our topic except to the extent that they confuse the attestation by disturbing somewhat the regular relations among the reflexes of PS E-, Ē-, Ā-, IE-, IĒ-, IĀ-. One can imagine that these weak sound changes reflect interference among different pronunciation types coming from different Common Slavic areas during the period of Slavic expansion, and perhaps they are amenable to detailed areal analysis. This makes them an interesting, though possibly not very fruitful, problem for future research.

The excursus in section 5.1.4 was motivated only by the history of the "*je- > *o- problem", but offered some new perspectives on the East Slavic *ju- > *u- merger.

Section 5.2 looked at a small number of etyma with PS, PB E- preceding a tautosyllabic liquid. Because of the Slavic metathesis of initial liquid diphthongs, these lexemes have traditionally been peripheral to the *e- > *a- problem, and justifiably so. One of these lexemes, PS ALK-UTI- ‖ PB ELK-ŪN-Ē- 'elbow' [14] was subsequently interpreted as a pair of doublets produced by Rozwadowski's change (section 5.3.3). But the other lexemes indicate no generalizations and were left for individual discussion in chapter 7.

5.4.2. Results

The remaining portions of the chapter were devoted to the question of "pre-existing" *e- ‖ *a- doublets, the problem of separating the results of the *e- > *a- merger from similar word-initial variation of older date, in particular qualitative ablaut and the results of Rozwadowski's change, by which PIE *a-, *o- came to be reflected as PS, PB E- besides the regular A- (section 5.3.3).

While the presentation in section 5.3.1 outlined the several kinds of initial doublets that have to be dissociated from the *e- > *a- question and argued for a specific methodological stance in the interpretation of multiple variants, the following sections presented a factor analysis of the lexical material, which treated as independent variables the properties "original initial vowel" and "eventual geographical distribution of initial-vowel reflexes".

This made it possible to infer with some confidence that none of the CS *e- ‖ *a- diversity in Slavic results from different geographical distributions of qualitative ablaut alternants (section 5.3.2).

After the identification of Rozwadowski's change in section 5.3.3 it was demonstrated that the PS, PB E- reflexes of PIE *a-, *o- were subject to the *e- > *a- merger, and that the lexemes in question were dispersed through the Slavic Migrations with outcomes quite similar to those of the other lexemes with PS E- (as shown in table 5.3).

This in turn allowed us to interpret a small number of lexemes which have normal *e- ‖ *a- diversity in part of Slavic, but solid *a- reflexes in several Slavic regions, as evidence that Rozwadowski's change produced areal variants in the former Slavic−Baltic dialect continuum (section 5.3.4). The analysis was extended to the Baltic data, and altogether seven lexemes were shown to have such doublets. These lexemes and the isoglosses their reflexes define will be discussed again in chapter 6.

Chapter 6

PIE *e-, *a-, *o- in Slavic and Baltic

In chapter 1 and in chapter 4 we reconstructed the lexical distribution of Proto-Slavic and Proto-Baltic initial E- and A-, applying one and the same procedure to the material of the two language groups: lexemes attested only with initial LCS *o- or Baltic *a- reflexes were taken to represent PS, PB A-; those with LCS *je- or *je- and *o- reflexes, respectively Baltic *e- or *e- and *a- reflexes, were taken to represent PS, PB E-. Although the actual modern distribution of these initial open-vowel reflexes is quite different from language to language − to some extent even from dialect to dialect − within the two language groups, this procedure yields a high degree of agreement between the lists of Proto-Slavic and Proto-Baltic lexemes representing these reconstructed initial vowels (as displayed in table 4.1). As mentioned, this agreement is a rather strong corroboration that the independently reconstructed lexical distribution of E- and A- is valid for each of the language groups, and it suggests that this lexical distribution is part of their shared heritage (cf. section 9.4).

In chapter 5 the results of this reconstruction were confronted with the Proto-Indo-European initials in the inherited part of the relevant material, and among many other details two significant facts were established. First, it was shown that in a number of lexemes the reconstructed PS, PB E- corresponds to Proto-Indo-European initial *a- and *o-. This is in sharp contrast with the regular correspondence between PIE *a, *o and PS, PB A which holds not only for all other environments, but also in word-initial position in the majority of inherited lexemes. But although this unexpected, irregular correspondence is represented only by a small number of lexemes, it shows a peculiar consistency between Slavic and Baltic which suggests that it is the result of a shared innovation, an apparently ancient, weak change of initial PIE *a-/*o- > *e- − Rozwadowski's change. The lexemes in question are briefly repeated in table 6.1 (a) (cf. section 5.3.4, and see further below).

Secondly, several of these lexemes and some additional ones with initial Pre-Slavic−Baltic *a- from other sources, must be reconstructed with E- ‖ A- doublets in Proto-Slavic and/or in Proto-Baltic (cf. table 6.1 [b]), which indicates that the change in question affected different parts of the

Table 6.1. Lexemes showing the effect of Rozwadowski's change, (a) with uniform reflexes in Proto-Slavic and Proto-Baltic, (b) with apparently heterogeneous reflexes

		PIE	PS	OPr.	La.	Li.	PB
(a)	[17]	*alu-ko- 'rancid'	E-	–	–	–	–
	[30]	*ak̂-eti- 'harrow'	E-	a-	e-	e-/a-	E-
	[31]	*ak̂-etro- 'sturgeon'	E-	e-	–	e-/a-	E-
	[27]	*os-eno- 'ash'	E-	–	–	–	–
(b)	[13]	*alisā- 'alder'	E-/A-	a-	a-	e-/a-	E-/A-
	[19]	*aspā- 'aspen'	E-/A-	a-	a-	e-/a-	E-/A-
	[29]	*ak̂-erā- 'awn; perch'	E-	–	a-	e-/a-	E-/A-
	[5]	*okʷ-eti- 'pool'	–	–	a-	e-/a-	E-/A-
	[6]	*olǝwo- 'lead'	E-/A-	e-/a-	a-	a-	E-/A-
	[14]	*ol-k-u- 'elbow'	A-	a-	e-	e-/a-	E-
	[20]	*or-ilo- 'eagle'	E-/A-	a-	a-	e-/a-	E-

(Pre-)Slavic–Baltic dialect continuum to different extents. This evidence is quite robust despite the opacity contributed by the more recent Slavic–Baltic *e- > *a- merger and later changes in initial vowels (section 5.3.4).

6.1. Rozwadowski's change: When and where?

The peculiar agreement between Slavic and Baltic in the derivatives of PIE *$h_2ek̂$- 'pointed' – PS ES-ERĀ-, ES-ETI-, ES-ETRA- versus AS-TRA- and PB EŠ-ERIA-, EK-ETI-Ā-, EŠ-ETRA- versus AŠ-TRA-, which was mentioned in section 5.3.3, is most naturally interpreted as evidence that Rozwadowski's change is an old, shared innovation, but how old it is is hard to tell. However, it is remarkable that most of the examples of this change actually show deep morphological and phonological differences among the Slavic and Baltic languages.

   Consider the difference in affixation between PS ALK-UTI- and PB ELK-ŪN-Ē-, both sharing several layers of affixation, and then, after the -*u*-formation, diverging. Or consider the differences between PS ELIX-Ā- ‖ ALIX-Ā- and PB ELS-NI- ‖ ALS-NI. In this lexeme, there is a difference between Slavic and Baltic in suffixation, but also between the shapes of the root, which presented different environments for the "*ruki* change", whence the -X- ‖ -S- correspondence; for a more detailed analysis, see chapter 7, s. v. Or consider the difference in root structure between PS

ELAUA- ‖ ALAUA- and PB ELUA- ‖ ALUA-, or the Lithuanian innovation in the root of PS EPSĀ-, PB (Li.) EPUŠĒ- ‖ (La., OPr.) APSĒ-. This Lithuanian by-form is thought to be due to a contamination of PB EPSĒ- with PUŠI- 'pine' (< PIE *puk̂-, cf. Gk. *peúkē* 'pine', OHG *viuhte*, Gm. *Fichte* 'idem'; cf. Fraenkel [1962−1965: s. vv.]), which seems plausible. But it should be noted that this hypothetical contamination implies a chronological stage when there was a (virtual) neutralization of /s/ and /š/ after /u/ (and /i r k/) − or, in other terms, a productive /s/ ∼ /š/ alternation − so that the /s/ of PB EPSĒ- and the /š/ of PB PUŠI- could be construed as functionally equivalent (conditioned variants or alternants). Observe also the different reflexes of PIE *k̂ in PS ES-ETI- and PB EK-ETI-Ā-.

All these differences point to the conclusion that Rozwadowski's change antedates the development of the dialect diversity exemplified by these different pairs of doublets. If one assumes the contrary, it is impossible to understand why a change in a word-initial vowel would have affected predominantly (seven out of eleven!) lexemes that had morphologically distinct by-forms in different Slavic−Baltic dialects; consider the many other lexemes with initial Pre-Slavic−Baltic *a- that remained unaffected (examples [1.3] and [4.1]). Since some of the differences we have observed go back to before the *ruki* change (which is the earliest definable phonological change differentiating Slavic and Baltic; cf. Andersen [1968]), we can infer that Rozwadowski's change is older than the merger of PIE *k̂ with the different variants of PIE *s in Slavic and Baltic.

This surely was a long time ago, and given the fact that the area in which this dialect differentiation occurred has long since become peopled with speakers of other languages, one should not expect to be able to form any conception of the space in which Rozwadowski's change took place. And so it is notable that precisely because the change gave rise to so relatively many doublets, one can actually discern (or construe) spatial relations among some of these which, in the aggregate, amount to a pale reflection of the change's occurring in the central region of the Pre-Slavic−Baltic dialect continuum − assuming the same relative locations of Slavs and Balts as in the previous chapters − in such a way that it left dialects in the north and the south, and perhaps also in the west, unaffected, and possibly spread from east to west; cf. table 6.2.

The possible east-to-west spread can be inferred in part from relations among the Slavic doublets. First, there is an evident southern versus northern A- ‖ E- distinction, which is clear-cut in the pair PS ALKUTI- ‖ PB ELKŪN-Ē- 'elbow' [14], as noted in section 5.3.4. Two other lexemes

Table 6.2. Slavic–Baltic lexical correspondences with reflexes of Rozwadowski's change, construed as spatial relations

	Southern periphery	Center		Northern periphery
	Proto-Slavic		Proto-East-Baltic	
(a)	ALK-UTI-		ELK-ŪN-Ē-	
	AR-ILA-	ER-ILA-	ER-ELIA-	
(b)	ALAUA-	ELAUA-		ALUA-
	ALIX-Ā-	ELIX-Ā-	ELS-NI-	ALS-NI-
	APS-Ā-	EPS-Ā-	EP(U)Š-Ē-	APS-Ē-
(c)	ES-ERĀ-		EŠ-ERIA-	AŠ-ERIA-
			EK-ET-Ē-	AK-ET-Ē-
(d)	ES-ETRA-		EŠ-ETRA-	
	ES-ETI-		EK-ETI-Ā-	

have doublets with a slightly different distribution defining a southern versus northern PS A- ‖ PS, PB E- dichotomy: the Sorbian E- reflexes of PS ERILA- ‖ ARILA- 'eagle' [22] seem to tie in with East Baltic ERELIA- (OPr. /arelis/ remains ambiguous); and the Bulgarian dialect forms with e- of PS ELAUA- ‖ ALAUA- 'tin; lead' [6] show affinity with OPr. /elwas/ (OPr. /alwas/ is ambiguous).

Secondly, there is an apparent western versus eastern A- ‖ E- distinction reflected in the doublets ELIXĀ- ‖ ALIXĀ- 'alder' [13], EPSĀ- ‖ APSĀ- 'aspen' [19], which have a clear western distribution of CS *a- reflexes — PS ALIXĀ- (in Sorbian, East and West Slovak, Czech, and Lechitic; only Central Slovak has CS *e-) and PS APSĀ- (in Sorbian, Slovak–Czech, Lechitic) contrasting with CS *e- and *e- ‖ *a- reflexes of PS ELIXĀ-, EPSĀ- elsewhere.

We have here the solution to the apparent paradox that the Sorbian languages, which have not generalized any *a- reflexes resulting from the Slavic–Baltic *e- > *a- merger (cf. tables 1.1, 3.1), have *a- in all the Slavic lexemes that retained PS A- doublets after Rozwadowski's change: the first wave of settlers in this region were pure "*e-speakers" (cf. section 3.3, figure 3.1), representatives, presumably, of a southern variety of ante-Migration Common Slavic which was peripheral in relation to both of these innovations. The route by which these settlers probably reached their new lands can be read out of the archaeological record, which demonstrates the importance of the Danube for the early settlement of the West Slavic regions; see figure 6.1 (and cf. section 9.2). This interpretation of the details of the **e-* and **a-* distribution is in full agreement with Trubačev's well-known theory of the "secondary occidentalization of Sorbian", the idea (derived from a study of their lexicon) that the features the Sorbian languages share with the other West Slavic languages are secondary and superficial, and that before the Migrations these dialects were fundamentally different from both Lechitic and Slovak−Czech (cf. Trubačev 1967, 1968b).

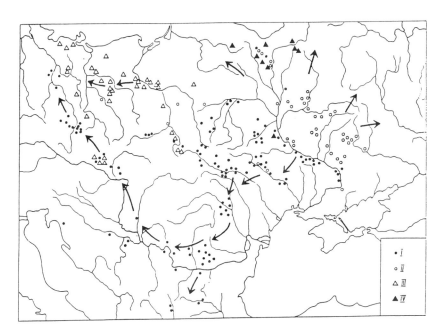

Figure 6.1. Slavic settlements ca. AD 400−800 and inferred settlement routes (Baran 1991: 78). I: Semi-subterranean houses having a stove. II: Semi-subterranean houses having a hearth. III: Other Slavic house types having a stove. IV: Above-ground houses.

If we compare the Slavic A- ‖ E- distinctions with the Baltic reflexes − PB A- doublets in Latvian, but E- doublets in Lithuanian (cf. table 6.2) − it appears that in the larger perspective, the (southern and western) ante-Migration Common Slavic A- areas and the (northeastern) Latvian A- areas can be construed as peripheral in relation to a central E- area with reflexes of Rozwadowski's change. Seen in this light, the Latvian A- forms *asars* 'perch' [29] and *akacis* 'pool' [5] can be interpreted similarly as peripheral, northeastern relic forms, comparable to PS ALKUTI-.

But in a few shared Slavic−Baltic lexemes (table 6.2 [d]), both Slavic and East Baltic know only Rozwadowski reflexes.

The toponymic evidence of Northwest Baltic appears to agree with the peripheral location of these areas. Unfortunately the attestation is really too skimpy to permit any firm conclusions. But it can be mentioned that while Curonian attestations have *e-* in PB EDLĒ- 'spruce' [4] and EZERA- 'lake' [35] (which have PIE *$*h_1e$-), the Rozwadowski lexemes PB ELSNI- ‖ ALSNI- and EP(U)ŠĒ- ‖ APSĒ- are attested with *a-* in Curonian, Latvian, and Lithuanian place names, and not with the Rozwadowski reflex *e-*; see chapter 7, s. vv.

If one were to take the Old Prussian *a-* forms of all or most of these lexemes at face value − /aketēs, alisknas, apsē, arelis/ − these would strengthen the appearance of Rozwadowski's change having spread from east to west and leaving the largest number of lexemes unaffected in the south, the southwest, the west, the northwest, and the northeast.

But it is important to remember that − beguiling though this hypothetical, ancient areal pattern may seem − it has been inferred *as if* the modern attestations can be taken at face value. In view of the fact that Old Prussian has many examples of *a-* for PIE *$*e-$ ($*h_1e$-), and considering that the modern Latvian reflexes are a composite of Northwest Baltic forms of speech (Curonian, Zemgalian, and Selonian) overlaid with Latvian (Latgalian), the attested forms from these areas obviously have to be taken with a grain of salt. In view of the considerable time depth involved and the muddling of the initial vowel reflexes that may have been produced by possibly repeated fusions of speech communities in this area during its thousands of years of prehistory, what we see may not in fact be a pale reflection of age-old dialect differences, but merely a semblance of an areal pattern.

But we have noted what can be observed. Perhaps something can be built on these observations in the future. (See for example the discussion of PS ELIXĀ- ‖ ALIXĀ- [13].)

6.2. Balto-Slavic *a- > *e-?

It was recognized a long time ago that the irregular initial-vowel correspondences between PIE *$*a-$, *$*o-$ and PS, PB E- constitute a problem

distinct from both the "East Slavic **je- > *o-* change" and the Baltic **e-
> *a-* merger (Bezzenberger 1897: 296−297; Zubatý 1903: 365).

Jan Rozwadowski was the first to devote a separate study to this problem. He observed that several of these deviant correspondences have **e*
in the second syllable − he contrasted PS ESERĀ- 'fishbone', ESETRA- 'sturgeon', EZERA- 'lake', ESENI- 'autumn', EMELA- 'mistletoe' and their Baltic
congeners with ASTRA- 'sharp', ASLĀ- 'adze', ASSI- 'axle', etc. (1915:
18−21). And on the basis of this regularity he hypothesized that in Balto-
Slavic (his term; HA), initial **a-* assimilated to an **e* in the immediately
following syllable.

Rozwadowski's explanation has not been embraced warmly by the
scholars who have concerned themselves with the reflexes of Slavic and
Baltic initial **e-* and **a-*. Such classics as Meillet (1934) and Vaillant
(1950) ignore it, and more recent treatments of the subject such as Arumaa (1964), Shevelov (1965), Lamprecht (1987) do likewise. The main
reason for this may very well be the general opacity of the data which
results from the Slavic−Baltic **e- > *a-* merger and the more recent
layers of innovation, which were discussed in chapter 5. But one must
reckon as well with a strong preference on the part of many scholars for
taking the available attestation at face value even when it is known to be
unreliable. Evidently anyone who is inclined to take a LCS **o-* or, say,
OPr. *a-* at face value, rather than getting involved with the multiple ambi-
guities described in chapter 5, would probably prefer leaving a number
of forms with, for the time being, unexplained initial vowel reflexes,
rather than hypothesizing several sound changes marching the same initial vowels first up the hill (**a-/*o- > *e-*) and then down again (**e- >
a-). Add to this the relative uncertainty that (generally speaking) continues to reign regarding Indo-European ablaut, which − far from motiva-
ting restraint − has made it easy for many scholars to suppose that any
word-initial vowel doublets might represent inherited ablaut alternations,
which removes the problem entirely from the purview of Common Slavic
(cf. section 8.1.3).

Unfortunately there are other reasons to feel uncertain about Rozwadowski's rule. The most important one, surely, is that when all the facts
are in − which they were not when Rozwadowski explored this problem
− his explanation just does not fit the data (see table 6.1 above). It is
somewhat surprising that Rozwadowski's old hypothesis − unques-
tioned, unsupported by any new argumentation, and unaccompanied by
a new analysis of the material − has recently found an advocate in Popowska-Taborska (1984: 83).

When all the relevant data are considered, it looks pretty doubtful whether the deviant Proto-Slavic and Proto-Baltic E- correspondences can be interpreted even in the spirit of Rozwadowski's proposal, that is, in simple phonological terms, as the result of an internally motivated evolutive change. Since the lexical material is so limited, and it varies somewhat between Slavic and Baltic to boot, it really is not a promising case for historical interpretation. The most one can reasonably do with such data, it seems, is to suggest some of the different interpretive perspectives in which they can be viewed. This is what I will do in the following few pages.

6.3. Non-Indo-European contacts?

If an internally motivated sound change is unlikely as the origin of PS, PB E- for PIE *a-, *o-, the alternatives evidently have to involve language contact of one sort or another.

Let us begin by noting that the putative change has to be envisioned as early enough that it could have largely identical consequences in Slavic and Baltic. An important illustration of this is the identical distribution of PS, PB E- and A- in derivatives of PIE *$h_2e\hat{k}$- 'pointed' (see section 5.3.3). This identity, of course, may have been characteristic of a majority area and does not preclude some dialect differences such as the ones highlighted in table 6.2.

One of the early contact situations one can imagine is with the non-Indo-European substratum in (parts of) the vast territories in Eastern Europe the linguistic precursors of the Slavs and Balts penetrated and settled from the second millennium before our era on − as documented by the archaeological record, by the distribution of Baltic hydronyms, and by the substantial body of ancient (North) Baltic loan words shared by the West Finnic languages and, to a lesser extent, the East Finnic languages (cf. Thomsen 1889 [1921]; Serebrennikov 1957; Toporov and Trubačev 1962: 3−12; Gimbutas 1963, 1971; Volkaitė-Kulikauskienė 1987: 147−152).

In this connection it is relevant to note that some of the troublesome E-lexemes have long been suspected of being borrowings from a substratum language − specifically a few that denote elements of European flora, e. g., PS ELIXĀ- 'elder', EMELA- 'mistletoe', EPSĀ- 'aspen'; cf. chapter 7,

s. vv. These could conceivably have been borrowed with different initial vowels in different parts of the Pre-Slavic−Baltic area. But since practically nothing is known about the substratum language(s), little is gained by invoking them. Besides, the majority of the Rozwadowski lexemes are in fact of Indo-European origin.

But if one considers the possibility that the aberrant PS, PB E- are due to interference from a substratum language, one must wonder whether this interference occurred before or after initial laryngeals were lost, yielding the qualitatively distinct initial vowels *e-, *a-, and *o-.

If one assumes that these dialects still had laryngeals at that time, the aberrant initial PS, PB E- reflexes could have resulted from inadequate transmission of initial laryngeals. If the substratum language had no initial segments similar to the Indo-European laryngeals, some lexemes derived from, say, PIE *$h_2e\hat{k}$- 'sharp' might have developed by-forms with and without *h_2-, the former eventually yielding PS AS-, PB AŠ-, the latter PS ES-, PB EŠ-. This is a slightly interesting possibility, for there is some other evidence that points to irregularities in the transmission of initial laryngeals − traditionally typified by the equation PS KOST-I- (LCS *kostĭ), Lat. *costa* 'rib' and Lat. *ōs, ossis* 'bone', Gk *ostéon*, Arm. *oskr*, Skt. *ásthi*, Hitt. *haštāi-* (< PIE *h_3est-); cf. Shevelov (1965: 233−234). Gamkrelidze and Ivanov (1984: 131−132) provide a survey of the relevant data (presented in support of a different hypothesis). However, in all such examples, it seems, the initial vowel has the quality corresponding to the lost laryngeal. This is consistent with the findings of Koivulehto (1991: 23−25), whose Finnic examples of Indo-European word-initial laryngeals show both vowel coloring and *k*- for *h_x- (e. g., Fi. *kesä* 'summer' < *h_1es- 'be', Fi. d. *kasa*- 'edge' < *$h_2e\hat{k}$- 'pointed', Fi. *koke*- 'experience' < *h_3ek^w- 'see; eye'). Of course one cannot exclude the possibility, under different circumstances, that laryngeals could be lost without leaving any qualitative traces in contiguous vowels. It is certainly a possibility to keep in mind.

6.4. Contact with other Indo-European dialects

On the other hand, if the irregular PS, PB E- correspondences have to be accounted for as results of language interference, such interference could just as well have occurred between different Indo-European dialects. Traditionally several episodes of this nature have been recognized – and debated – for the distant prehistory of Slavic and Baltic.

6.4.1. Gutturalwechsel

One of these is thought to have given rise to the well-known Slavic and Baltic fluctuation of velars (*Gutturalwechsel*), the irregular correspondences (and lexical doublets) in which several dozen Proto-Indo-European etyma reconstructible with a palatal stop (traditionally, $*\hat{k}$, $*\hat{g}$, or $*\hat{g}^h$) have centum reflexes, or both satəm and centum reflexes, in Slavic and/or in Baltic (and/or in other language groups); see table 6.3. Traditionally these centum reflexes have been thought to be the result of dialect mixture or as culturally motivated borrowing (cf. Gołąb 1972, 1992: 78–90). They have also been explained as the outcome of different leveling changes operating on earlier, regular patterns of neutralization (cf. Gamkrelidze and Ivanov 1984: 109–114). These different types of explanation are not mutually exclusive, and actually appear to apply with different success to different lexemes. Under the phonological (or morphophonemic) explanation, the lexical distribu-

Table 6.3. Gutturalwechsel. Slavic and Baltic lexical doublets with centum and satəm reflexes of Proto-Indo-European palatal stops

PIE	Centum reflexes	Satəm reflexes
$*\hat{k}leu$-	PB KLAUS-Ī-, Li. *klausýti* 'to ask', OPr. *klausiton* 'to hear'	PS SLEU-, SLĀU-Ā-, LCS **sluti* 'be known', **slava* 'fame' PB SLUU-Ē-, SLĀU-Ē-, La. *sluvêt* 'be known', Li. *šlóvė* 'fame'
$*\hat{k}weit$-	PS KUEIT-, KUAITA-, LCS **cvisti* 'to bloom', *cvětŭ* 'flower' PB KUIT-Ē-, La. *kvitêt* 'to bloom'	PS SUIT-Ē-, SUAITA-, LCS **svĭtěti* 'to be light', **světŭ* 'light' PB SUIT-Ē-, Li. *švitěti* 'to sparkle'
$*\hat{k}erm$-	PS KERM-UX-Ā, LCS **čermŭxa*, R. *čer'-ómuxa* 'bird cherry' PB KERM-(A)UŠ-, La. *cẽrmauksis* 'rowan', Li. *kermùšė* 'wild garlic'	PS SERMUX-IĀ-, Sn. *srêmša* PB SERMUŠ-, Li. *šermùkšnis* 'rowan'
$*\hat{g}^herd^h$-	PS GARDA-, LCS **gordŭ* '(fortified) city' PB GARDA-, Li. *gardas* 'pen'	PS AB-ZARDA-, R *ozoród* 'rack' PB ŽARDA-, Li. *žardas* 'rack; fence', OPr. *Sardis* 'fence'
$*\hat{k}oi$-u̯-	PS KAIUĀ-, LCS d. **kěva* 'bobbin'	PB ŠAIUĀ-, Li. *šaivà* 'bobbin'
$*\hat{g}^hans$-	PS GANSI-, LCS **gǫsĭ* 'goose'	PB ŽANSI-, Li. *žąsìs* 'goose'

tion of centum and satəm reflexes in the modern languages would be random except for a discernible imprint of the earlier phonological regularity. Under the contact explanation, some of the deviant reflexes might be assignable to specific semantic fields (e. g., animal husbandry, wood construction, tools; cf. Gołąb [1992: 86]) and correlate with plausible hypothetical differences in technology or in economic or spiritual values between the borrower and donor dialects.

6.4.2. Reflexes of syllabic sonorants

Another prehistoric episode of this kind may be responsible for the dual reflexes of syllabic sonorants in Slavic and Baltic, where PIE *$\mathring{n}$, *$\mathring{m}$, *$\mathring{r}$, *$\mathring{l}$ yielded PS and PB IN, IM, IR, IL (for short, -IR-) and UN, UM, UR, UL (-UR-); cf. Arumaa (1964: 133−137, 151−160), Shevelov (1965: 86−90), Stang (1966: 77−79); see table 6.4. Shevelov follows Kuryłowicz in trying to uncover a phonological conditioning correlating with the IR-reflexes and UR-reflexes, but even though he restricts his purview to Slavic data, he is forced to conclude that other factors must be involved, including borrowing (Shevelov 1965: 90). This conclusion recommends itself with greater force to the observer who considers Slavic and Baltic together. The only more or less firm phonological correlation, which Kuryłowicz observed, is a numerical predominance of -IR- reflexes after a Proto-Indo-European palatal (*$\hat{k}$, *$\hat{g}$, *$\hat{g}^h$). But this need not be taken as evidence of an original phonological conditioning of -IR- reflexes and -UR-reflexes (cf. Arumaa 1964: 137; Stang 1966: 79). Possibly this correlation merely indicates that the -IR- reflexes are characteristic of the ancestral satəm dialects of Slavic and Baltic, whereas the -UR- reflexes were introduced into the linguistic traditions of the ancestors of Slavs and Balts by speakers of slightly different dialects at some point after the satəm assibilation was in progress. This hypothesis has the advantage that it is compatible with three particulars Stang emphasized (1966: 79), viz. (i) that overall there are more -IR- reflexes than -UR- reflexes, (ii) that inflectional morphemes have -IR- reflexes, but not -UR- reflexes, and (iii) that -UR- reflexes are especially common in the expressive vocabulary.

6.4.3. Tememation

Most recently one more system of dual reflexes has been brought to light in Slavic and Baltic, namely of the Proto-Indo-European stop series. Besides the regular reflexes of traditional Proto-Indo-European (I) tenues,

Table 6.4. Slavic and Baltic doublets with -IR- and -UR- reflexes of original syllabic sonorants

PIE	Zero grade -IR-	Zero grade -UR-
en	PB IN-, Li. *į, iñ-* 'in'	PS UN-, LCS *vŭ(n)* 'in'
er-n̥-b-	PS ER-IM-BI-, LCS *jerębĭ* 'grouse'	PB ER-UM-BĒ-, Li. d. *jerumbė* 'grouse' [20]
slen-k-	PB SLINK-, Li. *sliñkti* 'creep; move slowly'	PB SLUNK-, Li. *sluñkius* 'slowpoke, la-zybones'
gʷʰen-	PS GIN-DLA-, LCS *žędlo, P ządło, R žalo* 'sting' PB GIN-TEI, GIN-TLA-, Li. *giñti* 'strike, drive', *giñklas* 'weapon'	PS GUN-A-TĒI, LCS *gŭnati* PB GUN-TUEI, OPr. *guntwei* 'drive'
temh-	PS TIM-Ā-, LCS *tĭma* 'darkness' PB TIM-SĀ-, La. *tìmsa* 'darkness'	PB TUM-SĀ-, Li. d. *tumsà* 'darkness', La. *tùmsa* 'idem'
gem-	PS GIM-ĀM, LCS *žĭmǫ* 'press, crum-ple'	PB GUM-, La. *gumstât* 'press', Li. *gù-multi* 'crumple'
gʷrem-	PS GRIM-Ē-TĒI, LCS *grĭměti* 'thunder'	PB GRUM-, La. *gruměti* 'thunder'
kʷer-	PB KIR-NA-, OPr. *kirno* 'bush'	PS KUR-A-, LCS *kŭrŭ* 'root; bush'
gʷʰerh₃-	PS GIR- ĀM, LCS *žirǫ* 'swallow, eat'	PS GUR-DLA-, LCS *gŭrdlo* 'throat' PB GUR-TLA-, Li. *gurklỹs* 'idem'
stel-bʰ-	PB STILBA-, La. *stiĺbs* 'forearm'	PS STULBA-, LCS *stŭlbŭ* 'post' PB STULBA-, Li. *stuĺbas* 'pillar', La. *stùlbs* 'shin'
gʷelhₓ-	PB GIL-, Li. *gìlti* 'hurt, intr.'	PB GUL-, OPr. *gulsennien* 'pain'

(II) mediae and (III) mediae aspiratae − Slavic and Baltic (I) tenues and
(II−III) mediae − there are several dozen only recently identified Indo-
European etyma having Slavic and, to a lesser extent, Baltic counterparts
with (I−II) mediae and (III) tenues; cf. table 6.5. Holzer, who discovered
these, has dubbed the unknown language which is the presumed source
of these vocables "Tememmatian" (for *tenuis* − *media, media aspirata* −
tenuis). The lexemes in which these irregular reflexes are found are for
the most part agricultural terms, which suggests that the speakers of Tememmatian played a certain role in the development of the early farming
technology of the ancestors of Slavs and Balts. It is indeterminate
whether these loans were adopted before or after the satəm assibilation

Table 6.5. Slavic lexical doublets with Tememantian stop reflexes and with regular Slavic and Baltic reflexes

PIE	Tememantian	PS and LCS	Compare:
*bʰr̥so-	**proso*	PS PRASA-, LCS **proso* 'millet'	PS BARX-INA-, LCS **boršĭno* 'flour'; Lat. *far* 'millet', Eng. *barley*
*dʰoiĝ-dʰo-	**toik̂-to*	PS TAISTA-, LCS **těsto* 'dough'	PS DAIG-IĀ-, LCS **děža* 'kneading trough'; Gk. *toikhos* 'wall', Lat. *fingō* 'shape', Eng. *dough*
*dʰu̯oro-	*tu̯oro-*	PS TUAR-Ī-TĒI, LCS **za-tvoriti* 'shut'	PS DUIR-Ī-, LCS **dvĭri* 'door'; Gk. *thúra* 'door', Lat. *forēs* 'door', Engl. *door*
*dʰe-l-	**te-l-*	PS TE-L-ENT-, LCS **telę* 'calf'	PS DĒ-T-Ī-, LCS **dě-ti* 'children'; Skt. *dharú-* 'nursing', Gk. *thēlus* 'nursing', Lat. *filius* 'son'
*ĝʰem-ro	**k̂em-ro-*	PS SEMBRA-, LCS **sębrŭ* 'farmer'	PS ZEM-IĀ-, LCS **zemĺa* 'land'; Av. *zamar-* 'earth', Skt. *jmán* 'ground'
*su̯o-poti-	**su̯o-bodi-*	PS SUA-BADI-, LCS **svo-bodĭ* 'free'	PB PATI-, Li. *pats* 'self'; Skt. *svá-pati-* 'free', Lat. *sui potens*
*kol-	**gol-*	PS GAL-ĒNI-, LCS **go-lěnĭ* 'calf of leg'	PS KAL-ĒNA-, LCS **kolěno* 'knee'; Li. *kelénas* 'knee', Gk. *kōlēn* 'shank bone', Lat. *calx* 'heel'
*kʷoi̯o-	**gʷoi̯o-*	PS GAIA-, LCS **gojĭ* 'peace'	PS KAIA-, LCS **po-kojĭ* 'quiet'; Av. *šāiti* 'joy', Lat. *quiēs* 'peace'

or the language contact which gave rise to *Gutturalwechsel*. But the fact that there are more Tememantian words in Slavic than in Baltic puts these apparent borrowings into a definite spatial perspective.

6.5. Slavic–Baltic *a- > *e- as a contact change

It goes without saying that each of the classes of irregular correspondences that have been mentioned here merits continued study on its own terms. The possibility that each of them may be the result of contact between Pre-Slavic and Pre-Baltic and other Indo-European dialects is only a possibility and not a final verdict. At the same time, there is no need to close one's eyes to the possible generalization that there was extensive contact among diverse early Indo-European dialects in this region and that collectively the several classes of irregular correspondences are a simple reflection of this prehistoric state of affairs.

It is obvious that when etyma with initial PIE *a- or *o- are represented by both ᴀ- forms and ᴇ- forms in Slavic and Baltic, the unexpected ᴇ- reflexes allow of precisely the same kind of interpretation as centum reflexes of Proto-Indo-European palatal stops, as nasal and liquid ᴜ-diphthongs for original syllabic sonorants, and as Tememátian stop correspondences. For an interpretation along these lines, no assumptions have to be made about the structure of unknown, non-Indo-European languages. And one does not have to suppose that the change was connected with the first contact between Indo-European speakers and a local non-Indo-European population, but can allow for the possibility that it occurred as a result of one of several contact episodes involving Indo-European dialects, perhaps some time during the first millennium or millennia after the initial penetration of Indo-European speakers into the East-European forest zone. Whether it occurred as the precursors of Slavs and Balts established themselves among earlier Indo-European settlers, or as a result of an intrusion of new-comers into Pre-Slavic—Baltic territory is impossible to say.

There is no possibility of dating this event in external terms except in relation to the eventually vast areas that were settled by speakers of the ancestral dialects of Slavs and, especially, Balts: since the Rozwadowski reflexes are shared by most of Slavic and Baltic, they must be due either to a substratum language which was in place when the precursor dialects of Slavic and Baltic were introduced in Eastern Europe — according to the archaeological record already in the second millennium before our era, or to an immigrant Indo-European dialect in contact with Pre-Slavic—Baltic dialects well before these dialects attained the wide geographical distribution attested in the archaeological record already in the first millennium before our era.

For a scenario for this kind of dialect interference there are two obvious possibilities. First recall section 1.3.3, where we considered the hypothetical situation in which the identical phonemic opposition of two open vowels, *æ and *a, would be implemented, say, as an [æ] versus [a] difference in one dialect and an [a] versus [ɑ] difference in another. This is all it would take for the *a [a] of the first dialect to be identified with the *æ [a] of the second. If on the whole the norms of the second dialect prevailed, one lasting effect of such a contact episode might be a small change in the etymological distribution of *æ and *a — some lexemes having *æ reflexes for expected *a reflexes — which to the language historian centuries later would appear as the result of a weak change of *a > *æ.

Precisely such a change would account for the aberrant lexemes with Slavic and Baltic ᴇ- for PIE *a- and *o-. To be sure, this hypothetical account would produce deviant reflexes of PIE *a, *o not only in word-initial position, but also non-initially, which is not part of the explanandum as we have understood it so far. But the inherited patterns of apophony, which remained productive in Slavic until the dawn of history and even longer in the different Baltic languages, would have minimized the likelihood of word-internal *a being reinterpreted as *e. And where by-forms with *e for apophonic *a might have arisen they would have been exposed to systemic pressure and might have been remade according to the productive ablaut patterns in the course of the subsequent millennia. Besides, there are in fact isolated instances of unexplained *e*-grade in these languages which would be compatible with such a hypothetical account: LCS *drebŭ 'clippings, hulls' beside *drobŭ 'crumb; numbil; fowl' (PS DREBA- ‖ DRABA-) and *teplŭ (largely North Slavic) beside *toplŭ (largely South Slavic) 'warm' (PS TEP-LA- ‖ TAP-LA-) are obvious examples; cf. Varbot (1984: 90–92).

But the other possibility, which corresponds to the scenario in section 1.3.2, is perhaps simpler: a contact of the precursor dialects of Slavic and Baltic with a group of Indo-European speakers that had merged the reflexes of initial PIE *e-, *a-, *o-, perhaps as the result of an early loss or merger of initial laryngeals. On the whole the attested Slavic and Baltic languages preserved the word-initial vowel distinctions of the former of these groups in the received lexical distribution. But the variant usage of the latter group, whose single initial vowel was identifiable with Pre-Slavic–Baltic *e-, gave rise to lexical doublets with *e-, which in the small set of lexemes listed in table 6.1 were codified at variance with the tradition.

6.6. Slavic, Baltic, and other Indo-European dialects

The advances in the study of the prehistory of Slavic and Baltic during this century have argued for an increasingly articulate conception of the genesis of these language groups. In the long debates over the origin of the Slavic and Baltic languages earlier in this century, different hypothetical accounts were put forward involving alternating periods of shared and separate developments among their ancestral dialects in order to explain the similarities and contrasts among their modern descendants. These hypotheses often seemed based on the unspoken assumption that there was a single wave of Indo-European settlement that covered Eastern Europe, after which the respective speech communities went through periods of changing relationships.

In more recent decades, it has become clear that this simple assumption will not do. As more attention has been focused on differences internal to Slavic and Baltic, the studies of the Baltic lexicon by, among others, Stang (1966, 1971) and Smoczyński (1981, 1986) and of the Slavic lexicon, for instance, by Martynov (1983, with further references), Gołąb (1992, with further references), and, especially, Trubačev (1991, with further references), have demonstrated with great weight that the vocabulary particularly of the ancestral dialects of the Slavs is composed of layers of elements from several linguistic traditions and allows us to infer both periods of convergent development shared with neighboring Indo-European dialects and contact episodes – with Italic, Iranian, Celtic, and Germanic. For instance, besides the layer of Common Slavic borrowings from Iranian, which seems to imply a period of significant cultural contact, there is the narrowly West Slavic body of Iranian loan words especially well represented in Lechitic (Trubačev 1967, 1968b). Such contact episodes as the Pre-West Slavic–Iranian one must have been intimate in character, that is, they must have involved groups of foreign speakers melding with a Slavic-speaking ethnic matrix.

The several examples of well-defined irregular phonological reflexes that were reviewed in section 6.4 above are an important part of this picture of the prehistory of Slavic and Baltic, for these examples too bear witness to the merging of diverse linguistic traditions in their precursor and ancestral dialects – even though the sources of these irregularities cannot be identified or labeled with ethnonyms, the way the more recent different ingredients of the lexicon can.

Admittedly the idea I have put forward here, that the Slavic and Baltic E- reflexes of Proto-Indo-European initial *a-* and *o-* arose the same way as the other irregular phonological reflexes – *Gutturalwechsel*, I/U-diphthongs for syllabic sonorants, and Tememation stop correspondences – does not move our understanding forward by a great deal. It is easy to fault this account with explaining one unknown by numerous other unknowns. But it seems reasonable to view the otherwise incomprehensible aberrant initial vowel correspondences of Slavic and Baltic in this perspective – it is after all a perspective that is demanded by other irregular correspondences dating from a similarly early period of Slavic and Baltic prehistory – at least until other, compelling evidence will support a more substantial hypothetical account.

Chapter 7

The material

The purposes of this chapter are to present documentation for the geographical distribution of Slavic and Baltic forms with initial PS, PB E- and to sketch the etymological connections of this lexical material, within Slavic, between Slavic and Baltic, and beyond Slavic−Baltic, with specific attention to the initial vowels.

7.0.1. Sources and conventions of presentation

The material is surveyed on the basis of the fuller data contained for the most part in (i) Popowska-Taborska (1984), Trubačev (1974, 1979, 1981 a, and Sławski (1974, 1991) for Slavic, (ii) Fraenkel (1962, 1965), Mažiulis (1988), and Toporov (1975, 1979, 1980, 1990) for Baltic, and (iii) Pokorny and others for Proto-Indo-European. To conserve space, point by point references to these works are for the most part omitted.

Furthermore, in the interest of brevity, the presentation omits many modern dialect forms and older attestations which shed no light on the Slavic *je- ‖ *o- isoglosses or Baltic *e- ‖ *a- isoglosses and focuses on those language areas in which doublet forms are attested. Consequently, sometimes a single Slavic or Baltic form (mostly a standard form) is allowed to stand for the whole panoply of regular and irregular reflexes descended from a specific by-form in a given language area. However, all local attestations which are not directly reducible to LCS *je- or *o- (or Baltic *e- or *a-), but may be relevant to their development are acknowledged.

The material is arranged alphabetically, except that doublet forms with PS, PB A- are listed under E-. Thus all the etyma with PS or PB E- precede the small number of etyma beginning with I- and L-.

Each entry is headed by the reconstructed Proto-Slavic and/or Proto-Baltic form(s), the original or basic sense(s), and in many cases a numbered list of significant secondary senses.

Next follow numbered paragraphs with a brief summary of the geographical distribution of the modern reflexes of the initial in Slavic and Baltic and more extensive accounts of the attestation in each of the two language groups, accompanied by commentary as needed. In these accounts, a number in parentheses following a cited form assigns to the form the sense of the same number listed in the head entry.

Table 7.1. List of the Slavic and Baltic lexemes analysed in chapter 7

	PS	PB		PS	PB
[1]	EDEINA-		[23]		ERKIĀ-
[2]	EDSKE		[24]	ERKXI-	ERŠKIA-
[3]	EDUĀS		[25]		ERŽILA-
[4]	EDLI-	EDLĒ-	[26]	ESE	
[5]		EKETĒ-	[27]	ESENA- ‖ ĀSENA-	
[6]	ELAUA- ‖ ALAUA-	ELUA- ‖ ALUA-	[28]	ESENI-	‖ ASENI-
[7]	ELBEDĀ- ‖ LABADĀ-		[29]	ESERĀ-	EŠERIA-
[8]	ELBEDI- ‖ LĀBANDI-		[30]	ESETI-	EKETI-
[9]	ELIKA-		[31]	ESETRA-	EŠETRA-
[10]	ELEITA-		[32]	ESMI	ESMI
[11]	ELENI-	ELENI-	[33]		EŠUĀ-
[12]	ELISĀ-		[34]		EŽ
[13]	ELIXĀ- ‖ ALIXĀ-	ELSNI-	[35]	EZERA-	EŽERA-
[14]	‖ ALKUTI-	ELKŪNĒ-	[36]		EŽIĀ-
[15]	‖ ĀLNĪ	ĒLNĒ-	[37]	EZIA-	EŽIA-
[16]		ELUEDĒ-	[38]	derivatives	
[17]	ELUKA-		[39]	IA GE	
[18]	EMELA	EMELA-	[40]	IA LAI	
[19]	EPSĀ- ‖ APSĀ-	EPSĒ- ‖ APSĒ-	[41]	IATERA-	
[20]	ERIMBI ‖ etc.	ERUMBĒ- ‖ etc.	[42]	IAUĪNĀ-	
[21]	derivatives		[43]	IEB-TĒI	
[22]	ERILA- ‖ ARILA	ERELIA-	[44]	LEMESIA-	

A final paragraph discusses problems of etymology, including the wider Indo-European perspective, and concludes with a statement of how the form(s) of the given lexeme may be interpreted in light of the theories put forward in this investigation.

Cited forms are intended to be faithful to the sources with one major exception: all attestations from Cyrillic sources, primary or secondary, are romanized; forms in a standard orthography are represented by phonemic notation, phonetic transcription is transliterated. This is done to evade an effect of some Cyrillic spelling conventions, which is to obscure the distinction between initial vowel and initial glide plus vowel.

7.0.2. The corpus

The material that is analysed below includes all Slavic lexemes with initial PS E- and all Baltic lexemes with PB E- which are attested in at least two

Baltic languages or at least one Baltic and one Slavic language. The lexemes with PS and/or PB E- appear as sections 7.1–7.37. Among these lexemes are some that begin with (tautosyllabic) liquid diphthongs (PS, PB EL-, ER-), which previous investigators have examined or ignored depending on their conception of the time of the "**je > *o-* change". The small number of lexemes with other initials are discussed in sections 7.38–7.44. A list of all the lemmas is displayed in table 7.1.

Table 7.2. The material discussed by Šaur (1982) and by Popowska-Taborska (1984)

PS	Šaur	P.-T.		PS	Šaur	P.-T.
[1] EDEINA-	*edinŭ	*jedinŭ		[24] ERKXI-		
[2] EDSKE	*ešče	*ješče		[26] ESE	*ese	*jese
[3] EDUĀS	*edŭva	*jedva		[27] ESENA-		*jesenŭ
[4] EDLI-	*edla			[28] ESENI-	*esenĭ	*jesenĭ
[6] ELAUA- ‖ ALAUA-		*jelavŭ		[29] ESERĀ-	*esera	*jesery
[7] ELBEDĀ-	*elbeda			[30] ESETI-		*jesetĭ
[8] ELBEDI-	*elbędĭ			[31] ESETRA-	*esetrŭ	*jesetrŭ
[9] ELIKA-	*elĭčĭ			[32] ES-MI	*esmĭ	
[10] ELEITA-	*elito	*jelito		[35] EZERA-	*ezero	*jezero
[11] ELENI-	*elenĭ	*jelenĭ		[37] EZIA-	*ežĭ	*ježĭ
[12] ELISĀ-				[38] derivatives		
[13] ELIXĀ- ‖ ALIXĀ-	*elĭxa	*jelĭxa		[39] IA GE		*ježe
[14] ‖ ALKUTI-				[40] IA LAI		*jeli,
[15] ‖ ĀLNĪ						*jeliko
[17] ELUKA-	*elŭkŭ			[41] IATERA-	*eterŭ	*jeterŭ
[18] EMELA-	*emela	*jemelŭ		[42] IAUĪNĀ-	*evnĭja	*jevĭja
[19] EPSĀ- ‖ APSĀ-					[sic!]	
[20] ERIMBI- ‖ etc.		*jerębĭ		[43] IEB-TĒI		
[21] derivatives				[44] LEMESIA-		*jemešĭ
[22] ERILA- ‖ ARILA-		*jerīlŭ				

This corpus includes all lexemes that have been considered relevant by previous investigators of the Slavic **je-* ‖ **o-* problem. The lexemes that are discussed by Šaur (1982) and Popowska-Taborska (1984) are indicated in table 7.2. Not included are a few lexemes Šaur mentions – (i) **egŭda* 'when' and (ii) **eriti* 'bustle' – neither of which he considers relevant to the **e- > *a-* change. I also ignore a few lexemes Popowska-Taborska briefly discusses – (i) Sn. *jekel ‖ okèl* 'ratchet', (ii) SC *jèktika ‖ òktika* 'fever', (iii) R d. *jer'ep'én'it'-sa* 'be annoyed', (iv) Cz. *jesep* 'sandbank', (v) R *ol'ábka*, Br. *al'ápka* 'dipper (Cinclus)', all of which she shows are of no relevance. It is apparent from table 7.2 that Popowska-Taborska's study did not include lexemes with initial liquid diphthongs, whereas Šaur's did. Such lexemes have been included here because they begin with PS E-.

7.1. PS ED-EIN-A-, ED-IN-A- − (0) 'one'; derivatives meaning (1) 'only', (2) 'once', (3) 'however'

The root is this lexeme occurs in both Slavic and Baltic, but the preposed part is known only to Slavic.

1. In East Slavic, CS *a- is general. *e- reflexes occur in Church Slavonic loans in all three East Slavic languages, but are well attested also in peripheral folk dialects of the Russian Northeast and the Ukrainian Southwest. In the other five regions, *e- is almost universal, but there are sporadic *a- forms in (proximal) Slovenian, in (proximal) Bulgarian, and in Old Church Slavonic.

1.1. LCS *jedinŭ: P *jeden*, d. *jeżiny* (1), o. *jednąc* (2), Sc. *jãděn*, Pb. *jadån, jidaịnə* (1); US *jedyn*, d. *jeden*, LS *jaden, jadny* (1); Sk. *jeden, jediný* (1), *eden, jednúc* (2), Cz. *jeden, jediný* (1), o. *jednúc* (2); Sn. *êden*, o. *jéden*, d. *édn, èn, ən, edíni* (1), d. *edĩn*, d. *jenǫk* (2), SC *jèdan, jĕdĩnī* (1), ča. *jedôn, edan*, d. *jednōć* (2); Bg. *edín*, d. *edén, ednóš* (2), M *eden, edin*, d. *ednəš*, OCS *jedinŭ, jedĭnŭ*; R d. *jed'ín, jad'ín, jadnó*, N-d. *jed'ín* (Perm'), *jédnyj* (Pskov, Arxangel'sk, Vologda, Perm', Rjazan', Jaroslavl', Vjatka, Samara, Kazan'), *jed'ínoj* (1), Br. d. *jednákovo* (3), *jednác'* (2), *jedýnyj* (1), U d. *jedýn, jedýnyj* (1), *jidén, jedén, jidnákyj* (Lemko), d. *jednáčy* (2).

1.2. LCS *odinŭ: Sn. o., d. *adən*, d. *odnok* (2) (Prekmurje); Bg. d. *adnŭč* (2), *adnoto, adnŭ, adín*, OCS *odĭnače* (2) (Ps., hapax); R *od'ín, odnáko* (3), Br. *aʒ'ín, odnák* (3), *aʒ'íni*, U *odén*, d. *odýn*.

1.3. Secondary ja-: P o., d. *jaden* (thought to be a hypercorrection; cf. section 5.1.3). Reduced forms of this lexeme are widespread, especially in some languages; they are characterized by consonant aphaeresis and elision; cf. the examples from Slovenian and Serbo-Croatian above. They are of recent date and have no bearing on the reconstruction of the initial.

2. The Baltic correspondences are not relevant: OPr. *ains*, La. *viens*, Li. *víenas*; East Baltic has a *w- 'distal deixis' contrasting with the Slavic ED-.

3. The initial element PS ED- 'near deixis' (PIE *ed; Pokorny [1959−1969, 1: 284]) seems to recur in PS ED-UĀS [3] and possibly in PS

ED-S-KE [2]. Its short vowel before Proto-Indo-European media is incompatible with Winter's Law (Winter 1978).

In any case, by their distribution among the Slavic languages, the modern *je-* and *o-*reflexes bear witness to a PS E- and the Slavic−Baltic *e-* > *a-* merger.

Literature: Popowska-Taborska (1984: 30−35); Trubačev (1979: 9−18); Sławski (1991: 13−30).

7.2. PS ED-S-KE − 'still; more'

This is a uniquely Slavic formation.

1. CS *e-* forms occur in all Slavic languages. *a-* forms occur in East Slavic, in both South Slavic regions and sporadically in (proximal) Polish. The numerous modern forms with initial *i-* (for LCS *je-* or *e-*) or *u-* (for LCS *o-*) or with aphaeresis, with -*š-* (or *š-*, -*š*), and/or with apocope are undoubtedly allegro-forms in origin; they are adduced alongside the full forms here only to illustrate the variety of reductions they exemplify. Some occurrences of initial *i-* and *j-* may represent the conjunction *i* 'and', as indicated below; among the *e-* forms such additions may not be distinguishable from straight *e-* reflexes with *j*-prothesis.

1.1. LCS *ješče*: P *jeszcze*, d. *ešče, iši*, Ka. *ješ, ješče, jiš*, Sc. *jeiš*, Pb. *jist*; US *hišče*, d. *šče*, LS *hyšći, hyšć, hešče, hešć, ješče, ješči, yšči*; Sk. *ešt'e*, d. *ešče, ešči, išče*, Cz. *ještě*, o. *ješče*, d. *ešče*; Sn. *še*, o. *ešče*, d. *šče, išče, iše* (< *i [je]šče*), SC d. *ješte*, kaj. *ihče*; Bg. *ešte*, d. *éščé, jéšte, ište* (< *i [e]šte*), M *ešte, ište* (< *i[e]šte*), *ešče, eš*, OCS *ješte*; R *ješčó*, d. *ješče*, Br. *jaščé*, d. *jaščý, jaščó, iščé* (< *o-?*), *ščé*, U *ščé*, d. *ješčé, ješčý, ješčo, iščé*.

1.2. LCS *ošče*: P d. *oščo*; Sn. d. *još, jošt, jošče* (< *i ošče*), SC *još, jošt, jošte* (< *i ošte*), d. *jošće*; Bg. *óšte*, d. *óše, oš, jošt, jóšte* (< *i ošt*[*e*]), M *ušte*, d. *ušče, ošte, još* (< *i oš*[*te*]); R d. *oščé, oščó*, Br. d. *aščé, iščé* (< *je-?*).

2. There are no known cognates in Baltic.

3. Some investigators posit protoforms with a variety of initials and finals (Sławski posits eight! [1991: 67]), but there is no reason to take all the attested allegro forms back to the protolanguage; one form with PS E- is sufficient. The accretion of *i* 'and' in South Slavic *j-oš(te), i-šte*, etc. is a lexicalization of a simple semantic strengthening. Possibly a deic-

tic PS E- (cf. ESE, ETERA- below) was similarly added to reinforce an earlier synonym; or it was expanded with the PS ED- of ED-EIN-A- [1], ED-UĀS [3], though this hypothetical PIE *ed (Pokorny 1959–1969, 1: 286) is as hard to see in LCS *ješče ‖ *ošče as in Lat. *ecce* 'look!' (< *ed-ce), where its reconstructed presence is disputed (Schrijver 1991: 35). The synonym that was reinforced with PS E(D) may well have been a syncopated allegro form (of the structure *sV-ke), the last element being the enclitic copulative particle (PIE *kʷe), the penultimate element (which Trubačev calls "infixed" and Sławski "mobile") perhaps being some form of the demonstrative of near deixis (PIE *k̂ī 'this').

The modern *je- and *o- reflexes of this lexeme exemplify the Slavic–Baltic *e- > *a- merger.

Literature: Trubačev (1979: 32–33); Popowska-Taborska (1984: 61–63); Sławski 1991: 67–69).

7.3. PS ED-UĀS — 'hardly'

This is a uniquely Slavic formation.

1. Slavic: *e- forms are indicated in all six regions of Slavic settlement — in some, though, only indirectly by forms in *le-* (see below); the initial *l-* is thought to be a substitution for LCS *j-* or due to contamination or composition with *lě- 'hardly' (CS *lě-edwā would be an additive formation parallel to *i oš(te) mentioned under PS EDSKE above). *a- forms are known from Russian dialects (but not from the rest of East Slavic), from (proximal) Slovenian, and from Eastern South Slavic; the attestation includes an isolated form in Old Church Slavonic.

1.1. LCS *jedva: P o. *jedwa, jedwo* (*ledwo*, etc.); (US *lědma*, etc., LS *lěbda*, etc., Sk. *ledva*, etc.), Cz. *jedva* (*ledva*, etc.); Sn. *jédva*, d. *jedvaj*, SC *jèdva*, ča. *jedvà*, kaj. *jedvaj* (*ledva*, etc.); Bg. *edvá*, d. *edváj, edvám*, M *edváj*, d. *edvám*, OCS *jedva, jedŭva*; R *jedvá*, o. *jedŭva* (S-d. *l'édv'e*, etc.), Br. d. *jedva* (d. *l'eʒ'v'e*, etc.), U o. *jedvá* (*lédve*, etc.).

1.2. LCS *odva: Sn. d. *odvo*, o. *odvaj*; Bg. d. *odvám, odváj*, M d. *odvaj*, OCS *odŭva* (for *odva); R NW-d. *odvá*, o. *odva*.

2. PB UĀS, Li. *võs* 'idem' corresponds to the second part of the Slavic word. Li. E-d. *advõs* is a blend of native *võs* and Br. o. *odva*.

3. The initial element is thought to be identical to the demonstrative in PS ED-EINA- in section 7.1 above.

This lexeme exemplifies the Slavic–Baltic **e-* > **a-* merger.

Literature: Fraenkel (1962–1965: 1274); Popowska-Taborska (1984: 35); Trubačev (1979, 16); Sławski (1991: 35–37).

7.4. PS EDL-I-, EDL-Ā-, PB EDL-Ē- – 'spruce; fir (Picea, Abies, Pinus)'

This lexeme has only **e-* forms in Slavic, but both *e-* and *a-* forms in Baltic.

1. LCS **jedla, *jedlĭ, *jedl'a*: P *jodła*, o. *jedl*, Pb. *jadlə*; US *jědla*, LS *jedła*; Sk. *jedl'a, jedlica*, Cz. *jedle*, o. *jedl, jedlice*; Sn. *jéla, jêl*, d. *jèdu̯a*, SC *jéla, jèlica*; Bg. *elá, elíca*, M *ela, elka*; R *jólka, jél'*, d. *jógla*, Br. *jólka*, U. *jalýna*.

2. PB EDL-Ē-: OPr. *Addle* – *Tanne* (E. 596), Cur. top. *Egel, Eglinen*, La. *egle*, top. *Egle, Ęgluoṇa*, Li. *ẽglė*, d. *ãglė*, top. *Ẽglė, Eglesỹs, Aglesỹs, Eglýnas, Ẽglinis, Ẽglis, Ẽglupis*.

All the Slavic and Baltic forms are phonologically compatible with Lat. *ebulus* 'elder' (< PIE **h₁edʰ-lo-s*), the Old Prussian *a-* being ascribable to the **e-* > **a-* merger; this is the simplest account. (The Old Prussian form may also agree with Gaul. *od-ocos* 'elder' [< PIE **h₁odʰ-*]. So may the Slavic and East Baltic forms if they are results of Rozwadowski's change. The Old Prussian form may be a product of both this and the Slavic–Baltic **e-* > **a-* merger.) The root PIE **h₁edʰ-* is thought to recur in Li. *ãdata*, La. *adata* 'needle', which is semantically compatible with the Slavic–Baltic names of the spruce or fir, but makes no sense at all in relation to the Italo-Celtic elder. This formation sheds no light on the original vocalism of PS, PB EDL-.

The lexeme is one of a handful of words with PS E- that show no evidence of the **e-* > **a-* merger in Slavic. The Baltic languages have reflexes of the merger in Old Prussian and Lithuanian.

Literature: Pokorny (1959–1969, 1: 289–290); Trubačev (1979: 14–15); Toporov (1975: 56–57); Mažiulis (1988: 48); Sławski (1991: 30–35).

7.5. PB EKETĒ ‖ AKETĒ — 'pool; ice-hole'

This derivative is attested only in Baltic. It occurs with *a*- in Latvian.

1. La. *akacis, akata*, Li. *eketė*, d. *aketė, ẽketis*.

2. These are derivatives of PB AK-I- 'eye', PIE *h_3ek^w-, with semantic parallels in Slavic. The Lithuanian initial *e*- appears to be due to Rozwadowski's change, and the *a*- variants in Lithuanian result from the **e-* > **a-* merger. The Latvian forms may have gone through both changes, but may simply have escaped Rozwadowski's change (cf. sections 6.1−6.2, and table 6.2).

Literature: Fraenkel (1962−1965: 120); Toporov (1975: 57−58, s. v. *agins*); Mažiulis (1988: 49, s. v. *agins*).

7.6. PS ELAUA- ‖ ALAUA-, PB ĒLUA- ‖ ĀLUA- — 'lead (Pb)'

Both Slavic and Baltic have **e-* and **a-* variants.

1. **a-* forms occur in all the Slavic languages, **e-* forms only in Bulgarian.

1.1. LCS **jelovo*: Bg. o. *élav*, o. *jelovo*, d. *élavo*.

1.2. LCS **olovo*: P *olów*, o. *olów*; LS *wóloj*, US *woloj*; Sk. *olovo*, Cz. *olovo*; Sn. o. *olôv, ólovo*, SC *ȍlovo, ȍlov*; Bg. *olovo*, M *olovo*, OCS *olovo*; R *ólovo*, o. *olovĭ*, Br. *vólava*, U *ólovo*.

1.3. Apparent aphaeresis in R d. *lov'*, but this might instead reflect a Southeast Baltic substratum form borrowed into dialectal Common Slavic as **alwi-*, with subsequent regular metathesis of the initial liquid diphthong and no trace of the Baltic vowel quantity or pitch accent. The Sorbian forms have regular prothetic *w*- and regular final -*j* for LCS -*vĭ*.

2. PB ĒLUA- ‖ ĀLUA-: OPr. *elwas* 'Zinnerz' (Mažiulis 1988: s. v.) 'tin (St)', *Alwis — Bley* (E. 527) 'lead (Pb)', La. *aȋvs, aȋva* 'tin', Li. *álvas* 'tin'.

3. Both the Slavic dialect variants − the *i*-stem feminine (in Sorbian, Lechitic, Western South Slavic) and the *o*-stem neuter (in East Slavic, Slovak−Czech, Western and Eastern South Slavic) − are hard to reconcile with the Baltic forms: the accent of Li. *álvas*, La. *aȋvs, aȋva* appears to show compensatory lengthening for a lost laryngeal (**aləw-?*) where the Slavic forms have their second vowel (PS ALAU-A-). The word is traditionally considered a derivative of PIE **el-* 'white' (Pokorny [1959−1969,

1: 303]; Gamkrelidze and Ivanov [1984: 783, 789]; cf. Li. *elvỹs* 'birch', OHG *elo* 'white', Lat. *lūridus* 'pale'), but it is more likely a borrowing.

Huld (in press) offers a shrewd hypothesis, based on the distinction between Lat. *plumbum album* 'white solder, tin' and *plumbum nigrum* 'black solder, lead', deriving the Slavic and Baltic words from an unattested Celtic term for 'white [solder]' (i.e. 'tin'), *poləuom [ploudʰom]*. While the noun *(p)loudʰom* yields the Germanic word for 'lead', the adjective *(p)oləuom*, is adopted by Slavic−Baltic (and substantivized) as the term for 'tin'; the root is otherwise known to Slavic as PS PĀLUA-, LCS *polwa-*, OCS *plavŭ* 'withish, yellow' and to Baltic as La. *pal̃ss*, Li. *pálšas, pal̃vas* 'sallow, pale', *pilkas* 'grey'. Huld's reconstruction is reconcilable with both the monosyllabic PB ĒLUA- ‖ ĀLUA- (with a prosodic reflex of the laryngeal) and the dissyllabic PS ALAUA- ‖ ELAUA- (with a segmental reflex). This hypothetical borrowing deserves to be integrated in a wider context of Celtic and Slavic−Baltic loan contacts.

Whatever the origin of the word, the exceptional initial *e-* of Bg. *elav(o)* and OPr. *elwas* point to E- doublets that can be ascribed to Rozwadowski's change. OPr. *Alwis* may reflect both this change and the later **e-* > **a-* merger, or it may be an old A- doublet. The solid *a-* attestation in East Baltic points to an A- doublet that escaped Rozwadowski's change. The same goes for the Slavic languages, where the consistent, invariant **a-* forms in five of six Slavic regions suggest a PS A- doublet. (Cf. sections 6.1−6.2 and tables 6.1 and 6.2.)

Literature: Popowska-Taborska (1984: 48−49); Toporov (1975: 81−82); Mažiulis (1988: 73).

7.7. PS ELBEDĀ- ‖ LABADĀ- − (0) 'goosefoot (Atriplex, Chenopodium)'; (1) 'horehound'

This Slavic lexeme has no cognates in Baltic.

1. Apparent CS **el-* forms occur in (proximal) Polish, in Slovak−Czech, (proximal) Slovenian, Bulgarian, and East Slavic. Apparent CS **al-* forms occur in (proximal) Polish, Sorbian, (proximal) Slovak, Western and Eastern South Slavic, and East Slavic − but in the South Slavic languages with what looks like the regular North Slavic reflex *lo-* rather than the normal South Slavic *la-*. The latter reflex does occur in

Bulgarian, but it also occurs in Polish dialects, where it is at variance with the normal North Slavic *lo-* reflex.

1.1. CS **elbedā*: P *lebioda*; Sk. d. *lebeda*, Cz. *lebeda*; Sn. d. *lebéda, leboda*; Bg. *lebeda*, R *l'eb'edá*, Br. d. *l'eb'adá*, U d. *lebedá*.

1.2. N-CS **albadā*: P *łoboda*; US *loboda*, LS *łoboda, łobeda*; Sk. *loboda*; (Sn. *lóboda*, SC *lobòda*; Bg. *lóboda*, M *loboda* are irregular **al-* reflexes in South Slavic, cf. paragraph 1.4); R d. *lobodá*, Br. *labadá*, U *lobodá*.

1.3. S-CS **albadā*: P d. *łabada*; SC *laboda*; Bg. *láboda*.

1.4. CS **labadā*: (P *łoboda*, US *loboda*, LS *łoboda, łobyda*, Sk. *loboda* are ambiguous, cf. paragraph 1.2); Sn. *lóboda*, SC *lobòda*; Bg. *lóboda*, M *loboda*.

2. Although there are no cognates in Baltic, Li. *balánda,* La. *baluoda,* d. *balanda* (with -*an*- from Curonian), apparently derived from *bálti* 'to become white', is a similar formation − like its Slavic counterpart motivated by the white powder on the plant's leaves.

3. PS ELBEDĀ- is held to be a derivative of PIE **h₂elbʰ-* 'white', just like the bird name PS ELBEDI- 'swan' (see section 7.8). If it is, then its modern reflexes show the effects of both of the two sound changes studied in this investigation, Rozwadowski's change explaining the PS E-, the Slavic−Baltic **e-* > **a-* merger accounting for the CS **e-* ‖ **a-* diversity.

3.1. But the diverse attested forms are difficult to reconcile. They can be reduced to a single proto-form PS ELBEDĀ- only under the assumption of the Slavic−Baltic **e-* > **a-* merger in some Common Slavic dialects and a later competition among the **e-* ‖ **a-* dialect variants, but only if this competition occurred after the metathesis of initial liquid diphthongs (that is, as northern LCS **le-* ‖ **lo-*, but southern LCS **lě-* ‖ **la-*) − especially in the South Slavic regions. This last assumption is hard to justify, for on the whole the Central Slovak and South Slavic leveling of quantity in initial liquid diphthongs gave rise to a pretty clear isogloss separating northern and southern Slavic dialects: in the north, CS **al-* versus **āl-* are metathesized as CS **la-* versus **lā-* (> LCS **lo-* versus **la-*), whereas in the south they merge in a two-mora diphthong CS **al-*, metathesized as CS **lā-* (> LCS **la-*). The changes in question occurred at a time (the 600−700s) when the Slavic migrations in the west and south were coming to an end, and it is hard to imagine not only why northern forms of precisely this lexeme would have become so popular in the Slavic south; one is hard put to guess how they could even have been introduced there in this late phase of the territorial expansion.

Shevelov posits a CS **lebodā* (I would write this CS I−II **lebadā* or LCS *⁺leboda*) and assumes that a variety of unsystematic vowel assimilations affected the first two syllables of the word (1965: 361), but he also allows for the possibility that the forms in paragraph 1.1 above derive from CS **elbedā* (representing the root of Lat. *albus*; [1965: 393]). This is tantamount to positing two different states of this Proto-Indo-European root, **h₂lebʰ-* and **h₂elbʰ-* to account for the internal Slavic diversity (cf. section 7.8). Boryś (1984) posits **elboda ∥ *elbeda*, but appears oblivious to the problematic geographical distribution of the reflexes (see Sławski [1991: 40−42]).

3.2. The recent proposal by Holzer (1989: 60−64), who interprets the word as the Tememate reflex (cf. section 6.4.3) of PIE **el-pod-ā*, lit. 'goose-foot', with Tm. **b* for PIE **p* and, crucially, Tm. **lo* for PIE **l̥* perhaps offers a solution. The root is the **h₁el-* of Lat. *olor, olōris* (< **el-ōr-*) 'swan'. A full-grade **el-pedā* (> Tm. **elbedā* > CS **elbedā*), in some areas subject to the **e- > *a-* merger, would yield northern LCS **lebeda* ~ **lobeda* and southern **lěbeda ~ *labeda*. The zero-grade PIE **l̥-ped-ā* (> Tm. **lobedā* > CS **labedā*) would yield LCS **lobeda*, which could have become disseminated across the Slavic territories irrespective of the development of initial liquid diphthongs − in North Slavic this would be indistinguishable from the reflex of CS **albedā*. Some of the attested forms must still involve irregular vowel assimilations. In favor of Holzer's etymology of the word is the fact that this plant name fits in among the rather numerous agricultural terms he has identified, which have Tememate reflexes in Slavic.

But the existence of a Proto-Slavic by-form LEBEDĀ- (< PIE **h₂lebʰ-*) cannot be ruled out; cf. section 7.8.

Literature: Trubačev (1979: 18); Sławski (1991: 40−42).

7.8. PS ELB-ED-I- or LEB-ED-I- ∥ LĀB-AND-I- − 'swan (Cygnus cygnus)'

Slavic has only CS **e-* forms. Baltic has a different word for the swan.

1. PS EL-/LE- forms are found in Eastern South Slavic and East Slavic; the PS LĀB-AND-I- reflexes occur in Lechitic and Slovak−Czech; both forms occur in Western South Slavic.

1.1. CS *elbedi- or *lebedi-: Sn. *lebę́d*, SC o. *lȅbūt*; Bg. *lébed*, M *lebed*; R *l'éb'ed'*, Br. *l'éb'eʒ'*, U *lébid'*.

1.2. CS *lābandi-: P *łabędź*; Sk. *labut'*, Cz. *labut'*; Sn. *labód*, SC *läbūd*.

2. OPr. *Gulbis* − *Swane* (E. 717) 'swan', La. *gùlbis*, Li. *guĩbė* are irrelevant to the issue of initial vowels. But the PB GULB-I(A)- had a dialectal Slavic correspondent PS KULP-I- ‖ GULB-I- which was disseminated in competition with the other Slavic doublets during the period of expansion: Ka. *kelp*, Sc. *køup*; US *kołp, kolpica* 'pen', LS *kołp*; SC d. *kup* (Hercegovina), o. *kuf* (Dubrovnik, kaj-d.), o. *gub, guf*; R *kólpik* 'spoon-bill heron', *kolpíca* 'young pen', U *kólpyk* 'spoon-bill', d. *kolpéc'* 'osprey'. See Toporov (1979: 330−334). Note that outside of East Slavic, none of the KULPI- ‖ GULBI- attestations are in proximal areas.

3. Among the closest relatives to Slavic, only Germanic seems to show a formation similar to PS ELBEDI-, OHG *albiz̧, elbiz̧*, OE *ielfetu*, ON *elptr, ǫlpt* 'swan', the root being represented more widely, cf. Lat. *albus* 'white', Gk. *alphós* 'white leprosy', Hitt. *alpa-* 'cloud'(?) (< PIE *h_2elb^h- 'white'). These forms are compatible with a PS ELB-, assuming the effects of Rozwadowski's change in Slavic. If CS *el- sequences were subject to the *e- > *a- merger (as suggested in section 7.7), this PS ELB-EDI- by-form must be considered one of the handful of lexemes that show no effects of the merger (cf. section 3.8).

The reflexes with *la-* in paragraph 1.2 might be taken to reflect the *e- > *a- merger. But this would not explain their different suffix, -AND-I-. Furthermore, the Slovak−Czech forms call for a long root vowel, which may also be reflected in South Slavic (in polysyllables, SC *lä-* is ambiguous between initial AL- and ĀL-). From within Slavic one would posit PS ĀLB-ANDI- (thus Sławski [1991: 40], who writes the form as *ólbǫdī*). However, Beekes compares Gk. *alōphoús: leukoús* (Hesych.) 'white' (< PIE *$h_2lōb^h$-) with these forms (1969: 40), which suggests the possible existence of an inherited by-form PS LĀB-ANDI-, as above. In Western South Slavic, blends of the two reconstructible forms occur, such as the segmental blend SC o. *lȅbūt* (with the root vowel of the first and the suffix of the second by-form) and the segmental-accentual blend Sn. *labód* (with the accent of the first, but the stem shape of the second by-form).

But it has to be noted as a possibility that the LCS *leb-* forms reflect not a metathesized CS *elb-, but a PS LEBEDI- (< PIE *h_2leb^h-) with the same root in state 2 just as in *$h_2lōb^h$- (cf. Anttila 1969).

If this is the case, LCS *lebedĭ* and *labǫdĭ* should be reconstructed as PS LEB-EDI- ‖ LĀB-ANDI-, both having no bearing at all on the topic of this study.

Literature: Trubačev (1979: 19); Sławski (1991: 39−40).

7.9. PS ELA-, EL-IKA- − (0) 'whitefish (Leuciscus idus, L. grislagine, L. 1., L. vulgaris)'; (1) 'Alburnus lucidus', (2) 'Alosa vulgaris', (3) 'roach'

This lexeme is limited to Slavic. There are no known *a-* forms of it.

1.1. LCS *jelĭčĭ: P *jelec*, Ka. *jel*; US *jelc, jĕlc* (2); Sk. d. *jelec*, Cz. *jelec*; R *jel'éc*, U d. *jeléc', veléc'*.

1.2. Secondary *ja-*: P d. *jalec*, Ka.-Sc. *jolc*; LS *jalc, jalica* (2); Sk. *jalec*, Cz. d. *jalec*; SC d. *jálac, jal* (Bosnia); Br. *jál'ec*, U *jaléc'* (1).

2. There are no known cognates in Baltic.

3. PS ELA- is traditionally thought to contain PIE *el-* 'light-colored'. It is one of the handful of lexemes that show no evidence of the Slavic−Baltic *e-* > *a-* merger anywhere in the Slavic languages.

Literature: Pokorny (1959−1969, 1: 31); Trubačev (1979: 22−23); Sławski (1991: 48, 50).

7.10. PS ELEITA- − 'gut', pl. 'innards'; modern meanings (0) 'intestine', pl. 'innards', 'belly'; (1) 'black pudding' or 'sausage', (2) 'animal's testicles', (3) 'cow's (third) stomach', (4) 'boil', (5) 'bruise'

This appears to be a uniquely Slavic word.

1. *a-* forms are attested in Western South Slavic and in Russian, but not in Belarusian or Ukrainian. *e-* forms occur in Belarusian and Ukrainian, in the three West Slavic regions, and in Western South Slavic. The lexeme is not attested in Eastern South Slavic.

1.1. LCS *jelito*: P *jelito* (0, 1); US *jelito* (3), LS *jelito* (0, 3); Sk. *jelito* (0, 1), Cz. *jelito* (1), dial. (5); Sn. *jelita* (1), SC *jĕlīto* (1), d. (0, 1, 3); Br. *jal'íti* (2), U o. *jelyta* (1).

1.2. LCS *olito*: Sn. *olīto* (0, 1), SC ča-d. *olito* (0, 1); R d. *ol'ítka* (4).

1.3. Secondary *ja-*: P dial. *jalito* (Silesia; possibly a hypercorrection), Sk. d. *jalito* (0, 1), SC *jalito* (1); Br. *jal'íti* (2), U *jalytý*. Some take these forms as evidence of a Common Slavic prefix *ē-/*ō-* (Popowska-Taborska 1984: 20), which would be absent in the East Slavic forms under 1.4 (fortunately with no ill consequences for the meaning). This prefix appears ex machina in discussions of other seemingly difficult etyma; cf. section 7.20; it is not very persuasive.

1.4. Apparent aphaeresis in Ka. *ä̀lèta* (0, 1); R N-d. *l'itóxá* (0, 1), *l'itóka* (3), C-d. *l'itón'ja* (3). These forms can be interpreted as results of a local (Old or Middle Russian?) metanalysis of *v(ŭ)* + *ol'ito* as *vo* + *l'ito*, regularized as *v l'ito* (independent of diverse, presumably expressive, derivatives); cf. R d. *ol'itka*. The forms in question cannot be reflexes of a LCS *jĭlito* (< PS *ILEITA-), as has been suggested (cf. Sławski 1991: 48); this would have yielded *ilito* in Russian.

2. There are no Baltic attestations outside of Old Prussian. OPr. *Laitian − Wurst* (E. 381) 'sausage' is thought to be derived from PB *lei- (PIE *leh_1i-) 'pour' and to exemplify the meaningless Common Slavic prefix *ĕ-/*ŏ- (see paragraph 1.3 above). Levin suggests the reading *"ialitan"* for the Prussian vocable (1974: 102), which makes the word look like an adaptation of Polish *jelito*, accidentally obscured by two letter transpositions. This is an astute analysis, but it implies the assumption that there was no capitalization in some earlier version(s) of the Elbing Vocabulary, which is hard to evaluate.

3. There are no certain cognates outside Slavic (not even OPr. *Laitian*, above). Trubačev's appeal to Gm. *Aal* 'eel' (1979: 22), barely possible semantically, leaves both the root vowel's quantity (PGmc. *ēl-ā, Skt. *āli- 'stripe, line') and the form and function of the supposed derivational suffix(es) in PS ELEITA- unexplained.

In the absence of a plausible etymology of this word, all one can do is note that its attestation points to PS E- and is compatible with the account of the Slavic−Baltic *e- > *a- merger proposed here.

Literature: Trubačev (1979: 21−22); Popowska-Taborska (1984: 19−21); Sławski (1991: 47−48).

7.11. PS EL-EN-I-, PB EL-EN-I- − (0) 'deer (Cervus elaphus)'; (1) 'reindeer', (2) 'moose'; derivatives mean (3) 'stag-beetle (Lucanus cervus)', (4) 'thyme'

This lexeme has *e- and *a- forms in Slavic. In Baltic it is attested with e-.

1. East Slavic basically has *a- forms, but *e- forms occur in dialects and in at least one Belarusian toponym. Eastern South Slavic basically has *e- forms, but there is one derivative with *a- attested in Bulgarian.

Elsewhere, basically only *e- forms occur, the Czech and Slovak *a-forms being recently borrowed zoological terms.

1.1. LCS *jelenĭ: P jeleń, jelonek (3); US jeleń, LS jeleń, d. heleń; Sk. jeleň, Cz. jelen (0, 3); Sn. jélen (0, 3), SC jèlen (0, 3), ča. jèlen; Bg. elén (0, 3), M elen, Gk. top. Ellēnitsa (Arcadia), OCS jelenĭ, ChS. jelenecŭ (3), R d. jel'én', jel'én'ec (3), Br. d. jél'en', top. Jal'én'i, U W-d. jel'ín', jelén', o. jelenĭ.

1.2. LCS *olenĭ: Sk. d. oleň (1), Cz. oleň (2) (zoological terms, borrowings); Bg. ólenica (4), R ol'én', Br. al'én', U ólén', olénka (3).

1.3. Irregular prothesis in P d. wjeleń.

2. PB EL-EN-I- in Li. o. elenis 'deer; elk', otherwise ĒL-N-I-, ĒL-N-Ē-, see section 7.15.

3. The Slavic forms point to an earlier n-stem, as does the lexeme āl-n-i- (OCS lanĭ) 'doe'; discussed below (cf. PB ĒL-N-Ē-, section 7.15). Gk. élaphos (< *el-n̥-bʰos), ellos 'fawn' (< *el-n-o-s), énelos (< *el-en-o-s): nebrós 'fawn' (Hesych.), OIr. elit (< *eln̥tī) W elain (< *elənī) 'roe', Arm. eɫn 'doe', Go. lamb, OHG lamb, OE lamb all point to PIE *h₁el-en-. The Slavic *a- forms are due to the *e- > *a- merger.

Literature: Toporov (1975: 77−78); Trubačev (1979: 20); Popowska-Taborska (1984: 40−44); Sławski (1991: 42−46).

7.12. PS ELISĀ-, PB ELISĀ- − (0) 'alder thicket'; (1) 'swampy place (in forest), swamp', (2) 'white hellebore'

The Slavic lexeme has both *e- and *a- variants, its Baltic counterparts, only a- forms.

1. Slavic *e- forms are known from eastern Poland; *a- forms occur in a large area reaching from the Ukrainian Polissja in the south, across central and northern Belarus, eastward beyond Smolensk to the Moscow area, and westward to Białystok, Augustów, and Suwałki in northeastern Poland.

1.1. LCS *jelĭsa: P jeleśnik (2), top. Jeleśnia (tributary of Czarna Orawa river).

1.2. LCS *olĭsa: P d. olesie (1), olesisty, oleśnik (2), top. Alsarbe (near Suwałki); R d. al'ós (0,1) (Smolensk region, Dniepr basin), top. Ol'sa (Upper Dniepr), Ol'safka, Aleksna (near Moscow), Br. al'sa (0, 1), al'ós (0, 1), U ol'ós, oles (0, 1), olesnyk (2).

2. OPr. top. *Alsitten*, etc., Cur. *Alxwalke, Alxnewadt*, La. *àlksna* (1), top. *Álksna, Aîksnene*, Li. top. *Álksna, Ãlksnė* all point to PB A-, but the Slavic forms give important testimony regarding the extinct Baltic languages.

3. The striking absence of the regular Slavic *s*-reflex PS -x- marks these Slavic dialect forms as substratum loans, semantically differentiated from the Slavic counterparts descended from PS ELIXĀ- 'alder', see section 7.13. Theoretically the Polish **je-* forms would be reconcilable with PS ELIXĀ- if they were construed as secondary modifications of dialect forms with mazurzenie (in which the x-reflex -*š*- merges with -*s*-, e. g., **jelešník > *-sń- > jeleśník*). This would modify the otherwise solid CS **a-* representation of PS ALIXĀ- in Lechitic. But taken at face value, these data simply reflect the geographical distribution of Southwest, South, and Southeast Baltic **e-* and **a-* reflexes of PB EL(I)S- such as this distribution was when the Slavs moved into these areas. Hence the data tie in with the Baltic forms under the next lemma. But note that the morphological structure of the substratum word is identical to that of Slavic ELIXĀ- ‖ ALIXĀ- (cf. section 7.13, paragraph 3.2).

Literature: Popowska-Taborska (1984: 44−46); Sławski (1991: 50−55).

7.13. PS ELIXĀ- ‖ ALIXĀ-, PB ELS-NI- ‖ ALS-NI- ‖ ALIS-NI- − (0) 'alder (Alnus)', the Slavic lexeme in part merged with the original derivative PS ELIX-IĀ- 'alder thicket'; (1) 'spruce'

Both Slavic and Baltic have **e-* and **a-* forms of this lexeme.

East Slavic has mainly **a-* forms, but **e-* forms are known from both (north)east Russian and Southwest Ukrainian. Sorbian, Slovak−Czech, and Lechitic have **a-* forms, except that Central Slovak has **e-* forms. Western South Slavic has **e-* forms, except that **a-* forms occur in Western Slovenian dialects and are attested in toponyms in Carinthia and in both the Western South Slavic language areas. Eastern South Slavic has only **e-* forms.

1.1. LCS **jelĭxa*: Sk. *jelša*, d. *jelcha*, top. *Jelšava*, Cz. d. *jelše*; Sn. *jélša*, d. *jólša*, SC *jèlša*, d. *jélha, jóha*; Rum. top. *Elešnica*, Bg. *elxá* (0, 1), d. *élšá*, M *evla*, d. *elxa* (1), Gk. top. *Élesna, Elésnitsa*; R d. *jél'xá*, NE-d. *jólxa*, NE-d. *jelóxa*, U d. *jil'xa*, top. *Jelyxovyči* (near Halyč).

1.2. LCS *olīxa: P olcha, d. olsza, Ka. olxa, Pom. top. *Wolsche, Wilsowe*, Pb. vilsă; US wólša, LS wolša; Sk. E-d. olcha, W-d. olša, top. *Olšovany*, Cz. olše; Carinthia top. *Olsa, Olschenitzen*, Styria top. *Olschnitz*, Sn. W-d. ólša, top. *Olšenica, Olšnik* (Prekmurje), SC top. *Olešev Jarak* (near Zagreb); R ól'xá, Br. vól'xa, d. al'xá, U víl'xá, o. ol'xa.

1.3. Secondary *ja*-: Sk d. jalcha, jalša, Sn. d. jálša, top. *Jalševnica*, SC kaj-d. jälša, jaha.

2. In Baltic, *e*- forms occur only in Lithuanian. OPr. *Abskande* – Erle (E. 602), read "Aliskands" for [aliskn̥ts] /alisknas/ < *aliksnas* 'alder', top. *Alxwangen, Alxowe, Alsitten*, etc., Cur. *Alxnewadt, Alxwalke*, La. àlksna 'alder thicket', top. *Alksna, Alksnene*, Li. eĩksnis, alksnis, d. alksnà, álksna, élksna, alìksnis 'id.', top. *Álksna, Aĩksnė.*

3.1. Lat. *alnus* (< *al-es-no*-) and part of Baltic (e. g., Li. eĩksnis, alksnis < *elsnis* with *k*-epenthesis) appear to have the same suffixal -*n*-, which may suggest that the collective meaning of 'alder thicket' (cf. section 7.12) is primary, but may simply be a device for adjusting the word to a productive declension.

The second vowel of the etymon, which is ambiguous in some languages, cf. OHG *elira, erila*, Gm. *Erle, Eller*, but must have been -*e*- in Latin (cf. Schrijver 1991: 41), has produced *u*-umlaut in ON *jǫlstr* (< *elustrā* 'laurel willow') and *ǫlr* (< *aluz*- 'alder'), but is -*i*- elsewhere, e. g., Fr. *alise* 'rowan-berry' (< Gaul. *alisia*), M. *áliza: hē leúkē tõn dendrõn* 'white poplar' (Hesych.). This vowel is absent in parts of Baltic, and the root shows contradictory prosodic reflexes (Li. aĩ-, La. àl- beside Li. ál-; see above; cf. Li. álvas 'tin' [6]), which may reflect loan adaptation at some stage; cf. Gamkrelidze and Ivanov (1984: 635); Huld (1990: 401 – 402); Schrijver (1991: 41).

3.2. There is an apparent morphological gradation in the prehistoric Slavic – Baltic dialect area: (i) *als*- (OPr. top. *Alx-wangen*, Cur. *Alxwalke*, La. *Alsvanga*), (ii) *als-n*- (Cur. *Alxnewadt*, La. àlksna, Li. aĩksnis, álksna, etc.), (iii) *alis-n*- (Li. d. *alìksnis*, etc.), (iv) *alis-ā* (South[east] Baltic > CS d. *alis-ā*, e. g. Br. al'sa, al'ós; cf. section 7.12), (v) LCS d. *olīxa*. Here (iii) looks like a compromise formation, mediating between (ii) and (iv). This gradation significantly weakens the suggestion of a particularly close relationship between the Baltic and Latin forms (as *n*- derivatives); thus Trubačev (1979: 24).

3.3. Germanic shows both initial *e*- and *a*-. So do Baltic and Slavic. The geographical distribution of the initial vowels in Slavic differs strikingly from that of most other *e*- || *a*- doublets. There is nothing unusual about the distribution of *e*- and *a*- doublets in South Slavic and East

Slavic; it is not significantly different from the reflexes of, say, PS EDEINA-[1], EDUĀS [3]; cf. tables 1.1 and 1.3. But the solid attestation of *a-* reflexes in Sorbian, Czech–Slovak (except Central Slovak), and Lechitic indicates that the total distribution is not the result simply of the dissemination of by-forms developed through the *e-* > *a-* merger, but presupposes the existence of Proto-Slavic doublets, as above, just as in the case of PS ELAUA- ‖ ALAUA-, ERILA- ‖ ARILA-, etc. (cf. sections 5.3.4 and 6.1–6.2). In Baltic, *e-* forms occur only in Lithuanian, but are reflected indirectly in Southwest Baltic, cf. section 7.12, paragraphs 1.1 and 3.

On the basis of the Latin and Celtic evidence for initial (dialectal) PIE *a-* (cf. Friedrich 1970: 70–73) it appears that PS ELIXĀ-, PB ELS-NI-, and ELISĀ- [12] owe their initial to Rozwadowski's change, which left unaffected A- forms both in Slavic and in Baltic (cf. sections 6.1–6.2). But the *e-* and *a-* forms in Germanic suggest the possibility of a wider Indo-European dialectal *e-* ‖ *a-* variation (though hardly the qualitative ablaut envisaged by Pokorny and others; cf. Pokorny [1959–1969, 1: 302–303]). In any case, the Slavic and East Baltic E- doublets were subject to the later Slavic–Baltic *e-* > *a-* merger.

Literature: Toporov (1975: 53–54); Trubačev (1979: 23–26); Popowska-Taborska (1984: 37–40); Mažiulis (1988: 44–47); Sławski (1991: 50–55).

7.14. PS AL-K-UTI-, PB EL-K-A-/-Ā- ‖ EL-K-ŪN-Ē- ‖ AL-K-ŪN-Ē- ‖ ŌL-(EK)-TI- — 'elbow'

Slavic has only *a-* reflexes, while Baltic has both *e-* and *a-* beside *ō-*.

1. CS *alkuti-:* P *łokieć*; US *łohć*, LS *łokś*; Sk. *loket'*, Cz. *loket*; Sn. *lakât*, SC *lâkat*; Bg. *lakŭt*, OCS *lakŭtĭ*; R *lókot'*, Br. *lókoc'*, U *lókot'*.

2. There are several formations which have initial *e-* and *a-* in Latvian and Lithuanian. They are arranged here according to the suffixes involved:

  (a) with the -K- suffix: La. *èlks, èlka*, Li. top. *Alk-ùpis*;
  (b) with a -T- suffix: OPr. *Woltis — Unterarm* (E. 112) 'forearm', *Woaltis — Ele* (E. 458) 'ell';
  (c) with -K- and -T-: La. *uôlekts*, Li. *úolektis*;
  (d) with -K- and a -VN- suffix: OPr. *Alkunis — Elboge* (E. 110), read /alk-ūn-ias/ 'elbow', La. *èlkuons, èlkuonis, èlkuone*, top. *Ęlkune*, Li. *alkū́nė*, d. *elkū́nė*.

If one supposes that the -κ- suffix has been lost through cluster simplification in (b) OPr. *Woltis* and *Woaltis*, the (b) formation is reducible to (c). The same root meaning 'bend' may occur in such river names as Li. *A͂lnė, Álnis, Álnupis, Elna*, mentioned under PB ĒLN-Ē- 'doe' in section 7.15.

3. The diversity of initial vowels in the other Indo-European languages matches both PS A-, Baltic *a-* in (2 a, 2 d), and PB ō- in (2 b, 2 c): Go. *al-eina*, OHG *elina*, Lat *ulna* (< **olenā*), OIr. *uilen*, W *elin* (< **ol-inā-*), Skt. *aratnís*, together with PS AL-, Baltic *al-* reflect PIE *h_xh_3-el-*; Gr. *oléné, õllon : tēn toũ brakhíonos kampén* 'the bend of the arm' (Hesych.) and PB ŌL- reflect PIE *h_xeh_3-l-*.

The East Baltic *e-* forms, which motivate the reconstruction of PB E-, are evidence of Rozwadowski's change, the *a-* forms in Lithuanian resulting from the Slavic−Baltic **e-* > **a-* merger. The Slavic and West Baltic forms probably escaped Rozwadowski's change (cf. sections 6.1−6.2); this is the simplest account. (It seems less likely − but the possibility strictly cannot be ruled out − that the forms of either or both these dialect groups went through both Rozwadowski's change and the later **e-* > **a-* merger.)

Literature: Fraenkel (1962−1965: 8); Toporov (1975: 75−76); Mažiulis (1988: 67−68).

7.15. PB ĒL-N-IA-*l*-Ē-, PS ĀL-N-Ī- − 'doe'

Slavic has only CS **ā-* reflexes, while Baltic has both **ē-* and **ā-* forms.

1. CS **āl-niā*: P *lani, lania*; Sk. *laň*, Cz. *laně, laň*; Sn *lânjec*, SC *làne*; OCS *alŭnii, lani*; R *lán'*, Br. *lán'*, U *lán', lán'a*. Cf. section 7.10.

2. OPr. *Alne − Tyer* (E. 647) 'deer', top. *Allenau*, La. *âlnis* 'elk', top. *Alnace, Elnẹni*, Li. *élnė*, d. *álnė* 'doe', *élnis*, d. *álnis, élnias* 'deer, elk', top. *Alnà, A͂lnas, A͂lnē, Álnis, Álnupis, Elna*.

3. W *elain* (< *elənī*), OIr. *elit* (< **eln̥-tī*), MIr. *ell* (< **elnā*), Arm. *eln*, Gr. *élaphos* (< **el-n̥-b^ho-s*), *éllos* 'fawn' (< **el-n-o-s*) all point to PIE *$h_1$el-en-*, PB EL-EN- (section 7.11).

The long-vowel forms PB ĒL-N-Ē-, PS ĀL-N-I- are possibly (i) Indo-European dialectal by-forms (ablaut variants in the style of Lat. *pēs*, Gk. *poũs* 'foot', Li. *piemuõ*, Gk. *poimén* 'herdsman'). Or they suggest either (ii) a shared Pre-Slavic−Baltic **ēl-*, preserved in East Baltic, but subject to the Slavic−Baltic **e-* > **a-* merger in Slavic and parts of Baltic; or (iii) a shared Pre-Slavic−Baltic **ōl-*, subject to Rozwadowski's change in (East) Baltic (**ōl-

> *ēl-), but apparently unaffected elsewhere. Note that the last mentioned possibility presupposes a different vowel system than the more recent one in which tautosyllabic -ōR- merges with -ūR- (e. g., *pùlti* < *pōltei, puolia* 'fall; inf., pres. 3'); Stang characterizes this stage in his discussion of three-mora diphthongs, where he views Li. *várna*, SC *vr̀ana* 'crow' as a vṛddhi formation (< PIE *wōrn-eh₂), subject to shortening earlier than the secondary three-mora diphthongs that arose through the loss of laryngeals (cf. 1966: 18 footnote 1, 52).

While the origin of the apparent Slavic–Baltic doublets remains uncertain, it seems clear enough that at least East Baltic shows evidence of a PB ĒLNI- affected by the Slavic–Baltic *e- > *a- merger.

Literature: Fraenkel (1962–1965: 8); Toporov (1975: 77–78); Mažiulis (1988: 68–70).

7.16. PB ELU-EDĒ – 'hasp; switch; peg'

This lexeme is known only to Baltic, where it has both *e-* and *a-* variants.

1. OPr. *Aloade – Haspe* (E. 541) 'door-hasp' /alwadē/, La. *elvede* 'spruce rafter', *elvete* 'switch', Li. *elvėdė* 'swing beam', *elvýtė, alvýta, alvỹtė* 'willow switch'.

2 There is no reliable etymology for these vocables, not even real confidence that the Prussian lexeme is related to the East Baltic ones. It is difficult to choose between the possible connections with PIE *el(u̯)- 'turn, roll' (< *u̯elhₓ-u-; thus most recently Toporov) and PIE *ol-u 'bend', the root of PS ALK-UTI- ‖ PB ELK-ŪN-Ē- [14], etc.; thus Mažiulis).

Whatever their (Indo-European or other) ancestry, the attestations appear to exemplify the Slavic–Baltic *e- > *a- merger.

Literature: Fraenkel (1962–1965: 120–121); Toporov (1975: 77–78); Mažiulis (1988: 70–71).

7.17. PS EL-UKA- – (0) 'bitter'; (1) 'rancid'; (2) 'bile'

This is a specifically Slavic formation. It has no known *a-* forms.

1.1. LCS *jelŭkŭ: P E-d. *jełki*; Sn. *jérek*; R *jólkij* (0, 1), d. *jólč, jóloč* (2), Br. *jólki*, U d. *jilkyj, jelkýj*.

1.2. Note P d. *iłki* (1), R NE-d. *ilkój*, U d. *ylkýj* (0, 1). For the semantically similar words Cz. *žluknouti* 'turn rancid', Sn. *žérek, žolhek*, SC kaj-d. *žuhkek*, ča-d. *žlkak, žuhkak* 'bitter, rancid' Trubačev proposes Common Slavic pre-forms such as LCS **jĭz-jĭlŭknǫti, *jĭz-jĭlŭkŭ*, etc. (1979: 22), but this is contrary to Slavic sound laws. In Serbo-Croatian and Slovenian LCS **jĭz-* regularly yields *iz-*; no Common Slavic dialects develop prothetic *j-* after consonant (cf. SC *ùzēti, ùzmēm* 'to take; Inf., Pres. 1 sg.', not ***užmēm* < LCS *vŭz-ę-ti, vŭz-ĭm-ǫ*, not ***vŭz-jĭm-ǫ*); and then there is Havlík's law. The geographical distribution of these *ž-* forms suggests a local, Late Common Slavic origin. Their relationship with CS **zĭlčĭ*, later **žĭlčĭ*, 'bile' needs to be reconsidered.

1.3. Polish and Ukrainian appear to have zero grade, the other Slavic languages seem to show *e*-grade (!) of the root otherwise known from the words for beer, PS ALU-, R d. *ól*, o. *olŭ*, Sn *ôl., ôlovina* 'yeast', Bg. *olovína*.

2. The adjective has no counterpart in Baltic, but the root seems to recur in PB ALU-, OPr. *Alu − Mete* (E. 389) 'mead', La. *alus*, Li. *alùs* 'beer'.

3. While ON *ǫl*, OE *ealu* mean 'beer, ale', the meaning of Lat. *alūmen* 'alum' and Gr. *alúdoimon: pikrón parà Sóphroni* (Hesych.) (i. e. 'sharp, pungent, bitter') suggest that the meaning of the Slavic adjective is primary, and the name of the beverage, PS ALU- and its congeners, derived. Since the Latin and Greek words point to PIE **h₂elu-*, either the initial of PS ELU-KA- is a secondary *e*-grade, created within Slavic, or it is the result of Rozwadowski's change. The apparent fact that the meaning of the adjective is not derived, speaks in favor of the second of these alternatives. However, the relationship of PS ELUKA- with PS ALU- is considered doubtful by some (cf. Sławski 1991: 49).

Whatever the origin of its initial, PS ELUKA- is one of the small number of Slavic lexemes with E- that show no evidence of the Slavic−Baltic **e- > *a-* merger.

Literature: Trubačev (1979: 22); Sławski (1991: 49).

7.18. PS EMELĀ-/-A-, PB EMELA- − 'mistletoe (Viscum, Loranthus)'; modern meanings, (0) 'mistletoe'; (1) 'ivy'; (2) 'dizziness'

Both Slavic and Baltic have **e-* and **a-* variants.

1. There are three Common Slavic by-forms, with **i-*, with **e-*, and with **a-*. **e-* forms occur in West Slavic and in Slovenian, Bulgarian, and

Ukrainian. **a-* variants occur in Slovak−Czech, in Western South Slavic and Bulgarian, and in East Slavic.

1.1. LCS **jemela*: P *jemioła*, Pom. top. *Gemelnicza* (1294), Pb. top. *Gemel*; US *jemjel*, LS *jemjoł, jemjelica*; Sk. d. *jemelo*, Cz. d. *jemela*; Sn. d. *jemêla*; Bg. d. *émila*; Br. d. *jem'alá*.

1.2. LCS **omela*: Sk. d. *omela, omola, omalo*, Cz. d. *omelo*; Sn. d. *omêla, omel*, SC d. *òmela*; Bg. d. *omel*; R *om'éla*, Br. *am'éla*, d. *am'alá*, U *omélá*.

1.3. LCS **jĭmela*: P. d. *imioła*, Sk. *imelo*, d. *jmelo, mel*, Cz. *jmelí*, d. *melí*, Sn. *imêla*, d. *mêla*, SC *ìmela*, d. *mèla*, Bg. *ímél* (1), d. *ímela* (2), M *imela* (0, 2); R o. *imela*, Br. d. *im'alá*, U d. *imelá*.

1.4. Prothetic *h-* in LS *hemjoł*, Sk. d. *hemelo*, U d. *homela, hamélo, hemela* (see section 5.1.1). Secondary *ja-* in P d. *jamioła*, Ka. *jamèlna*; LS *jamola*; Sk. d. *jamelo, jamola, jamalo*, Mor. d. *jameł, jamela*; U d. *jamelýna, jámela* (see section 5.1.3).

2. OPr. *Emelno* − *Mispel* (E. 646; German dialect for 'Mistel'), top. *Amelung* (1357), *Ammelink* (1359), *Omolowo* et al., Cur. *Amulle, Amelen*, La. *ãmuls, ãmals, ãmulis, ęmuols* 'mistletoe, clover', Li. *ãmalas*, d. *ēmalas* 'mistletoe', top. *Amaĺvas, Amãlis, Amãlė*. The *-uo-* in the Latvian forms can be due to contamination with *abuols* 'apple tree', *azuols* 'oak' (Mažiulis 1988: 252). The second vowel of Li. *ãmalas* shows the common vowel retraction before sonorant (like *vãsaras* < PIE **wes-er/n-*, OCS *vesna* 'spring', and *vãkaras* < PIE **wekʷ-ero-*, OCS *večerŭ* 'evening').

3. There are no known cognates outside Slavic and Baltic. A derivation from PIE **h₁em-* 'take' (cf. PS IM-Ā-TĒI, EM-IĀ-M, OCS *imati, jemljǫ*, Li. *im̃ti, ìma, ẽmė* 'to take; inf., 1 sg.pres. 1 sg.pret.') + *-el-* (cf. LCS *bĭč-el-a* 'bee', *čĭm-el-ĭ* 'bumble-bee') with the original meaning 'taker, catcher' is possible, with by-forms based on zero grade (PS IM-EL-Ā-) and full grade (PS EM-EL-Ā-). Alternatively, this is a non-Indo-European substratum borrowing, just as several other plant names, **emel-*, possibly **amel-* (> Slavic−Baltic **emel-* by Rozwadowski's change). In that case, the zero-grade PS IM-EL-Ā- may be a (local) Common Slavic popular etymology linking the name of the plant with the function of the bird-lime produced from its sap (cf. Mažiulis 1988: 252).

If the Pre-Slavic−Baltic form was **amel-*, it would make sense to interpret the solid *a-* reflexes in the Baltic toponyms (see paragraph 2) as evidence that Rozwadowski's change was limited in its range. The PS, PB E- forms it produced were subject to the Slavic−Baltic **e-* > **a-* merger.

The geographical distribution of CS **i-*, LCS **jĭ-* forms (see paragraph 1.3) shows that these were disseminated at the time of the Slavic territorial expansion side by side with the **je-* and **o-* forms.

Literature: Popowska-Taborska (1984: 21−24); Trubačev (1979: 26−27); Mažiulis (1988: 252−253); Fraenkel (1962−1965: 9); Sławski (1991: 55−56); Toporov (1979: 26−28).

7.19. PS EPS-Ā- ‖ APS-Ā-, PB EPUŠ-Ē- ‖ APS-Ē- − 'aspen (Populus tremula L.)'

Baltic has *a*- variants, but *e*- occurs in Lithuanian; North Slavic and Bulgarian have LCS *o- forms, whereas South Slavic (including Bulgarian) has *je- and *ja- reflexes.

1.1. LCS *jes-ika: Sn. *jesíka*, SC. *jèsika*, top. *Jesikovac*.

1.2. LCS *os-al-ina: P *osa, osina*; US *wosa, wosyna*, LS *wósa*; Sk. *osika*, Cz. d. *osa, osina*; Bg. *osíka*; R *os'ína*, Br. *as'ína*, U *osýna, osýka*.

1.3. LCS *jas-ika: Sn *jasíka*, SC *jàsika*, Bg. *jasíka*, M *jasika*.

2. OPr. *Abse* − *Espe* (E. 606) /apsē/, top. *Absmedie, Absowe, Abswangen*, La. *apse*, top. *Apsa*, etc., Li. *ãpušė, ēpušė* (with -*u*- like *pušìs* 'pine'; cf. sections 6.1−6.2), top. *Apsìngė, Ãpusinas, Ãpšė*, etc.

3. The South Slavic forms with *ja*- are likely secondary to *je*- forms (pace Skok [1971: s. v.]). But a fuller examination of these forms in relation to the local reflexes of PS ESENA-, ĀSENA- 'ash' would seem well motivated. On the early relationship between these tree names, see Gamkrelidze and Ivanov (1984: 625−627).

The Slavic and Lithuanian forms with *e- are isolated. They find no support in the related languages, cf. OHG *aspa*, MHG *espe*, OE *æspe*, ON *ǫsp*, which point to *asp- or *osp-, with possible cognates outside Indo-European, but possibly of Indo-European origin (Friedrich 1970: 49−53; Nepokupnyj 1989). They are best understood as evidence that Rozwadowski's change affected only part of the Pre-Slavic−Baltic area (cf. section 6.2, table 6.2); note that Lithuanian place names derived from this root show *a*-, suggesting that Northwest Baltic retained the original initial *a-, just like the Pre-Latvian and, presumably, the Pre-Prussian dialects; particularly instructive are such forms as the river name *Ãpšė*, which can only be a Lithuanized substratum form *apsė (contra Nepokupnyj [1989: 38]). And note that the Sorbian *a- forms reflect the opposite, southern periphery of ante-Migration Common Slavic that was unaffected by Rozwadowski's change.

The Slavic and Baltic E- forms were subsequently subject to the Slavic–Baltic **e-* > **a-* merger.

Literature: Fraenkel (1962–1965: 14); Sławski (1974: 159); Trubačev (1974: 80–81); Toporov (1975: 51–52); Mažiulis (1988: 42); Nepokupnyj (1989: 35–42).

7.20. PS ER-IM-B-I-, ĒRB-I-, ĪRB-Ī-, R-EM-B-I-, PB ER-UM-B-Ē-, ĒRB-Ē-, ĪRB-Ē-, R-UM-B-EN-IA- − (0) 'hazel-grouse (Bonasa bonasia)'; (1) 'partridge (Perdix)', (2) 'crane (Grus)'

This lexeme has **e-* and **a-* variants in both Slavic and Baltic in addition to reflexes with other initial vowels. It cannot be discussed without reference to the derivatives meaning 'rowan tree', examined in section 7.21.

1. CS **a-* forms are attested in East Slavic, in (proximal) Polish, and in (distal) Serbo-Croatian. **e-* forms are known from Slovak–Czech, Western South Slavic, and Eastern South Slavic.

1.1. LCS **je-*: P d. *jerząbek*; US *jerjab*, LS *jerjeb*; Sk. d. *jerebic* (1); Cz. *jeřábek* (0), o. *jeřáb* (2); Sn. *jerêb* (0, 1), *jerebíca* (1), SC *jerèbica* (0); Bg. *érebica* (1), *érembica* (1), M *erebica* (1); R o. *jerjabĭ* (1).

1.2. LCS **o-*: P E-d. *orzębica*; SC d. *orèbica* (0, 1), ča. *ȍrēb*; R o. *orjabĭ* (1), d. *or'ábka*, Br. d. *órabka* (0), U ór'abka* (0).

1.3. Secondary **ja-*: P *jarząbek* (0); Sk. *jarabica* (1); Sn. d. *jarebíca* (0), SC d. *jarèbica* (1), *jȁrēb* (1); Bg. *járebica* (1), M d. *jarebica* (1); cf. section 5.1.3. Note the prothesis in US *wjerjabka* (0), LS d. *heŕabc* (0).

1.4. LCS **jĭ-*: Bg. d. *érbica* (1).

1.5. Ø-: Sn. d. *rêb* (1), *rebíca* (1), SC d. *rebica* (1); R *rjábčik*, d. *r'abók* (0), Br. *rábčik* (0), U *r'ábčyk* (0).

2. La. *i(e)rube, iřbe, virba*, Li. *jerbė̃, íerbė, jeru(m)bė̃, jerũbė, (j)ãrubė*, S-d. *vẽrubė, ìrbė, vìrbė*.

3. Traditionally the Slavic lexemes have been reconstructed as an *r*-initial root **rV(m)b-* with freely omissible, meaningless prefixes (**ě-*, **ŏ-*, cf. Popowska-Taborska [1984: 24–28]; Trubačev [1974: 73–75, s. v. **arębŭ*]; Sławski [1991: 132 s. v. **ěrębŭ*]) and an equally meaningless nasal infix. The data suggest rather the following:

3.1.1. In some Common Slavic dialects, an original PS ĒRB- has undergone regular initial liquid-diphthong metathesis (LCS **rěb-*) to yield the stem of U *ríba* 'rowan'; see section 7.21, paragraph 1.5.

3.1.2. In some Common Slavic dialects, the corresponding zero-grade form PS ĪRB-, has been generalized, cf. the monosyllabic root shapes in Bg. d. *érb-ica* 'partridge' and Ka. *jerzbina* (< Pre-Ka. **jĭ́rb-ina*), *jarzbina* (with secondary *ja-*), US d. *jerbina* 'rowan', Sn. d. *rbika* 'blackberry' (< Pre-Sn. **ŕb-ika*).

3.1.3. In most Slavic dialects, this bird name is based on a longer stem which includes an *en*-suffix (denoting the young of animals?). The *-ę-* of LCS **erębĭ-* is ambiguous, but the East Baltic correspondents with *-um-* point to a zero grade. This formation, PS ER-IM-B-I-, which was not subject to the metathesis of initial liquid diphthongs, accounts for the forms under 1.1. It is morphologically parallel to Gk. *elaphós* 'deer' (< PIE **h₁el-n̥-bʰo-s*) mentioned in section 7.11 (cf. Vaillant [1958: 158], [1974: 487], who construes the root differently).

3.1.4. From the CS **e-* forms, the **e-* > **a-* merger produced the LCS **o-* forms under 1.2.

3.1.5. The forms with *ja-* under 1.4 may all be secondary reflexes of LCS **je-* (cf. section 5.1.3) < CS **erimbi-*, but they are compatible as well with a Common Slavic **ērimbi-*, a conceivable contamination of CS **ērb-i-* and **er-im-b-i-* (or homologous Pre-Slavic forms).

3.1.6. The zero grade variant PS R-IM-B-I- appears to underlie the Western South Slavic and East Slavic forms in 1.4. It motivates the adjective LCS **rębŭ* 'speckled' just as **golǫbĭ* 'dove' motivates **golǫbŭ* 'light blue'.

3.2. In the Baltic languages, an original PB ĒRB-Ē- continues into Li. d. *ierbė* and *(j)erbẽ*, whereas the formation with the *n*-suffix has produced forms of the type Li. *eru(m)bẽ, erū̃bė*, later subject to the change of **e-* > **a-* and prothesis. Zero grade is in evidence in La. *ir̃be*, Li. *ìrbė* and is pre-vocalic in La. *rubenis* 'heath-cock' (< **r-um-b-en-*).

3.3. The extensive parallelism between the Slavic and Baltic forms is obviously no coincidence. It is evidence of an ancient morphological variation, and a generalization of diverse variants that acquired different areal extensions in the prehistoric Slavic–Baltic dialect continuum.

The shorter Slavic and Baltic variants ĒRB-V-, ĪRB-V-, point to an original **h₁erb-* comparable to OHG *erpf* 'dark', ON *iarpr* 'dark', *iarpi* 'grouse'. If the meaning 'dark' is primary, the bird-name may be viewed as originally a taboo circumlocution ('Darkness bird').

The morphological analysis of the longer variants must either recognize a nasal infixed before the root-final consonant or hypothesize a different (secondary, renewed) circumlocution, possibly based on PIE **h₃er-* 'bird' ('birdie'; cf. section 7.21). To understand this prehistoric neologism requires reference to the mythological bond between the chthonic hazel-grouse and the celestial rowan tree (see section 7.21), a topic I address elsewhere (Andersen in press). Note that this etymological possibility is available because of Rozwadowski's change.

The forms in paragraphs 1.2 and 2 exemplify the Slavic−Baltic *e- > *a- merger. Note that in some of the Slavic areas in which the LCS *je- and *o- forms were disseminated, they were in competition with variants with LCS *jĭ- and Ø-; still, their geographical distribution is quite similar to that of other *je- ‖ *o- lexemes.

Literature: Fraenkel (1962−1965: 193−194); Trubačev (1974: 73−76); Popowska-Taborska (1984: 24−28); Sławski (1991: 132−139); Andersen in press.

7.21. PS ER-IM-B-Ī-NĀ-, ĒRB-Ī-KĀ-, ĒRB-Ī-NĀ-, ĪRB-Ī-KĀ, R-IM-B-Ī-NĀ-, PB ĪR-B-EN-Ē- − (0) 'rowan tree (Sorbus aucuparia), rowan berries'; (1) 'bird-cherry (Bonosa silvestris)'

These derivatives of the name for 'grouse' discussed in section 7.20 have *e- and *a- variants in Slavic, but not in Baltic.

1. CS *a- forms occur in East Slavic, in (proximal) Polish, and in (proximal) Slovenian. *e- forms are found in Polish−Kashubian, in Sorbian, in Slovak−Czech, and in (proximal) Slovenian. The combined geographical distribution of the *e- and *a- variants is somewhat wider for the tree name than for the 'grouse' word, in part because the latter has been replaced in the Sorbian languages.

1.1. LCS *je-: P d. *jerzębina*; US d. *jerjabina*, LS *jerjebina, jerjebk* (1); Sk. *jerab, jerabina*, Cz. *jeřáb*; Sn. *jerebika*; Br. *jarab'ina*.

1.2. LCS *o-: P d. *orzębina*; Sn. d. *obrika* (< *orbika* < *orebika* × *rbika*?); Br. *arab'ina*, U *horobýna*, d. *or'ábyna*.

1.3. Secondary *ja-: P *jarząb, jarzębina,* Ka. *jarzbina* (cf. 1.4); LS d. *jařebina*; Sk. *jarabina*, Cz. d. *jařabina*; SC *jarebina* (botanical term, borrowing); Br. *jarabína*. Note the prothesis in US *wjerjebina*, LS *herjebina*, Br. *verab'ina*, U *horobýna, verebýna*; assimilation in Cz. *řeřáb*.

1.4. LCS *jĭ-: Ka. *jerzbina*, US d. *jerbina*.

1.5. Ø-: Sn. d. *rebika, rbika*, SC *rebika*; R d. *r'ab'ika, r'ab'ina*, Br. *rab'ina*, U *r'abýna, ríba*.

2. In the Baltic area, the rowan tree is named for the grouse also in Latvian: d. *irbene* beside *sērmūk(l)is* (cf. Li. *šermùkšnis*) and standard *pîlādzis*; the last mentioned term is a borrowing from Livonian *pī'ləG*, 'rowan tree', cf. Fi. *pihlaja* 'idem'.

3. The relationships among the variants in paragraphs 1.1−1.5 were discussed in section 7.19 and need not be repeated here. The relation of PS, PB ĒRB-V- to the PS BĒR-KĀ- which underlies the names for 'beam tree (Sorbus torminalis)' or 'hawthorn (Crataegus)' − P *brzek*; US *brěkowc, břekowka*; Sk. *brekyňa*, Cz. *břek, břekyně*; Sn. *brę̃, brę́ka*, SC *brèkinja*; Bg. *brekín'a*; R *b'er'óka, b'ér'ek*, U *beréka* − will not concern us here.

Although originally a transparent derivative from the same root as the name of the grouse, the name of the rowan tree has become differentiated from the bird name in many Slavic dialects and the etymological connection lost. Evidently, in many parts of the Slavic territories the Migrations gave rise to coexisting by-forms of the two words which had different initials, and the existence of these variants has been exploited − differently in different areas − to reinforce the morphological differences between the two names, which originally resided solely in the suffixes. For the purpose of examining the **je-* ‖ **o-* isoglosses it makes sense to present these two sets of lexemes jointly, as has been done in this study since their first mention in chapter 1.

Literature: Trubačev (1974: 73−76); Popowska-Taborska (1984: 24−28); Sławski (1991: 132−139); Andersen in press.

7.22. PS ERILA- ‖ AR-ILA-, PB ER-ELIA- − (0) 'eagle'; (1) 'varieties of hawk (Buteo)'

Both Slavic and Baltic have **e-* and **a-* forms.

1. All the Slavic languages document **a-* forms. LS in addition has **e-* forms.

1.1. LCS **jerīlŭ*: LS *jerjeł, jerjoł*, o. *jerol* (1), o. *jörel* (2).

1.2. LCS **orīlŭ*: P *orzeł*, Ka. *wözeł*, Pb. *viråł*; US *worjoł*, LS o. *horal*; Sk. *orol, orel*, Cz. *orel*; Sn. *orel*, SC *òrao*; Bg. *órél*, M *orel*, OCS *orīlŭ*, Rum. top. *Orlea*, Gk. top. *Arlíska, Orla*; R *or'ól*, Br. *aról*, U *orél*.

1.3. Note prothesis in LS d. *herjeł*, d. *herjoł*.

2. OPr. *Arelie* − *Are* (E. 709) 'eagle', La. *èrglis*, d. *ereļi*, Li. *erẽlis*, d. *arẽlis*.

3. Go. *ara*, OHG *aro, aru* 'eagle', Gm. *Adl-er* 'idem', Eng. *earn* 'idem', Gk. *órnis* 'bird', Hitt. *ḫaraš, ḫaranaš* 'eagle' indicate PIE **h₃er-*. OIr. *irar*, Welsh *eryr* < **eriro-*, Bret. *er* < **ero-* have secondary front vowels (cf. Cowgill 1965: 146). As suggested in section 7.19. PIE **h₃er-* 'bird' may occur also in PS ER-IM-B-I-, PB ER-UM-B-Ē-, etc. 'grouse' and their derivatives.

The East Baltic and Lower Sorbian forms appear to reflect Slavic−Baltic E- doublets, evidence of the limited geographical range of Rozwadowski's change (cf. section 6.1). Old Prussian may well reflect both this change and the later Slavic−Baltic **e-* > **a-* merger. (So, conceivably, might all of the Slavic languages.) But the solid **a-* attestation in all but the Sorbian region speaks in favor of a Proto-Slavic doublet with A- (cf. 5.2.3); the effects, if any, of the Slavic−Baltic **e-* > **a-* merger in Slavic are impossible to gauge.

Literature: Fraenkel (1962−1965: 122); Toporov (1975: 101−102); Popowska-Taborska (1984: 49−51); Mažiulis (1988: 90).

7.23. PB ER-K-IĀ- 'tick; woodbeetle'

Initial *e-* and *a-* only in Lithuanian. This lexeme has no known correspondences in Slavic.

1. La. *ērce*, Li. *érkė, árkė* 'tick, woodbeetle'.
2. These words are plausibly interpreted as agentive derivatives of *ìr-ti* 'disintegrate', causative Li. *ar-d-ýti* 'unravel, break, destroy', cf. PS AR-Ī-TEI in OCS *raz-oriti* 'destroy' (PIE **h₁erh_x-*).

They exemplify the Slavic−Baltic **e-* > **a-* merger.

Literature: Fraenkel (1962−1965: 122).

7.24. PS ERKX-I-, PB ERŠK-IA- 'thorn; sting'

Initial CS **e-* in Slavic, and both *e-* and *a-* in Lithuanian.

1. Sn. *rȇšek* 'goose-thistle' (with suffix substitution from CS **erš-ĭć-ĭ*, PS ERKX-IKA-) shows the expected metathesis of the word-initial liquid diphthong.

2. La. *ẽršķis, ẽrkšis, ẽrkšķis* 'thorn-bush; sting', Li. *erškẽtis, erškẽtỹs, arškẽtis, aĩškẽtỹs* 'thorn; sloe-bush'.

3. Other correspondences are Skt. *ŗṣáti* 'pierces', *ŗkṣára* 'thorn', Gk. *árkeuthos* 'juniper', indicating PIE *$h_2erk̂$-.

Both Slavic and Baltic reflexes of this lexeme appear to exemplify Rozwadowski's change. Lithuanian additionally reflects the Slavic−Baltic *e- > *a- merger.

Literature: Fraenkel (1962−1965: 122−123).

7.25. PB ERŽ-IL-A- 'stallion'

Initial *e-* and *a-* in Lithuanian. No relevant correspondences in Slavic.

1. La. *èrzelis*, Li. *eržilas*, d. *aržilas* 'stallion', *eržilúotis*, d. *aržilúotis* 'be in heat (of mares)', *eržùs, aržùs* 'libidinous; obstreperous'.

2. R *jórzat'* (LCS *jĭrzati, PS IRZ-Ā-TĒI) 'fidget; copulate' has the zero grade; ON *argr* 'indecent, bad, libidinous', Gk. *órkheis*, Arm. *orjik^c*, Av. *ərəzi* 'testicles' and Ir. *uirge* 'penis', the *o*-grade (PIE *$h_1orĝ^h$-).

3. The original initial vocalism of PB ERŽ-IL-A- is uncertain, *$h_1erĝ^h$- or, more likely, *$h_1orĝ^h$-. In the latter case, the modern reflexes show the effect of Rozwadowski's change.

In either case, the Lithuanian variation results from the Slavic−Baltic *e- > *a- merger.

Literature: Fraenkel (1962−1965: 123−124).

7.26. PS E-SE − 'look!; here!; who knows, perhaps'

This thinly attested discourse marker has *a-* forms in East Slavic and *e-* forms in South Slavic and in East Slavic, unless OR *jese* is a Slavonicism. It is unknown to Baltic.

1.1. LCS *je-: Sn. *esej, esa, eso, esi, esode*; Bg. *esé*, OCS *jese*; R o. *jese*.

1.2. LCS *o-: R *vos'é, vós'e, vós'*, o. *ose*, Br. *vós'*, U *osé*, d. *jese*.

2. PS E-SE appears composed of the inherited PS SE 'look, behold' and a preposed deictic particle E-, which originates as a paralinguistic pho-

netic gesture and has been lexicalized at different times in the history of the Slavic languages, both prior to the Common Slavic prothesis (as illustrated by PS ESE and possibly PS E-S-KE [2] and subsequent to it, as shown by R *étot* 'this', *étakij* 'this kind of', d. *èvon* 'there!', *èvot* 'here!', SC *èvo* 'there!', etc.

Literature: Trubačev (1979: 8); Popowska-Taborska (1984: 51−52); Sławski (1991: 59).

7.27. PS ES-EN-A- ‖ ĀS-EN-A-, PB ŌS-I- − 'ash-tree (Fraxinus excelsior, ornus)'

This lexeme has CS **e-* and **a-* variants in Slavic in addition to a CS **ā-* variant corresponding to the Baltic **uo-*.

1. The Slavic variant with **ā-*, PS Ā- (see below) appears to occur in all the six regions. The **e-* variant is found in (proximal) Polish, (proximal) Slovak, and Western and Eastern South Slavic. Eastern South Slavic also has **a-* forms, mostly isolated dialect variants or toponyms. In Bulgarian dialects where **e-* and **a-* forms coexist, the **a-* forms are evaluated as older, except in localities where the two by-forms denote distinct tree species (cf. Popowska-Taborska 1984: 30).

1.1. LCS **jesenŭ*: P *jesion*, N-d. *jesień*, Pb. *jisin*; Sk. d. *jeseň*, Cz. d. *jeseň*; Sn. *jesện*, SC d. *jèsēn*; Bg. d. *ésen*, top. *Ésenište*, M top. *Esen*.

1.2. LCS **osenŭ*: P d. *u̯eśón* (Wielkopolska); Sn. top. *Osenca*, SC top. *Osenik* (Bosnia); Bg. d. *ósen*, top. *Ósenovo, Ósinite, Osenski dol, Osinkovica*.

1.3. LCS **ja-*: P o., S-d. *jasień*, Ka. *jasón*, Sc. *jãsòṷn*, Pb. *josin*; US *jasen*, LS *jasen*; Sk. *jaseň*, Cz. *jasan*; Sn. d. *jásen*, SC *jàsēn*; Bg. *jásen*, M *jasen*; R *jás'en'*, Br. *jás'en'*, U *jásen*.

2. OPr. *Woasis* − *Esche* (E. 627) 'ash', La. *uôsis*, Li. *úosis*.

3. Sławski (1977: 159) derives the LCS **o-* forms from **je-* forms, and these from **ja-* forms "by assimilation", overlooking that the two Proto-Slavic variants of this lexeme differ in vowel quality, quantity, and accent, contrast Sn. d. *jásen* and st. *jesên*. Both variants have correspondences in other Indo-European languages, PS ĀS-EN-A- differs by its secondary suffix from the Baltic counterparts, PB ŌS-I- (< PIE **h_xeh₃-s-*, a former *s*-stem). The short-vowel variant PS ES-EN-A- has the same root quantity as the correspondents in Italic (cf. Lat. *ornus* < **os-eno-s*; cf. Schrijver

[1991: 77–78]), Celtic (cf. OIr. *huinnius*, W *onnen*, Bret. *ounnenn* < **os-no-*), Germanic (cf. OHG *asc*, MHG *esche*, ON *askr* < **os-k-*), Albanian, and Armenian (Alb. *ah* 'beech [Fagus]', Arm. *haçi* 'ash [Fraxinus]' < **os-ka-*), but all these show PIE **os-* (< **h$_x$h$_3$-es-*).

Evidently PS ES-EN-A- is a product of Rozwadowski's change; its modern reflexes exemplify the Slavic–Baltic **e-* > **a-* merger.

The geographical distribution of the PS ĀS-EN-A- by-forms is an independent illustration of the dissemination of lexical variants during the Slavic expansion (see also PS ELBEDI- [8], EMELA- [18], ERIMBI- [20–21], LEMĒXIA- [44]); but many of the attested *ja-* forms may in fact be secondary modifications of LCS **je-* forms (cf. section 5.1.3).

It is interesting to note the complete absence of PS ES-EN-A- reflexes in East Slavic (where secondary *ja-* from LCS **je-* is unusual outside Ukrainian). Here there is an apparent congruence of PS ĀS-EN-A- with the initial of PB ŌS-I-. Perhaps there was a Southeast Baltic substratum effect here, parallel to the one hypothesized in section 3.7, favoring that Common Slavic by-form which had the initial vocalism most compatible with the corresponding substratum word.

Literature: Fraenkel (1962–1965: 1167); Sławski (1974: 159); Trubačev (1974: 79–80); Popowska-Taborska (1984: 28–30).

7.28. PS ES-EN-I-, PB AS-EN-I- — (0) 'autumn'; adverbs (instrumental case forms) meaning (1) 'in the autumn' or 'last autumn'

Slavic has both **e-* and **a-* forms. Old Prussian has the only Baltic correspondent, with *a-*.

1. East Slavic mainly has **a-* forms, but **e-* forms occur in southeast Russian dialects and southwestern dialects of Ukrainian. The Slovak-Czech region basically has **e-* forms, but **a-* forms are known from Eastern Slovak dialects and eighteenth century Moravia. Elsewhere only **e-* forms are attested.

1.1. LCS **jeseňĭ*: P *jesień*, Pb. *jisin*; Sk. *jeseň*, Cz. *jeseň* (Pan-Slavicism, poetic for *podzim*), o. *podjesen*; Sn. *jesẹ̑n, jesẹ̑nes* (1), SC *jèsēn, jesènas* (1); Bg. *ésen*, d. *esenés* (1), M *esen, eseneska* (1), ChSl. *jesenĭ*; R d. *jés'en'* (Rjazan'), *jes'en'á* (Rjazan'), *jes'énn'ij, jes'en'ás'* (1) (Tambov), *jes'en'jú* (1), U o. *jeseňĭ*, SW-d. *jesen'*.

1.2. LCS *oseně: Sk. E-d. *ośiń*, Mor. o. *oseň*; R *ós'en'*, d. *os'en'és'* (1) (Arxangel'sk, Volodga, Perm', Jaroslavl', Tver', Tobol'sk.), *vos'en'és'* (1) (Rjazan'), Br. *vós'en'*, U *ósin'*. The isolated Czech (Moravian) *oseň*, recorded as a Moravianism in the 1700s is perhaps the last evidence of the kind of variation discussed in section 3.7. The fact that the general local word for 'autumn' is *podzim* gives this isolated *o*- form the appearance of an archaism; it is hard to see any basis for disregarding it; one certainly cannot set it aside merely by stating that "its provenience is unclear"; thus Popowska-Taborska (1984: 54). It is an open question whether such lexemes as P *osienie* 'seeding', d. *u̯ośiń* 'winter seed', LS *wósenina* 'seeding, a seeded field' (< **woseń* 'seed'), Cz. d. *oseň* 'seeded field', widespread in West Slavic dialects, are made of whole cloth (i.e. derived from a LCS **ob-sějati* 'sow') or have resulted from resegmentation and semantic reinterpretation of inherited **o*- doublets of PS ESENI- (cf. Popowska-Taborska 1984: 54).

1.3. Secondary *ja*-: P o. *jasień*, Sk. W-d. *jaseň*, Sn. d. *jasen*, Bg. d. *jasen*. Prothetic *v*- in Sc. *vjìęseń*.

2. OPr. *Assanis − Herbist* (E. 14) 'autumn' is the only Baltic attestation.

3. Go. *asans* 'harvest time, summer', OHG *aran* 'harvest', Gm. *Ernte* 'harvest', Gk. *opōra* (< **op-os-ar-ā*) all point to PIE **h₁os-en/r-*, *o*-grade of **h₁es-* 'to be'. But the recent analysis of Fi. *kesä* 'summer' and congeners (Koivulehto 1991: 36−38) attests to the existence of a formation with the *e*-grade in some northern Indo-European dialects.

The Slavic attestations may reflect either of these vocalisms, assuming the *o*-grade variant would have been subject to Rozwadowski's change, but it is quite unlikely that Slavic would reflect both (cf. section 5.3.1−5.3.2). Whatever the source of the PS E-, Slavic evidently illustrates the later Slavic−Baltic **e*- > **a*- merger.

The Old Prussian form is compatible with three different interpretations: (i) *o*-grade preserved (PIE **o*- > PB **a*- > OPr. *a*-); (ii) *o*-grade, Rozwadowski's change, and the Slavic−Baltic **e*- > **a*- merger (PIE **o*- > PB **e*- > OPr. *a*-), and (iii) *e*-grade affected by the **e*- > **a*- merger (PIE **e*- > PB **e*- > OPr. *a*-); cf. section 5.2.3.

Literature: Toporov (1975: 130−131); Trubačev (1979: 27−29); Popowska-Taborska (1984: 52−57); Mažiulis (1988: 103−104); Sławski (1991: 60−62).

7.29. PS ES-ER-Ā- − (0) 'awn, beard on grain, hulls, thorn'; (1) 'fishbone', (2) 'fish scales'; PB EŠ-ER-IA- ‖ AŠ-ER-(I)A- − 'perch (Perca fluvialis)'

Both Slavic and Baltic have **e-* and **a-* forms.

1. The Slavic lexeme is attested only in Lechitic. **a-* forms occur in the proximal ([north]eastern) parts of the region.

1.1. LCS **jesera*: P d. *jesiora* (1), o. *jesiory* (1), Ka. *jesora* (1), Sc. *jìęsǝră* (1, 2), Pb. *jeserǻi̯*.

1.2. LCS **osery*: P NE-d. *osiory* (0, 1, 2).

2. La. *asers, asars, aseris*, Li. *ešerỹs*, d. *ašerỹs* 'perch (Perca fluvialis)'.

3. These Slavic and Baltic lexemes are descriptive formations meaning 'prickly thing(s)', cf. PS AST-RA- (< PIE **h₂ek̂-ro* 'pointed') and Li. *aštrùs-*, a secondary *u*-stem. Some scholars think the relic distribution of the Slavic reflexes of this lexeme puts the Common Slavic character of the word in doubt (cf. section 8.2.3). But its original basic meaning makes it clear this is an old formation, apparently an independent parallel to its Baltic counterpart with a distinct semantic specialization. The apparent Germanic parallel (OHG *ahira*, Gm. *Ähre* 'ear [of grain]' is ambiguous between < PIE **h₂ek̂-er-ā* and **h₂ek̂-es-ā*).

Both these Slavic and Baltic continuants of PIE **h₂ek̂-er-* exemplify Rozwadowski's change, but the Baltic dialects reflected in Latvian may have escaped this (cf. section 6.1 and tables 6.1). The Lithuanian and Slavic forms attest to the later Slavic−Baltic **e-* > **a-* merger.

Literature: Fraenkel (1962−1965: 125), Trubačev (1979: 29−30); Popowska-Taborska (1984: 55−57); Sławski (1991: 62).

7.30. PS ES-ETI-, PB EK-ETI-Ā- − (0) 'harrow'; (1) 'grain sieve', (2) 'rack for drying grain; drying shed'

Both Slavic and Baltic have **e-* and **a-* variants of this etymon.

1. In Slavic, **e-* forms occur in most of Poland, **a-* forms in Wielkopolska and East Slavic.

1.1. LCS **jesetī*: P d. *jesieć, jesiótka* (1).

1.2. LCS **osetī*: P E-d. *osieć* (2), W-d. *osiótka*; R *os'ét'* (2), Br. *as'éc'* (2), *as'ótka* (2), *vós'ec'* (2), U *os'it'* (1).

2. OPr. *Aketes* − *Egde* (E. 255) (0), La. *ecḗsas, ecêkšas* (0), Li. *akė̃čios,*
d. *ekė̃čios,* (0) *akė́ti,* d. *ekė́ti* 'to harrow'. The *-ē̆-* in the East Baltic nouns
has been carried over from the verb (Toporov 1975: 68). PB E- is confirmed by Fi., Est. *äes* 'harrow' (< **äγesi* < **äkesi* < **äketi* < **äkete*).
    3. Despite the semantic difference, these Slavic and Baltic lexemes are
convincingly argued to be *Gutturalwechsel* by-forms of one and the same
Pre-Slavic−Baltic formation (cf. Borýs 1984), having apparent parallels
in Germanic and Italo-Celtic and a near-parallel in Greek: OHG *egida,*
OE *eg(e)ðe,* Lat. *occa* (< **otekā* < **oketā*), OldW *ocet,* Gk. *oksína:*
ergaleĩon ti geōrgikón, sidēroũs gomphoũs ékhōn, helkómenon hupò boõn
'an agricultural implement with iron teeth, drawn by oxen' (Hesych.), all
derived from PIE **h₂ek̂-* ~ **h₂ok̂-* 'pointed'. The earlier, semantically
implausible, attempt to link the Baltic words with PIE **hek^w-* 'eye' (cf.
Toporov 1975: 67) is incompatible with the *-s-* of the Slavic correspondents. Toporov considers the *-k-* (< PIE **-k̂-*) of the Baltic forms evidence
of a western technological borrowing.
    Borýs thinks the Slavic **o-* forms (paragraph 1.2) are "older" than the
*je- forms (paragraph 1.1) (cf. Sławski 1991: 65); this is possible in principle, but it is much more likely that the modern Slavic diversity (which
includes dialect variation within Polish) is due to the relatively recent
Slavic−Baltic **e-* > **a-* merger, and that both Slavic and Baltic reflect
equally the much earlier Rozwadowski's change, which appears to have
preceded the stabilization of *Gutturalwechsel* variants. For the general,
methodological aspects of this reasoning, see sections 5.3.1 and 6.2.
    Thus, both Slavic and East Baltic forms presuppose Rozwadowski's
change, the OPr. *a-* being ambiguous (cf. sections 5.3.4 and 6.1). Both
Slavic and Lithuanian attest to the Slavic−Baltic **e-* > **a-* merger.
    Literature: Fraenkel (1962−1965: 119); Toporov (1975: 67−68); Po-
powska-Taborska (1984: 58−61); Mažiulis (1988: 59−60); Sławski (1991:
64−65).

7.31. PS ES-ETRA-, PB EŠ-ETRA- − 'sturgeon (Acipenser sturio)'

Both Slavic and Baltic has **e-* and **a-* forms of this lexeme.
    1. East Slavic has mainly **a-* forms. Older **e-* attestations in Russian
may be Church Slavonicisms, but the Ukrainian *ja-* (for LCS **je-*) is
surely a vernacular form. In the other regions, only **e-* forms are known.

1.1. LCS **jesetrǔ*: P *jesiotr*, Ka.-Sc. *jesoter*; US o. *jesetr*, LS *jesotr*; Sk. *jeseter*, Cz. *jeseter*; Sn. *jeséter*, SC *jèsetra*; Bg. *esétra*, M *esetra*; R o. *jesetrǔ*, U d. *jásétr*.

1.2. LCS **osetrǔ*: R *os'ótr, os'et'ór*, Br. *as'étr*, d. *as'ac'ór*, U *osetér*.

1.3. Secondary *ja-*: P o. *jasiotr*, Ka.-Sc. *jasoter*, US *jasotr*. Upper Sorbian *ja-* for LCS **je-* is unusual; Popowska-Taborska (1984: 58) suspects this form is a loan (from Polish?).

2. OPr. *Esketres* − *Stoer* (E. 567), read /esketras/, Li. *erškẽtras*, d. *erškẽtas, arškẽtas*, o. *ešketras*.

3. PS ES-ETRA- appears to be a transparent continuant of a PIE **h₂ek̑-etro-* 'pointed or prickly (one)', a formation contrasting with **h₂ek̑-er-* 'prickly thing(s)' > Slavic 'awn; fishbone', Baltic 'perch' [29]). The Baltic forms of the 'sturgeon' word are supposed to be blends of **ešetras*, which can be extrapolated from Slavic, and Li. *erškẽtis* 'thorn, thornbush', La. *ẽrkšķis* 'thorn, prickle' (< PIE **h₂erk̑-* 'pierce' [24]). Perhaps the older, *r*-less root shapes of OPr. *esketres*, OLi. *ešketras* are blends of *Gutturalwechsel* by-forms (i. e. < **ešetras* × **eketras*).

In any case, to the extent that these forms continue etyma with initial PIE **h₂e-*, they exemplify Rozwadowski's change, as well as the later Slavic−Baltic **e-* > **a-* merger.

Literature: Fraenkel (1962−1965: 123); Toporov (1979: 88−91); Trubačev (1979: 30−32); Popowska-Taborska (1984: 57−58); Mažiulis (1988: 288−289); Sławski (1991: 63−64).

7.32. PS ES-MI, ES-SEI, ES-TI…, PB ES-MI… − Present tense forms of 'to be'

Slavic has only **e-* forms, Baltic both *e-* and *a-* forms of this lexeme.

1. LCS **jesmǐ, *jesi, *jestǐ…:* P *jest*, Pb. *jis, jǎ*; US *je*, LS *jo*; Sk. *je*, Cz. *jest, je*; Sn. *jè*, SC *jěst, je*; Bg. *e*, M *e*, OCS *jesmǐ, jesi, jestǔ…;* R *jest'*, Br. *jósc'*, U *jé*.

2. OPr. *asmai* '1sg.'s, *assai, essei* '2sg.', *ast, est* '3sg.pl.', *asmai* '1pl.', *astai, estei* '2pl.'; La. *esmu, esi*, OLi. *esmì, esì, est(i), esme, estè*, d. *asti, esmà, asmà*.

OPr. *astin* /astis/ 'thing', Li. *esìmas* 'idem'.

3. This is PIE **h₁es-* 'to be'. The Baltic *a-* forms reflect the Slavic−Baltic **e-* > **a-* merger. Slavic shows no evidence of the merger in the forms of this lexeme.

Literature: Fraenkel (1962−1965: 124); Toporov (1975: 122−128, 134−135); Trubačev (1979: 32); Mažiulis (1988: 101−103); Sławski (1991: 66).

7.33. PB EŠU-Ā- − 'mare'

Baltic has both *e-* and *a-* forms. Slavic has **a-* in toponyms.

1. R top. *Osv'ica, Osva, Osovka, Osv'eja, Osv'ej* presumably continue Baltic substratum names; Trubačev (1991) suggests they represent PIE **ak̂wā-* 'water'.

2. OPr. *Aswinan − Kobilmilch* (E. 694) 'mare's milk', top. *Asswene, Asswin, Asswaylen, Eswiten,* La. top. *Asva,* Li. o. *ešvà, ašvà, ašvíenis* 'work horse', *ašvis* 'foal', top. *Ašvà, Ašvijà, Ašvìnė.*

3. The other Indo-European languages indicate initial **e-,* cf. OS *ehu-skalk* 'groom', OE *eoh* 'horse', Lat. *equus,* OIr. *ech,* Skt. *áśva-,* etc. (< PIE **h₁ek̂u̯-o-*).

The Baltic (and Slavic) forms with **a-* appear to reflect the Slavic−Baltic **e- > *a-* merger.

Literature: Fraenkel (1962−1965: 20); Toporov (1975: 135−138); Mažiulis (1988: 106).

7.34. PB EŽ 'I'

Baltic has both *e-* and *a-* forms. Slavic has only **ā-* reflexes.

1. OPr. *as* (46×), *es* (2×), La. *es,* Li. *aš,* d., o. *eš.*

3. The other Indo-European languages indicate original **h₁eĝ-* or **h₁eĝʰ-,* extended or not with an additional syllable: Lat. *egō,* Gk. *egō,* Go. *ik,* OHG *ihh-ā,* Skt. *ahám,* Av. *azəm,* etc. The Slavic forms LCS **ja, *jazŭ* seem to point to an *o-*grade alternant (**h₁oĝ-om >* PS ĀZ-AM with length from Winter's law). Trubačev's reconstruction of the phrasal origin of this pronoun (**e ĝo eme* 'Here I am!' [1974: 102]) pertains to a much earlier (pre-proto-) phase of Indo-European.

The Baltic attestation reflects PB E- and shows the effect of the Slavic−Baltic **e- > *a-* merger.

Literature: Fraenkel (1962–1965: 18); Trubačev (1974: 100–103), Sławski (1974: 166–167); Toporov (1975: 113–120); Mažiulis (1988: 98–99).

7.35. PS EZ-ERA-, PB EŽ-ERA- — (0): 'lake'; (1) 'swamp'

Both Slavic and Baltic have **e-* and **a-* forms of this lexeme.

East Slavic has almost exclusively **a-* forms now, but the Russian toponym *Jezar'išče* and U *jázer* are indubitable vernacular archaisms with **e-*. The other regions have **e-* forms, but isolated **a-* forms are known from Slovak–Czech and in toponyms in the formerly Slavic areas of Pannonia, Carinthia, Rumania, and Greece (cf. section 3.6). See also Udolph (1979: 97–110).

1.1. LCS **jezero*: P *jezioro*, Sc. *jĩęzoro̶*, Pb. top. *Jehser*; US *jĕzor*, LS *jazoro*, o. *jezoro*; Sk. *jazero*, E-d. *jezér*, Cz. *jezero*; Sn. *jézero*, d. *jêzer*, Carinthia top. *Jesêrz, Jezerce*, SC *jȅzero*, d. *jȅzēr*; Rum. *iezer*, top. *Iezeris, Iezerul*, Bg. *ézero, ézer*, top. *Ezerovo, Ezerec, Ezerata*, M *ezero*, Gk. top. *Ezerós*, OCS *jezero, jezerŭ*; R NW-d. *jéz'ero*, top. *Èzirišče* (near Pskov), U o. *jezero*.

1.2. LCS **ozero*: Sk. o. *ozero* (Kott 1910: s. v.), Cz. o. *ozero* (Kott 1910: s. v.); Carinthian top. *Asserz* (1410); Rum. top. *Ozero*, Gk. top. *Ozeros*; R *óz'oro, óz'or*, top. *Ošm-ozero*, Br. *vóz'era*, U *ózero*.

1.3. Secondary *ja-*: Sk. *jazero*, U SW-d. *jazero*. Prothetic *w-* in LS *wjazor, wĕzor*.

2. OPr. *Assaran* — *See* (E. 60) 'lake', top. *Azara* etc., Cur. *Eezeryne, Esser Semmen, Aserowischen*, La. *ezers*, Li. *ẽžeras*, d. *ãžeras*.

3. Connections with Gk. *Akhérōn* 'river in the underworld', *akheroúsia: húdata helōdē* 'swamp water' (Hesych.) and with the Illyrian *Oseriātes* and the Pannonian (Pliny) *Asseriates* 'lake dwellers?', might point to PIE **a-* or **o-*, but the source languages of these ethnonyms are not well known, and it is uncertain whether their initials can be taken at face value. In any case they may be compatible with the hypothetical derivational relationship of PS EZ-ERA-, PB EŽ-ERA with PS ĒZ-A-, PB EŽ-Ī-/IĀ- (see section 7.34), which implies a PIE **h₁eĝʰ-ero-*.

This is one of Rozwadowski's examples (he posited **aĝʰ-* on the basis of Gk. *akhérōn*, etc.). Whether it is a valid example of Rozwadowski's change or not, the variation in both language groups exemplifies the later Slavic−Baltic *e- > *a- merger.

Literature: Fraenkel (1962−1965: 125); Toporov (1975: 131−133); Trubačev (1979: 33−34); Popowska-Taborska (1984: 64−67); Mažiulis (1988: 104); Sławski (1991: 73−76).

7.36. PB EŽ-Ī-/-IĀ- − 'balk, border, property line'

Baltic has *e-* and *a-* forms. The Slavic correspondents have PS Ē-, CS *ē-.

1. OPr. *Asy − Reen* (E. 241; *Reen* is dialect for 'Rain') /azī/ 'balk', top. *Aseniten, Aselauken*, Jatv. *Starozyny* (< *stār-az-in-is*), La. *eža*, top. *Aža, Ažēni, Ažēns*, Li. *ežė, ežià*, d. *ažià*, top. *Ežupė, Ežmalis, Ežas*.

2. PB EŽ-Ī-/-IĀ- and PS ĒZ-A- (P *jaz*, Cz. *jez* 'levee', R, Br., U *jáz* 'fish weir', etc.) derive from different alternants of a PIE $*h_1\bar{e}\hat{g}^h$-, $*h_1e\hat{g}^h$-, reflected also in Arm. *ezr* 'bank, border, limit'.

The Baltic *a-* forms result from the Slavic−Baltic *e- > *a- merger.

Literature: Fraenkel (1962−1965: 125); Toporov (1975: 120−121); Trubačev (1979: 59); Mažiulis (1988: 101); Sławski (1991: 166−169).

7.37. PS EZ-IA-, PB EŽ-IA- − 'hedgehog (Erinaceus europaea)'

Both Slavic and Baltic have *e-* and *a-* forms.

1. *e-* forms occur in all Slavic regions, *a-* forms only in East Slavic. Contrast the distribution of *e-* and *a-* forms in the derivatives of PS EZ-IA- in section 7.38.

1.1. LCS *ježĭ: P *jeż*; Sc. *jëiž*, Pb. *jiz*; US *jěž*, LS *jež*, d. *jaž, ježyk*; Sk. *jež*, Cz. *ježek*, d. *jež*; Sn. *jéž*, SC *jêž*, d. *jêža*; Bg. *ež*, M *ež*; R *jóž, jóžik*; Br. d. *jéžik*, d. *jóžik*, U *již, jižák*.

1.2. LCS *ožĭ: R o. *ožĭ, ožikŭ*, d. *ož, ožik*; Br. *vózik*; U d. *ož*.

1.3. Prothesis in P d. *wież, wjiž*.

2. La. *ezis*, Li. *ežỹs*, d. *ažỹs, ēžis, ėžỹs*.

3. OHG *igil*, Gm. *Igel*, Gk. *ekhĩnos* point to PIE $*h_1e\hat{g}^h$-, but *o*-grade is apparent in Arm. *ozni*.

PS, PB E- may reflect the original *e*-grade form or it may be the result of Rozwadowski's change applying to the *o*-grade alternant. In either case, the Slavic and Lithuanian forms evidently reflect the later *e- > *a-merger.

Literature: Fraenkel (1962–1965: 1330); Trubačev (1979: 37); Popowska-Taborska (1984: 68–69); Sławski (1991: 80–82).

7.38. PS EZ-IA- derivatives

All derivatives appear to be formed from a CS *ezj- or *ež-. Meanings: (0) 'hedgehog's pelt, rough pelt, prickly peel'; (1) 'hedgehog's nest'; (2) 'she-hedgehog; other prickly animals'; (3) 'blackberry (Rubus) or other bramble-like plants', 'meadow grass (Dactylis glomerata)', or the like.

1. *a- forms occur more widely than in the base word: East Slavic, (proximal) Slovak and Moravian, and (proximal) southern Polish.

1.1. LCS *jež-: P *ježyna* (3), d. *jezina* (3), d. *jażyna* (3); Cz. *ježice* (2), *ježina* (3), *ježiník* (3), *ježovina* (0); Sn. *ježíca* (0, 3), *ježevíca* (0), *ježevína* (0), *jéžinja* (2), SC *jéževica* (3), *jèževina* (0, 3), *jéžica* (0, 1, 2), *jèžika* (3), *jèžina* (3); Bg. *éževína* (0); R *ježóv'ina* (0, 1), *ježev'íka* (3), E-d. *ježev'íga* (3), N-d. *ježev'íca* (3), NE-d. *ježev'íxa* (3) *ježíxa* (3), U *ježevýka* (3), *ježýna* (3), *ježovnýk* (3), *jižovýna* (0), *jižýc'a* (2).

1.2. LCS *ož-: P S-d. *ożyna* (3), d. *ożyniarki* (3) (near Cieszyn); Sk. N-d. *ožina* (3), Mor. d. *ožina* (3); R *ožíka* (3), S-d. *ožína* (3), *ožev'íka*, W-d. *ožev'ína*, Br. *ažíka* (3), *ažína* (3), *ažav'ína* (3), U *ožýna* (3).

1.3. The West Slavic occurrences of *o- forms, which cover northern Slovakia and southern Poland all the way to Silesia have been explained as the result of a secondary colonization by Ukrainian speakers (cf. Popowska-Taborska 1984: 68), but in view of all the other stable West Slavic linguistic features of these diverse dialects, this is not very convincing. There is no evidence that *o- forms of this word are of recent provenience in these areas, and there is no more reason to refer to Ukrainian settlers in this connection than in the several other cases where proximal regions have more *o- forms than corresponding distal regions.

Note that the differences in geographical distribution between the LCS *ježǐ ‖ *ožǐ forms and the derived plant names are comparable to what is seen in the case of the doublet forms of the 'grouse, partridge' and the 'rowan tree' words (PS ERIMB-I- [20–21]).

Literature: Trubačev (1979: 35−37); Popowska-Taborska (1984: 68−69); Sławski (1991: 76−80).

7.39. PS IA-GE- – 'that; since; if'

This Slavic conjunction, historically developed from the relative pronoun has CS *je- reflexes in two of the West Slavic regions, in Western South Slavic, and in East Slavic. It has apparent *a- attestations as well in East Slavic.

1.1. LCS *ježe: P o. *ež(e), hež(e)*, Ka. *ježe*; Cz. o. *(j)ež, ježe*; SC *jêr(e)*; R d. *ježe, ježda (l'i)*, o. *ježe*.

1.2. LCS *ože: R o. *ože, ožĭ*, Br. o. *ože*, U *ož(e)*.

Note that both Polish and Czech have early attestations without the etymological *j-*, in Polish subject to the medieval *h*-prothesis (cf. section 5.1.1). Like the indefinite PS IA-TERA- (see below), PS IA-GE may have developed reduced forms (CS *eže*) at an early date, which in the "*a-dialects" of Common Slavic (see section 3.3) would have been exposed to the CS *e- > *a- merger.

Literature: Popowska-Taborska (1984: 67−68).

7.40. PS IA LAI- − (0) 'if'; (1) 'when', (2) 'while', (3) 'whereas', (4) 'otherwise'; PS IA-LEI- KA- − (5) 'how much'

*je- forms are known from all Slavic regions; apparent *a- forms, only from South Slavic and East Slavic.

1.1. LCS *jeli: P o. *jele*; US *jeli*, LS *joli až*; SC *jĕl* (3); Bg. *éle* 'nevertheless'; OCS *jeli*; R *jéle* 'barely', o. *jeli* (0−3).

1.2. LCS *oli: Sn. o. *òli*, SC *oli* 'or'; R o. *oli* (0, 1, 2, 4), d. *oli*, U *óly* 'till', o. *oli*.

2.1. LCS *jeliko: P o. *jeliko* (5); LS d. *jolik* (0); Cz. *jelikož* (3), o. *jelik* (5); OCS *jeliko*; R o. *jeliko* (5), U *jelýko-moha* 'as much as possible'.

2.2. LCS *oliko*: Bg. d. *olku* 'so much', d. *olko* 'only'; R o. *oliko* (5).

3. These two lexemes are built on the relative pronoun LCS *je 'which' and *jelikŭ 'as great or much as', and are not expected to have *a-

forms. Some of the attestations could perhaps be explained away. For one thing, the Slovenian and Serbo-Croatian forms may be variants of *ali* 'or' (cf. Bezlaj [1977: s. v.]). For another, the Old Russian attestations are a handful of isolated forms scattered over a variety of texts, all bookish. But as in the case of the **a-* forms of PS IA-GE [39] and IA-TERA- [41], it seems simpler to assume that some Common Slavic variants occurred without the inherited initial CS **j-*.

The geographical distribution of LCS **je-* and **o-*forms of these lexemes is nothing out of the ordinary for lexemes subject to the **e-* > **a-* merger.

Literature: Trubačev (1979: 7−8), (1981 a: 186); Popowska-Taborska (1984: 46−48).

7.41. PS IA-TER-A- − 'someone; another'

This indefinite pronoun derived from PS IA-, attested with the expected **je-* form in Old Church Slavonic, appears to have a counterpart with **a-* in Sorbian.

1.1. LCS **jeterŭ*: OCS and RChS *jeterŭ* 'some, a certain'.

1.2. LCS **oterŭ*: US *wotry, wotery* 'another', LS *wótery*, d. *wótary, wótory* 'some, several'.

2. The relationship between the apparent **a-* forms in Sorbian and the Church Slavonic **e-* form may seem enigmatic. The Sorbian forms may look like blends of an original **jeterŭ* and **vŭtorŭ* 'other, second', "influenced by *kótary, kótery* 'which'" (thus Vaillant [1958: 489]). It is simpler (so Trubačev [1981 a: 187]) to suppose a (geographically limited?) loss of initial CS **j-* (possibly first in allegro speech?) preceding the **e-* > **a-* merger.

The resulting distribution of LCS **je-* and **o-* forms looks different from most other lexeme doublets with this variation. This is perhaps only because of the very skimpy attestation of this pronoun, which was evidently renewed in most Slavic dialects before the migrations. But in terms of the correlation established in section 6.1 between ante-Migration CS **a-* dialects (section 3.4, figure 3.1) and Rozwadowski E-doublets (table 6.2), this lone Sorbian **a-* lexeme is quite like LS *heŕol, jerol* (PS ERILA-) 'eagle' [22].

Literature: Trubačev (1981 a: 187); Popowska-Taborska (1984: 63−64).

7.42. PS IAU-ĪNA-, IAU-IIĀ, IAU-INIĀ-, PB IAU-ĪNA-, IAU-IĀ- − 'granary, drying shed'

Three different East Slavic loan adaptations of two Southeast Baltic words, **jawĭnas* and **jáujā*, dialect synonyms meaning 'granary, drying shed' and the like, occur with overlapping geographical distributions. Forms with LCS **je-* predominate in eastern areas of Belarus (Avanesov 1963: map 233), widely adapted with the suffix *-n'-* (PS -INIĀ-). Both the *-j-* and *-n'-* variants must be younger than the Jer Shift − or at least its initial phase, the phonetic omission of weak jers − for it was only through this phonetic process that *-vj-* and *-vn'-* sequences became admissible. The LCS **o-* forms have no distinct distribution; perhaps they are older.

1. LCS **javĭja*: P d. *jawia*, d. *jewje*, R *jev'ja, jévn'a, jóvn'a*, Br. *jóvn'a*, d. *jávja, jévn'a*, U *jevja, jévn'a*.

1.2. LCS **ovinŭ*: R *ov'ín*, Br. *av'ín*, U *ovýn*.

2. OPr. *Jauge, Jawyge* /jaujə/ 'meeting hall; gathering' (seventeenth century), (Gm. d.) *Jauge* /jaujə/ or with hypercorrect /g/, /jaugə/ 'barn', La. *jauja* 'threshing floor', Li. *jáuja* 'granary, drying shed', derived from PB IAU-AI, Li. *javaĩ* 'grain'.

3. Trubačev (1981 a: 187) reconstructs LCS **jevinŭ*, which is at variance with the attestation (see immediately above) and alludes to Li. *javienà* 'grain field' (which has a different suffix, is feminine, and has a different meaning). Although it is easy enough to reconstruct Proto-Slavic shapes for these lexemes, there is no reason to think they are not regional borrowings from Southeast Baltic.

These LCS **o-* and **je-* forms probably have no direct bearing on the Slavic−Baltic **e-* > **a-* merger, but are best understood as alternative ways of adapting the initial **ja-* sequence of the source language to the early Slavic phonological patterns − omitting the initial [i] as an unmotivated prothesis before the back vowel (Southeast Baltic **ja-* ⇒ CS **a-*) or recognizing the initial /j/ and adjusting the vowel after it from back to front (Southeast Baltic **ja-* ⇒ (L)CS **je-*; this progressive umlaut is productive in Common Slavic from CS-II through CS-III).

The *o*- form was borrowed with its suffix from the source dialects, where it evidently meant 'grain place, granary' (Southeast Baltic **jawaĩ* 'grain' : **jawĩnas* 'granary' are like Li. *mẽšlaĩ* 'manure' : *mẽšlýnas* 'dung-hill', *úoga* 'berries' : *uogýnas* 'berry patch', *ẽglė* 'spruce' : *eglýnas* 'spruce stand', and *žõdis* 'word' : *žodýnas* 'dictionary' (cf. Otrębski 1965: 199). The **je*- forms keep the Baltic *-iĀ-* suffix as *-j-* or replace it with the Slavic suffix *-n'-*'place' (PS -INIĀ-; cf. LCS **staj-ĭńa* 'stable', **paš-ĭńa* 'plowed field'). If there is a chronological difference between the CS **a*- and LCS **je*- adaptations, as it seems, it presumably correlates with the different tenacity with which Baltic speech was maintained in different parts of the South Baltic territories.

Literature: Fraenkel (1962–1965: 192); Toporov (1980: 21–22); Trubačev (1981 a: 187–188); Laučjute (1982: 12); Popowska-Taborska (1984: 73–75).

7.43. PS IEB-TĒI, IEB-ĀM- — 'copulate with'; other meanings are 'move', 'strike', 'curse', 'cheat'

All the Slavic languages show **je*- reflexes of this lexeme.

1.1. LCS **je*-: P *jebác*, Sn. *jâbac*; US *jebać*, LS *jebaś*; Sk. d. *jebat'*, Cz. *jebati*; SC *jèbati*; Bg. *ebá*; R *jet'í, jebát', jebú*.

1.2. LCS **jĕ*-: Sn. *jébati*; U *jibáty*.

3. This lexeme is relevant to the topic of the **e*- > **a*- merger only in so far as it shows that PS IE- normally was not subject to it. Several modern forms are ambiguous between LCS **je*- and **jĕ*- and Trubačev erroneously reconstructs PS **jĕbati* for **jeti* (1981 a: 188). One source of confusion is that in some Slavic dialects the received infinitive may have been remade as LCS **jebati* (e. g., SC *jèbati*), in others it has been replaced by the regularly formed iterative LCS **jĕbati* (thus U *jibáty* < PS IĒB-Ā-TĒI). Cf. Skt. *yábhati* 'futuit', Gk. *oíphō* 'futuo' (< **h₁ieb^h-* ~ **h₁ei̯b^h-*).

This lexeme was first introduced into in the discussion of the "**je*- > **o*-" question by Fortunatov (cf. section 8.1). It seems not to be relevant except as an indication that words with initial **je*- were in fact not subject to the change, which was an **e*- > **a*- merger.

Literature: Trubačev (1981 a: 188).

7.44. PS LEM-ĒX-IA-, LEM-ĒG-IA-, PB LEM-EŽ-I- — (0) 'coulter, plowshare'; (1) 'plow'

This word has two sets of Common Slavic variants, one with initial *l*-, and one without. The latter is attested in Lechitic, in South Slavic and in East Slavic, in all these regions in competition with the *l*- variant. The vowel-initial variant mostly occurs in *e- forms, but *a- forms are found in northwest Russian (cf. section 3.7). In addition to the initial variation, the suffix consonant appears as -*ž*, -*š*, and -*x*.

1.1. LCS *jemešĭ: P d. *jemiesz*; SC *jèmješ, jèmlješ*; Bg. *émeš, éméž, ímež*, M d. *émeš*; R o. *jemešĭ*.

1.2. LCS *omešĭ: R *óm'eža, óm'éž, óm'ex, om'éš*.

1.3. LCS *lemešĭ: P *lemiesz*; Sk. *lemeš*, Cz. *lemeš, lemech*; Sn. *lémež*, SC *lèmeš, lèmješ, lèmež*; Bg. *leméž*, M *lemeš*; R *l'em'éx, l'ém'éš*, Br. *l'am'éš, l'am'éx*, U *lemíš*.

2. La. *lemesis*, Li. *lḗmežis*, d. *lãmežis*.

3. This deverbal noun seems isolated in most of the Slavic languages, which have generally lost *e*-grade alternants of the root of LCS **lomiti,* *lamati 'break' (but note US *lemić*, SC *lijèmati* 'break', cf. Li. *lémti* 'break'). The Slavic -*x*- and -*š*- formations may be (expressive) derivatives of a PS LEM-EN- (cf. Bg. d. *lemen* 'plow' and LCS *grebenĭ 'comb', diminutive *grebešĭkŭ), but the suffix variation LCS *-*ěš*- ‖ *-*ěž*- is difficult to interpret. It seems to occur also in Baltic, but the vocalism does not match. Other LCS formations in *-*ež*- (such as *pad-ež-ĭ 'fall; case') have PS -EG-, which does not match Li. -*ež*- unless this is a borrowing from Slavic.

The apparent loss of the initial *l*- is somewhat odd. Some scholars describe it as a change of *l'* > *j* (thus Popowska-Taborska [1984]). But an initial *j*- would have blocked the *e- > *a- merger.

Accepting the loss of the initial *l*- as a possible idiosyncratic phonetic alteration (cf. section 5.3.2) that occurred in some Common Slavic dialects, it is clear enough that either the CS *e- and *a- forms arose before the Slavic Migrations and were disseminated during the period of expansion (*e- being generalized everywhere but in East Slavic), or the *a- form arose within East Slavic as a result of language contact in the Southeast Baltic area (cf. section 3.7).

Note that the forms with and without initial *l*- have been dispersed side by side through the Slavic Migrations.

Literature: Fraenkel (1962−1965: 354); Sławski (1974: 69−77); Popowska-Taborska (1984: 71−73); Trubačev (1987: 106−111); Vaillant (1958: 203).

Chapter 8

Alternative approaches

This investigation differs from all previous scholarship dedicated to the Slavic and Baltic *e-* ‖ *a-* diversity by the basic assumption that the actually attested geographical distribution of the reflexes of *e-* and *a-* doublets in these languages is an important explanandum.

This assumption does not just make certain data available for analysis which were there all the time, but were ignored in the past. It entails the use of a wider range of methods of analysis, as well as access to a greater variety of patterns of explanation. I will return to these points in the final section of this chapter (section 8.5).

It would seem unfair to claim that previous scholarship concerning this issue has been based on the contrary assumption that the geographical distribution of *e-* and *a-* doublets was of no significance. Previous investigators have simply been oblivious to the spatial dimension of the problem and have made no assumptions one way or the other. This is particularly evident in the writings of the few scholars, such as Filin (section 8.3.2.1) and Xaburgaev (section 8.3.1.5), who have actually tried to view the East Slavic "*je-* > *o-* change" in terms of the dialectalization of Common Slavic: they do not reveal even an inkling that this is a perspective that might be explored in concrete, detailed terms. It is actually only through the study of Popowska-Taborska (1984) that it became apparent that there were significant gains to be made if one took this aspect of the attestation seriously.

But the difference in initial assumptions does mean that − apart from the data that have been compiled, especially by Popowska-Taborska − I have not been able to use any of what has been contributed in the past in discussions of the Slavic and Baltic *e-* ‖ *a-* doublets in the present study. This is why I felt, as I stated in the Introduction, that it would be reasonable to put off all discussion of the scholarly tradition until a later point, when this tradition could be evaluated against the background of the results achieved here.

That point has now been reached. And so, in the following pages I will review some of the salient points − in initial assumptions, of method, and regarding patterns of explanation − that characterize the earlier scholarship on this topic. I do not intend to provide a blow-by-blow account of the scholarly dialog in the past; there are materials for such an account in Ekblom (1925) and Popowska-Taborska (1984); the latter in particular offers an excellent bibliography on the topic. My aim is merely to highlight the relationship between the different approaches that have been taken by others and the mostly implicit, initial assumptions that have underlain these approaches (section 8.1–8.3). Since such a great proportion of the previous scholarship has been focused exclusively on the Slavic side of the **e- ‖ *a-* question, I will discuss the Baltic issues separately (section 8.4).

In the final section I will then try to sum up what I consider the main assumptions and central points of method in this investigation and contrast them with weaknesses inherent in earlier accounts (section 8.5).

8.1. The geographical dimension

Previous scholarship has chosen between two distinct approaches in trying to account for the **je-* and **o-* doublets in the Slavic languages and their dialects. The majority opinion has long been that there was a specifically East Slavic sound change responsible for the **je- ‖ *o-* correspondences. A minority of scholars have taken the widespread distribution of **o-* by-forms in West and South Slavic as evidence that there was no special, East Slavic development, but that the change, whatever it was, was generally Slavic.

Both these opinions originated in the nineteenth century and were formed at a time when detailed information on the occurrence of **je-* and **o-* by-forms in the dialects of the Slavic languages was scant. Both therefore seemed more reasonable then than they do now.

Fortunatov (1890), for instance, mentions just three secure etyma showing an East Slavic change of **je- > *o-* before *-e-* or *-i-* (R *óz'oro* 'lake' [35], *od'ín* 'one' [1], *ov'ín* 'drying shed' [42]). The last of these he thinks proves that the change affected not just LCS **je-* from PS E-, but also LCS **je-* from PS IE- and IA-, which leads him to conclude that such examples as the inflectional forms of PS IEB-TĒI 'to copulate with' [43] (R 1sg. *jebú*, 3sg. *jeb'ót*) are the result of analogical leveling from earlier "Proto-Russian" **jebú*, **ob'ót*, and the like). Regarding three other examples (non-East Slavic **ošče* 'still' [2], **odŭva* 'hardly' [3], **olĭxa* 'alder'

[13]), Fortunatov acknowledges that there are "other sources" of the LCS *je- ‖ *o- variation. In his contemporary lectures on Old Church Slavonic he argues the matter on the basis of a dozen examples, LCS *jezero [35], *jelenĭ [11], *jesenĭ [28], *jesetrŭ [31], *jemelo [18], *jerębĭ [20−21], *jelito [10], *jedinŭ [1], *ježina [37], *jeli [40], *jeliko [40], R *ovín* [42], but the documentation he provides is almost entirely limited to standard language forms (Fortunatov 1919 [1972]: 278−281).

8.1.1. The East Slavic hypothesis

The East Slavic hypothesis has always been the *communis opinio*, in this century represented, among many others, by such scholars as Šaxmatov (1915: 138−140), Durnovo (1924−1925: 152), Jakobson (1929 [1962]: 44−52), Meillet (1934: 124 [1965: 134]), Jakubinskij (1941 [1953]: 134), Vaillant (1950: 180), Bulaxovskij (1958: 80−81), Horálek (1962: 106), A-rumaa (1964: 102), Borkovskij and Kuznecov (1965), Shevelov (1965: 422−427), and Lamprecht (1987: 36) − in addition to many others.

Among the advocates of this view, some have sought to see a relationship between the "East Slavic *je- > *o- change" and certain details in the development of other Slavic dialects. This variant of the "East Slavic doctrine" is first expounded by Fortunatov in his lectures in the 1880s (1919 [1972]: 278−281) and later modified and elaborated by Ekblom (1925: 25) and by Jakobson (1929 [1962]: 48−50).

Jakobson's version subsumes under the same rule that is posited for the "East Slavic *je- > *o- change" also Lower Sorbian dialect forms (with *he-* for LCS *je-) and Slovak and Czech forms (with Sk. *ja-*, Cz. *je-* for LCS *je-), as well as certain Old Church Slavonic spellings (of «e» for LCS *je-). However, the Lower Sorbian attestation of *je-* and *he-* is much less regular than Jakobson thought (cf. section 5.1.1); the Slovak *ja-* and *je-* likewise do not correlate well at all (cf. section 5.1.3); and the Old Church Slavonic «e» spellings actually reflect the beginning of the general Bulgaro-Macedonian change of LCS *je- > e- (see section 5.1.2) and have not a thing to do with the "East Slavic *je- > *o- change".

Although these extensions of the East Slavic hypothesis early on appeared too weak to be generally accepted, this did not diminish the standing of the East Slavic hypothesis, which, on the contrary, remained the mainstay of textbook accounts and eventually attained the status of standard doctrine. It forms the basis for the recent study by Šaur (1982), and it is tacitly assumed to be unassailable − in fact, unquestionable − in the more recent monograph by Popowska-Taborska (1984).

8.1.2. The East Slavic doctrine

It is interesting to note how much may hinge on initial assumptions — in this instance, what are the consequences of an initial assumption that the change at issue was a general Slavic change rather than a specifically East Slavic change.

If one assumes that this was a general Slavic change, then the uneven geographical distribution of *je- and *o- doublets naturally stands out as a primary explanandum — at least to anyone who is attuned to the spatial dimension of linguistic diachrony. The geographical distribution calls for the application of the methods of historical dialectology, and this, in turn, makes it important to *include* for consideration all potentially relevant lexemes with *je- and *o- forms. For it stands to reason that the ampler the data, the more reliable the inferences drawn from them. This initial assumption determined the approach in drawing up the list of lexemes investigated here (cf. chapter 7) and in working out the account in chapters 3 and 4.

If one assumes, to the contrary, that the *je- ‖ *o- correspondences are due to a narrowly East Slavic change, then the geographical distribution of *je- and *o- forms is implicitly presumed to be unproblematic, and the primary explanandum will be the phonological conditioning that motivated the putative East Slavic sound change. Under this assumption, attestations that contradict the assumed, basic "East Slavic versus West and South Slavic" distribution appear as "noise" in the data, as individual deviations which may be explained away or, if they are intractable, may be left for the diversion of future investigators. And with the goal in mind of determining the original phonological conditioning of the change, the investigator who chooses this approach will want to *exclude* from consideration any lexemes with *je- and *o- doublets which might conceivably have a nonphonological explanation.

This is the approach of Šaur (1982), who explicitly undertakes to settle the issue of the phonological conditioning of the „East Slavic *je- > *o- change" (which he understands as an *e- > *a- change; see further below). He begins his examination of the issue by identifying sixteen etyma with Common Slavic *e- which merit consideration (8.1 a); for references to chapter 7, cf. table 7.2. Some other lexemes are found to be difficult to reconstruct unambiguously, and hence have to be left aside; see (8.1 b).

(8.1) a. *edla, *edinŭ, *edŭva, *egŭda, *elenĭ, *elito, *elĭčĭ, *elĭxa, *elŭkŭ, *esenĭ, *esetrŭ, *esmĭ, *eterŭ, *ezero, *ežĭ
     b. *elbeda, *elbędĭ, *emela, *eriti, *esera, *evnĭja [sic!]

   c. *egŭda, *eterŭ, *ese* [missing from the list in (8.1 a)]
   d. *esmĭ*
   e. *elĭxa*
   f. *ešče*
   g. *edla, *elĭcĭ, *elŭkŭ*
   h. *edŭva, *elito*
   i. *ežĭ*
   j. *edĭnŭ, *elenĭ, *esenĭ, *esetrŭ, *ezero*

Some lexemes on the (8.1 a) list are considered East Slavic loans from Church Slavonic; see (8.1 c). One lexeme, it is noted, served grammatical functions, and hence it is alleged to have been immune to the change; see (8.1 d). Another lexeme is said to have had qualitative ablaut in Proto-Indo-European; see (8.1 e). One lexeme does not have a clear etymology and so has to be left aside; see (8.1 f). Eleven lexemes remain, of which three do not have LCS *o-* forms anywhere (8.1 g), two have an irregular geographical distribution of *je-* and *o-* forms (8.1 h) — "they must have developed by a different path from that of their East Slavic counterparts" (1982: 383), one occurs with both *je-* and *o-* reflexes in East Slavic (8.1 i), and only the remaining five have a regular (i. e. East Slavic) geographical distribution; see (8.1 j). These five little lexemes then serve as the basis for the formulation of a rule, Šaur's putative sound change (see section 8.3.3.1). In fact, however, only their citation forms are considered; most of their inflectional forms do not satisfy Šaur's rule, but they are tacitly ignored. The net effect of this approach is that it tries to explain away a greater number of lexemes with *je-* and *o-* doublets than it undertakes to explain; and in fact, among the lexemes with an *o-* doublet which it does try to explain, more inflectional forms are left unexplained than the author even claims to account for.

   Exactly the same approach is followed in Popowska-Taborska (1984), less blatantly perhaps, but more remarkably, considering that this study (unlike Šaur's) provides documentation for the full range of data that actually have to be accounted for. In her presentation the author repeatedly acknowledges attested forms that contradict the "expected" geographical distribution of the "East Slavic *je-* > *o-*" reflexes. But then in the end (in her "Final conclusions" [1984: 104−105]), she cuts loose from these troublesome data and returns to the comfort of the textbook opinion, concluding (as she obviously assumed all along) that only a few of the many lexemes with *je-* ‖ *o-* doublets have to do with "the East Slavic change"; see (8.2 a). The rest can be eliminated ("*wyeliminowano*") because they can be interpreted by "facts of a morphological character" (8.2 b), they exhibit alternations that existed already in Proto-Slavic (8.2 c), or they are limited to small areas, and their *je- forms can be considered secondary (8.2 d).

(8.2) a. *jedinŭ, *jelenĭ, *jesenĭ, *jesetrŭ, *jezero, *ježe, *ježĭ, probably *jevĭja, *jeměšĭ
   b. *jese, jeterŭ
   c. *jelito, *jelĭxa, *jemelŭ, *jerębĭ, *jesenŭ, *ješče, possibly *jedva, *jelavŭ, *jeli, *jeliko, *jerīlŭ
   d. *jesery, *jesetĭ

Only by "eliminating" the major part of the attestation which documents the actual geographical diversity of the *je- ‖ *o- correspondences can the author reconfirm the traditional conception of the change as being "East Slavic". She does this in two steps: (i) she glosses over the non-East-Slavic attestations of the lexemes in (8.2 a) (for the details, see chapter 7); and (ii) she closes her eyes to the fact that each lexeme in (8.2 b−d) − which she has chosen to consider irrelevant to her "East Slavic" change − is in fact attested with *o- variants in East Slavic if it occurs there at all.

It seems too bad that with all the critical data that have been brought together here − documenting in detail the attestation of *je- and *o-doublets in appellatives and in toponyms, in East and West and South Slavic, in modern dialects as well as in older sources − this study is unable to offer the reader anything more inspired by way of explanation of the putative change than Fortunatov's observation from a hundred years ago (that the "East Slavic *je- > *o- change" occurred when the following vowel was -i-, -e-, or -ę-, but not -ĭ-; see further section 8.3.1.1) jazzed up with Jakobson's proposal from 1929 (that the change was conditioned by the place of accent; see further section 8.3.1.2).

It seems too bad, but it is certainly not surprising that the autor does not get more mileage out of her efforts: if you follow the beaten path in analysing these data, it will take you to the self-same explanatory dead end our predecessors reached.

8.1.3. The Common Slavic approach

All the scholars who have adopted the East Slavic hypothesis (or doctrine) have had to assume that lexemes with *o- by-forms outside East

Slavic have developed from "other sources" (as Fortunatov put it; cf. section 8.1; cf. Popowska-Taborska's lists [8.2 a] versus [8.2 b] and [8.2 c]). But other scholars have taken precisely these non-East Slavic *o-doublets as evidence that there is no basis in the lexical material for such a division, and that all the relevant lexemes with *je- and *o- doublets should be examined and explained together.

These are the scholars who might have taken an interest in the geographical distribution of *e- and *o- doublets among the Slavic languages. Unfortunately, none of these people seems to have been oriented towards historical dialectology.

Some of them have considered the *je- ‖ *o- variation the remains of Indo-European ablaut alternations – thus Sobolevskij (1907: 31–34), Il'inskij (1923) and, most recently, it seems, Bernštejn (1961).

> Here [Sobolevskij, Il'inskij and a number of other scholars] saw the effects of ancient Indo-European o ‖ e alternations … [and] not a Common Slavic phonetic change. To explain a phonetic change of [je] to [o] in *ozero* etc. is impossible. … Why were the old alternations not preserved in this position, but leveled, differently in different groups of Slavic languages? This is not a difficult question to answer. The thing is that these alternations were maintained in morphemes in which they had some sort of grammatical function. Here however they had none. It is precisely in such instances that divergent generalizations would occur (1961: 227–228; my translation, HA).

Others have hypothesized that the *je- ‖ *o- doublets developed in the Common Slavic period as sandhi variants conditioned by preceding word-final consonants (Meillet [1934], section 8.3.1.4) or vowels (Georgiev [1963], section 8.3.3.4), or due to a more or less random development of prothesis (Calleman [1950], section 8.3.2.3; Mareš [1969], section 8.3.3.2; also Moszyński [1989: 196]).

Like the adherents of ablaut explanations, the authors of these phonetic explanations have been content to posit some prehistoric origin of a general *e- ~ *o- variation and a subsequent stochastic leveling with a geographically random outcome. But this lack of concern for the actual geographical distribution of *je- and *o- doublets is not immediately compatible with the data. Recall the most obvious generalization regarding the geographical distribution, which any tabulation of the data will show, viz. that every lexeme that has *je- and *o- doublets anywhere in Slavic is attested with *o- in East Slavic if it is attested there at all. To set aside this obvious generalization one would surely have to offer some explicit, cogent justification.

8.2. Categorizing the lexical data

If one assumes, as I do, that the geographical attestation of **je-* and **o-* doublets is to be taken seriously as a primary explanandum, it immediately follows that the traditional, *a priori* (East Slavic versus non-East-Slavic) sorting of the data is ruled out, and that all potentially relevant lexemes with **je-* and **o-* doublets must be examined on an equal footing so that genuine geographical generalizations can be made.

Now that the result of this approach have been presented, it is appropriate to comment on some of the divisions in the material that previous investigators have thought important, in order to see if the considerations they appealed to might contribute to a deeper understanding of the data. As a matter of convenience, and because they are the most recent investigations of the issue, I will refer in the following remarks just to the categories of lexemes with LCS **je-* ‖ **o-* doublets which Šaur (1982) and Popowska-Taborska (1984) exclude from their accounts (listed above in [8.1] and [8.2]). I do not wish to get too deeply involved in the etymology of individual lexemes at this point, but will try to focus on questions of principle. Section 8.2.4 reviews the divisions I myself see in the data and the special considerations these divisions motivate.

8.2.1. Ablaut

Both Šaur and Popowska-Taborska set aside as irrelevant certain lexemes which they think exhibit an initial ablaut alternation; cf. (8.3).

(8.3) a. LCS **jelĭxa, *olĭxa*, PS ELIXĀ- ‖ ALIXĀ- 'elder (Alnus)' [13]
     b. LCS **jese, *ose*, PS ESE 'look!' [26]
     c. LCS **jeterŭ, *oterŭ*, PS IATERA- 'which' [41]

It is extremely doubtful whether the roots of CS **elĭxa* (Šaur) or **ese, eterŭ* (Popowska-Taborska) were ever subject to qualitative ablaut. CS **elixā* is probably of non-Indo-European origin and occurs with **a-* in Lat. *alnus*, two particulars which speak against qualitative ablaut. Its **e-* ‖ **a-* diversity more likely shows the effect of Rozwadowski's change in Slavic and Baltic (cf. sections 5.3.3—5.3.4). The deictic **e-* in CS **ese*, which originates in a phonic gesture (cf. Ekblom 1925: 16—17), is quite likely an independent Slavic innovation. And the demonstrative CS **jetera-* surely cannot be separated from PS IA-. Since it does not have original

PS E-, it evidently calls for special consideration (see section 7.41). But in any case, even assuming that these lexemes had qualitative ablaut in initial position, "eliminating" them from discussion makes no sense. What needs to be emphasized, under the assumption of a regional Common Slavic (East Slavic) sound change (CS *e- > *a-), is rather that in the dialects affected by such a change, the resultant LCS *o- would be ambiguous between inherited (apophonic) PIE *o- (> CS *a- > LCS *o-) and inherited PIE *e- (> CS *e- > *a- > LCS *o-); and furthermore, that any lexeme attested with LCS *o- outside the area in question is a witness against the supposed geographical limitation of the change *unless* there is good reason to believe its *o- is apophonic.

It is pretty obvious that when Popowska-Taborska removes her two items (8.3 b) and (8.3 c) from the list of lexemes she wishes to account for, she does so because of the well attested initial LCS *o- in the Sorbian reflexes of CS *etera-, which does not conform to the "East Slavic doctrine". Šaur is undoubtedly motivated by the same interest. But additionally, by excluding CS *elixā from the evidence he removes an obstacle to his ostensibly inductive identification of the conditioning of his *e- > *a- change (see section 8.3.3.1). In order to disregard this counterexample to his generalization, he (implicitly) claims that the *o- of East Slavic (LCS) *olĭxa is apophonic. But he does not explain what would motivate this noun's having both *e*-grade and *o*-grade alternants to begin with, nor why its *e*-grade variant would not be attested in East Slavic, or, in other words, how one can be sure East Slavic *olĭxa is not an *e*-grade variant his sound law should be reformulated to cover.

8.2.2. Proto-Slavic dialect variation

Popowska-Taborska excludes from consideration a number of lexemes which had by-forms with different initial vowels "already in Proto-Slavic".

The Slavic word for 'ash (Fraxinus)' mentioned in sections 5.3.1 – 5.3.2 can serve as an example. This lexeme can be reconstructed with at least three initial vocalisms in Late Common Slavic, *ja-, *je-, *o-; see (8.4). Forms with *ja- occur in all Slavic regions. Forms with *je- and *o- are found in (proximal) Polish, (proximal) Slovak, and Western and Eastern South Slavic; the *o- attestations are mostly isolated dialect variants or toponyms, but in Bulgarian dialects where *je- and *o- forms coexist, the *o- forms are evaluated as older, except in localities where the two by-forms denote distinct tree species (cf. Popowska-Taborska 1984: 30).

It is a legitimate question whether this lexeme should be reconstructed with three Proto-Slavic variants (ESENA-, ASENA-, ĀSENA-) or with two (ESENA-, ĀSENA-).

(8.4)   PS ESENA- ‖ ĀSENA- 'ash (Fraxinus excelsior, ornus)' [27]
        *je-: P *jesion*, N-d. *jesień*, Pb. *jisin*; Sk. d. *jeséň*, Cz. d. *jesen*; Sn. *jésen*, SC d. *jèsēn*; Bg. d. *ésen*, top. *Ésenište*, M top. *Esen*
        *o-: P d. *u̯eśòn* (Wielkopolska); Sn. top. *Osenca*, SC top. *Osenik* (Bosnia); Bg. d. *ósen*, top. *Ósenovo, Ósiniti, Osinski dol, Osinko-vica*
        *ja-: P o., S-d. *jasień*, Ka. *jasòn*, Sc. *jãsôu̯n*, Pb. *josin*; US *jasen*, LS *jasen*; Sk. *jaseň*, Cz. *jasan*; Sn. d. *jásen*, SC *jȁsēn*; Bg. *jásen*, M *jasen*; R *jás'en'*, Br. *jás'en'*, U *jásen*

Occam's Razor favors the second option (cf. section 5.3.1), and so does comparison with other Indo-European languages, which document two distinct root variants (see chapter 7, s. v.). Popowska-Taborska opts for the first alternative, evidently because the attested *o-* forms are embarrassing to the "East Slavic doctrine". This is the case with each and every one of the eleven lexemes listed above under (8.2 c). On the other hand, in the parallel case of LCS *jeměšī, *oměšī, *leměšī* 'plowshare' [44], which could also be reconstructed with three (or more) Proto-Slavic variants (see again section 5.3.1), Popowska-Taborska finds two are enough; cf. (8.2 a). Significantly, the *o-* forms of this lexeme are attested only in East Slavic (see chapter 7, s. v.).

Evidently lexemes with multiple by-forms force the investigator to choose among a number of assumptions regarding the relative age of the variant forms, as was acknowledged in section 5.3.1. But when one looks closely at the work of the adherents of the "East Slavic doctrine", one can see that its built-in bias obscures these choices and prevents the investigators from even considering what their different consequences would be.

8.2.3. Relic forms

Popowska-Taborska "eliminates" some lexemes because they are geographically thinly distributed, thus *jesera* and *jesetĭ*; cf. (8.5).

LCS *jesetĭ* has recently been convincingly analysed as an inherited Slavic lexeme, semantically changed, but morphologically homologous to Li. *ekēčios*, La. *ecēšas* 'harrow' (cf. Boryś [1984]; see further chapter 7, s. v.). The fact that these Slavic and Baltic parallel formations exemplify *Gutturalwechsel* (both centum and satəm reflexes of PIE *$\hat{k}$) is an indication of their considerable age (cf. sections 5.3.3 and 6.1). Consequently, the fact that the Slavic lexeme has a relic distribution in modern times does not mean that it can be discounted as evidence for the development of PS E-, for one must assume that wherever the lexeme occurred when the "*je-* > *o-* change" took place, it would be subject to that change if it satisfied its conditions.

(8.5) a. PS ES-ETI- (*'harrow' > '(lattice) sieve; grain-drying rack; drying shed' [30]
  je-: P *jesieć, jesiótka*
  o-: P (Wielkopolska) *osieć, osiótka*; R *os'ét'*, Br. *as'éc', as'ótka, vós'ec'*, U *os'it'*

  b. PS ES-ER-Ā- 'awn, beard on grain, hulls, thorn', 'fishbone', 'fish scales' [29]
  je-: P d. *jesiora*, o. *jesiory*, Ka. *jesora*, Sc. *jìęsǫrǎ*, Pb. *jeserǻį*
  o-: P NE-d. *osiory*

LCS *jesera*, too, is obviously an inherited lexeme in Slavic. Its semantic diversity within Slavic (Pb. 'awn', but P d. 'fishbone') and the meaning of its Baltic counterpart (Li. *ešerỹs* 'perch') suggest that these lexemes too are parallel formations (< *'prickly thing(s)'; PIE *$h_2e\hat{k}$- 'pointed') of considerable age. In view of this, the fact that LCS *jesera* is not widely attested does not make it untrustworthy as evidence for the *je-* ‖ *o-* problem at all, as both Šaur and Popowska-Taborska claim. What is clear is that the Polish attestations with *o-* of both *jesetī* and *jesera* offend against the "East Slavic doctrine". This, and not their thin geographical distribution, seems to be the real motivation behind their investigators' decision to "eliminate" them.

Šaur's and Popowska-Taborska's diverse reasons for excluding the majority of lexemes with *je-* ‖ *o-* doublets from consideration in relation to the putative "East Slavic *je-* > *o-* change" – he excludes fourteen out of twenty-two such lexemes, she "eliminates" fifteen of twenty-four items – in point of fact have no basis in rational principles of analysis, but appear motivated by a desire to fit the data to the "East Slavic doctrine". The procedure these language historians follow in excluding two thirds of the relevant material from discussion is like a travesty of a jury-selection process – except that they are not rejecting potential jurors, but throwing out the very evidence that should be weighed.

8.2.4. Other criteria

In table 3.1 I presented the relevant Slavic lexical material categorized according to the geographical distribution of CS *e-* and *a-* reflexes and according to the number of regions known to have *o- forms. If one considers the reflexes themselves, there are in the set of lexemes we can reconstruct with PS ᴇ- three clear-cut subsets: (a) lexemes known only with *je- in the Slavic languages; (b) lexemes with *je- ‖ *o- doublets in some regions and *je- forms elsewhere; and (c) lexemes with *je- ‖ *o-doublets in some regions and *o- forms elsewhere. I repeat the data of table 3.1, reorganized for present purposes, in table 8.1.

An interpretation of the difference between subsets (a) and (b) was offered in chapter 3. It was pointed out there that it is really not knowable whether the lexemes with invariant LCS *je- did not a one time in some Slavic dialects have by-forms with CS *a- which have since been superseded by *e- forms. But it is not implausible to assume that they did retain CS *e- in all dialects, for a few lexemes could have escaped the stylistic *e- ~ *a- variation, and there might be no principled reason why precisely these four lexemes were the ones to retain CS *e- (see section 3.8).

The lexemes in subset (b) in table 8.1 can be divided, as Šaur's and Popowska-Taborska's approach suggests, into (b'), those attested only with CS *e- and *a- reflexes, and (b″), those which are found also with another initial segment. The latter subset contains at least the lexemes identified in table 8.1 (for the details, see chapter 7). A comparison between the geographical distributions in these two subsets shows no significant differences. This suggests that the origin of CS *a- by-forms is the same in both, and that there is no reason to separate these two subsets of lexemes as Šaur and Popowska-Taborska both do.

The lexemes in subset (b) are attested with CS *e- and *a- by-forms in one or more regions and with CS *e- reflexes elsewhere, whereas the lexemes in subset (c) are attested exclusively with *a- by-forms in several regions. They stand out by their small number and especially by their consistent representation with *a- by-forms in the West Slavic regions. Their solid *a- attestation in several regions naturally raises doubt whether the provisional reconstruction of their Proto-Slavic forms with PS ᴇ- is correct. As it happens, these are lexemes with PIE *a- or *o-, which cannot be interpreted without recourse to Rozwadowski's change, and which are best understood, it seems, as evidence that this change left isoglosses that cut through the Common Slavic dialect area prior to the *e- > *a- merger. That is to say, they can be reconstructed with Proto-Slavic doublets, as proposed in section 5.3.3 and discussed in section 6.1, PS ᴇʟᴀᴜᴀ- ‖ ᴀʟᴀᴜᴀ- [6], ᴇʟɪxᴀ̄- ‖ ᴀʟɪxᴀ̄- [13], ᴇᴘsᴀ̄- ‖ ᴀᴘsᴀ̄- [19], and ᴇʀɪʟᴀ- ‖ ᴀʀɪʟᴀ- [22]; see chapter 7, s. vv.

Table 8.1. Initial LCS **je-* ‖ **o-* variation by region and doublet category

		LCS	Sorbian	Sk. & Cz.	Lechitic	Sn. & SC	Bg. & M	East Slavic
a.	[4]	**jedlĭ*	e-	e-	e-	e-	e-	e-
	[32]	**jesmĭ*	e-	e-	e-	e-	e-	e-
	[9]	**jelĭčĭ*	e-	e-	e-	e-		e-
	[17]	**jelŭkŭ*			e-			e-
b'.	[31]	**jesetrŭ*	e-	e-	e-	e-	e-	e-/a-
	[26]	**jese*				e-	e-	e-/a-
	[11]	**jelenĭ*	e-	e-	e-	e-	e-/a-	e-/a-
	[30]	**jesetĭ*			e-/a-			a-
	[29]	**jesera*			e-/a-			−
	[28]	**jesenĭ*		e-/a-	e-	e-	e-	e-/a-
	[1]	**jedinŭ*	e-	e-	e-	e-/a-	e-/a-	e-/a-
	[3]	**jedva*	e-	e-	e-	e-/a-	e-/a-	e-/a-
	[36−37]	**jež...*	e-	e-/a-	e-/a-	e-	e-	e-/a-
	[2]	**ješče*	e-	e-	e-/a-	e-/a-	e-/a-	e-/a-
	[35]	**jezero*	e-	e-/a-	e-	e-/a-	e-/a-	e-/a-
b''.	[44]	**jemešĭ*			e-	e-	e-	e-/a-
	[10]	**jelito*	e-	e-	e-	e-/a-		e-/a-
	[20−21]	**jereb-...*	e-	e-	e-/a-	e-/a-	e-	e-/a-
	[27]	**jesenŭ*		e-	e-/a-	e-/a-	e-/a-	−
	[18]	**jemelo*	e-	e-/a-	e-	e-/a-	e-/a-	e-/a-
c.	[19]	**jesika*	a-	a-	a-	e-	e-/a-	a-
	[13]	**jelĭxa*	a-	e-/a-	a-	e-/a-	e-	e-/a-
	[6]	**jelovo*	a-	a-	a-	a-	e-/a-	a-
	[24]	**jerelŭ*	e-/a-	a-	a-	a-	a-	a-

Lexemes with (a) invariant CS **e-*; (b') with **e-* ‖ **a-*; (b'') with **e-* ‖ **a-* ‖ some other initial; (c) with **e-* ‖ **a-*. In (b') and (b'') some regions have only **e-*; in (c) some regions have only **a-*.

8.3. The phonological change

The phonological account proposed in this investigation of the Common Slavic change of **e-* > **a-* differs from previous accounts so significantly that it is really incommensurate with them (cf. section 8.5). Hence it may seem an idle exercise to offer a critique of earlier attempts to explain the origin of the LCS **je-* ‖ **o-* variation. For instance, it would seem that any hypothetical account of the sound change which is tailored to a specific, assumed relative chronology, would cease to be interesting the moment it is shown that the assumed chronology is wrong. However, things are often not that simple in diachronic linguistics. Most explanations in historical phonology which appear at all plausible have their appearance of adequacy because they fit their explanandum, not completely and in every respect, but more or less in a sufficient number of ways. And so it is worthwhile reviewing at least some of those accounts which practitioners in the field have found more or less credible in the past. In any case, only such a patient examination of earlier investigators' ideas will allow us to document the implicit assumption most of them shared, which has been rejected in the account offered in this study.

In the following pages we will pass in review accounts of three types. First, there are accounts which posit a detailed segmental and/or suprasegmental conditioning that supposedly motivated the putative change in word-initial position; all of these additionally assume more or less sweeping subsequent analogical levelings. These accounts have an appearance of observational precision, but none of them is particularly plausible. And, it must be recalled, each of them is designed to account only for a very limited subset of the actual data.

In the second place there are accounts which invoke a very simple conditioning and implicitly put a greater burden on the assumed processes of analogical stem unification. None of these accounts is based on anything observable in the data now, they are purely speculative, and some of them actually rather fanciful.

And finally there is one account which ascribes the East versus South and West Slavic *je- ‖ *o- doublets to influence from the (Southeast) Baltic substratum with which the Slavic settlers mixed in the areas that later became Belarus and Southern Russia.

Many statements and even discussions of the change that gave rise to the LCS *je- ‖ *o- doublets, unfortunately, are presented by their authors without a realistic, or even an explicit chronological frame of reference; this is particularly true of textbook statements, which are typically laconic. The accounts that will be reviewed here will be categorized in something like chronological terms (cf. section 1.2) according to whether they presuppose the prior development of prothesis and/or of the qualitative differentiation of Common Slavic long and short vowels, that is, a state of affairs with a distinction between initial (LCS) *je- and *o- (section 8.3.1), *e- and *o- (section 8.3.2), or (CS) *e- and *a- (section 8.3.3). But it must be acknowledged that many of the scholars who have contributed to the *je- ‖ *o- debate have made no explicit distinction between allophonic prothesis ([i̯e-] is /e-/) and phonemic prothesis ([i̯e-] is /je-/), and hence the distinction between the first and second kinds of accounts is in some instances difficult to draw.

8.3.1. The *je- versus *o- stage

The most widely accepted accounts of the CS *e- > *a- change assign it to a period in the development of Slavic when both the qualitative differentiation of the Second Common Slavic Vowel Shift and the development of prothetic glides had taken place (the stage labeled CS-III in section 1.2). As mentioned in section 1.2, this period begins some time before AD 800. At the end of this period, the vocalism − and the syllable structure − of the Slavic dialects change radically in the Third Common Slavic Vowel Shift, the so-called Jer Shift, which occurs perhaps as early as the mid 800s in the center of the Slavic language area (it is attested in the 800s in what is now Slovenia; cf. Ramovš [1936: 35]), at later dates in the deep south and in the northwest, and as late as the 1100s on the northeastern periphery. Some of the accounts that have been proposed refer to phonological states of affairs that arise only in connection with the Jer Shift.

8.3.1.1. Fortunatov

Fortunatov's formula posited a dialectal Common Slavic loss of initial *j-* before *e* when this preceded a dental or labial consonant followed by LCS *e* or *ę* (OR *ä*), or it preceded any consonant followed by *i*; thus OR *olenĭ, orăbĭ,* and *odinŭ, ožina,* but *ježĭ* and *ježevika*; cf. Fortunatov (1919 [1972]: 278−281).

The set of front vowels that comes into play here (*i, e, ę,* but not *ĭ*; there are no examples with *ě*) is not a natural class (cf. section 1.2), but if one imagines the allophonic variation of Early East Slavic *e* at the time after vowels were somehow adjusted to the occurrence of a (weak) jer (*ĭ* or *ŭ*) in the following syllable, as Šaxmatov did (1915: 138−139), this segmental conditioning is not really implausible. However, the role assigned to the intervening consonants is odd, to say the least. And there are neither articulatory nor perceptual reasons why these different environments would motivate the loss of an initial *j-*. Šaxmatov (1915: 139) thought it reasonable that *j-* was assimilated (that is, absorbed into) precisely a following [e], but not a following putative [ö] allophone of *e* that was conditioned by a subsequent back vowel (for *j-* was too different from [ö] to be assimilated to it), nor to a following putative [ê] that was conditioned by a subsequent *ĭ* (for *j-* and [ê] were too similar to be assimilated!). But no one has offered a typological parallel to such a peculiar conditioning anywhere.

Why the change of **je-* > **e-* would be followed by an additional change of **e-* > **o-* is left unexplained in this account. Fortunatov and many later scholars have been content to point to the treatment of borrowings (from Norse and Greek; cf. section 1.1), which document that in Early East Slavic, **e-* was constrained from occurring in word initial position. But to explain a sound change by the phonological constraint to which it gives rise is circular.

Considering that this account leaves the occurrence of lexemes with LCS **o-* variants in West and South Slavic unexplained, and that even within East Slavic it must regard the *actually* attested occurrence of **je-* and **o-* forms the joint result of sound change and analogical leveling and borrowing from Church Slavonic, the net contribution this account makes to our understanding is pretty slim. The most noteworthy feature of the Fortunatov account now, a hundred years after it was first put forward, is the glorious contrast between its detailed phonetic conditioning and its total lack of explanatory value, which makes this account such a wonderful example of High Positivism in historical phonology.

8.3.1.2. Jakobson

Jakobson found Fortunatov's segmental conditioning artificial and implausible and proposed a different generalization: *j-* was lost before *e* if the next syllabic was a front vowel, and if the accent was on the first or second syllable of the word. By claiming a significant affinity between segmental high tonality (*j*, front vowels, and the palatalized consonants that precede these are characterized by high-frequency resonance) and the high tonality (high F_0) of the Common Slavic pitch accent, Jakobson was able to construe the loss of *j-* as dissimilative rather than assimilative: *j-* is lost before *e* when the third high-tonality segment in a row coincides with the low-tonality pitch trough after a falling accent on the first syllable or before a rising one on the second (1929: 47). This account is vastly superior to Fortunatov's (and Šaxmatov's) in sophistication, but it is not more persuasive.

Jakobson's theory gives a detailed account of the vaguely similar Old Church Slavonic and Sorbian and Slovak peculiarities which were first descried by Fortunatov (cf. sections 5.1.1–5.1.3), and the theory includes an explicit relative chronology. For instance, to be compatible with the preservation of the initial in (the unaffected) LCS *jelĭ 'fir, spruce', the relevant change must be earlier than the cluster simplification that applied to PS EDLI-. And to produce the loss of the posited initial *j-* in LCS *jedinŭ ‖ *odinŭ, the change must be later than the rise of the neo-acute accent, which shifted the pitch accent from the third to the second syllable in words of this shape. Of course, Jakobson's appeal to accent in 1929 was made in terms of the contemporary conception of Common Slavic prosody, which has long since been abandoned, in part thanks to Jakobson's own contributions. Such examples of the "East Slavic *je-* > *o-* change" als LCS *ozero, *osenĭ actually had no accent in the Common Slavic period; they were enclinomena, as Jakobson taught in later years (Jakobson [1963 (1971): 671−672]; cf. Dybo [1975, 1981: 7, 52, *passim*]); hence they did not have a "pitch trough" between the first and the second syllable.

It is really surprising to see this valiant, but now antiquated attempt at an explanation invoked in recent writings (e. g., Galton [1973], Popowska-Taborska [1984: 105]).

8.3.1.3. Shevelov

The most recent independent variant of the Fortunatov account is Shevelov's (1965: 423−426) which does not differ in its basic approach from the old masters. Assuming, like his predecessors, the existence of prothetic *j-*, Shevelov posits two stages in the change: *je-* > *jo-* > *o-* (e. g., LCS *jezero* > *jozero* > *ozero*). While the first change is supposedly quite general, the second one unfortunately has to be constrained, and here we come back to the old problem of a suitable conditioning: according to Shevelov, *j-* is retained if the following syllable contains ĭ (or ŭ).

Shevelov admits in a footnote that it is "hard to determine precisely" why *j-* would be maintained in this environment. He suggests the reason may be some sort of adjustment to the following (weak) jer vowel (1965: 426). He also notes laconically that the resulting *o-* for original *je-* is usually attested in a stressed or pretonic syllable (1965: 423). These are obvious echoes of Šaxmatov and Jakobson, but with an unmistakable, however muted, acknowledgement that these scholars' ideas have really explained nothing.

8.3.1.4. Meillet and Vaillant

Meillet achieved as much (or as little) explanation thirty years before Shevelov by noting (i) that in initial position LCS *je-* and *o-* form a (front versus back) pair, by claiming simply (ii) that in Russian (*"grand russe"*) **je-* becomes **o-* unless it is maintained by analogy (*jegó* like *negó*) or bookish influence (from Church Slavonic), and then supposing (iii) that "this hardening [i. e., retraction; HA] of initial *je-* to *o-* must be due to sentence phonology", parallel to "the hardening of *i* to *y* after a hard [i. e., non-palatalized; HA] consonant, *e. g., obyskat'* from *ob* + *iskat'*..." (1934: 134 [1965: 124]).

Meillet's account assumes that the "Russian **je-* > **o-* change" occurred after the Jer Shift, prior to which the word final consonants he refers to were not final (see also [1934 (1965): 39]). This is quite impossible, for **o-* variants are attested already in texts from the 1000s, well before the Jer Shift. Meillet also neglects to consider that subsequent to the rise of this putative sandhi variation, there would have had to be a random process of paradigm leveling to account for the stabilization of stems. This would surely have lasted for centuries in the attested period, but − not surprisingly − there is no trace of it in the textual record.

Vaillant (1950: 180) repeats Meillet's account almost verbatim, but additionally claims than when the change occurred, LCS **e* and **o* were pronounced *(C')a* and *(C)a*, in other words, that the qualitative differentiation of the Second Vowel Shift had not occurred at the time of the Jer Shift. This is part of Vaillant's well-known theory of the origin of the Russian and Belarusian *"akan'e"* vowel reduction (propounded in the same place), which was based on a confused conception of the chronological development of Common Slavic.

8.3.1.5. Xaburgaev

Xaburgaev tries to exploit the observed similarity between the initial *e-* ‖ *a-* correspondences in Baltic and the **je-* ‖ **o-* correspondences in Slavic, and hypothesizes that the Slavic ones arose thanks to the Baltic-speaking substratum in modern-day Belarus adopting Slavic speech in the early Middle Ages. Crucial to this process, according to Xaburgaev, was the absence of prothesis before **e-* in Baltic, which was transferred into Slavic in the many lexemes the Balts shared with their Slavic neighbors.

> [U]nder the influence of the native language of the bilingual Balts a tendency might have arisen in the newly formed Russian dialects toward the loss of initial *j-* before *e-*, which would naturally lead to a change of initial *e-* > *o-*, which thus became the norm of pronunciation ... (Also the initial *a-* in the corresponding Baltic doublets like *ežer-* : *ažer-* 'lake' had to be rendered by *o-* in this period.) (Xaburgaev 1976: 216)

Xaburgaev does not explain why the substratum Balts, who probably had a phonemic distinction *e-* versus *je-*, would not identify the Slavic **je-* with their own *je-*. Nor does he offer any explanation of the subsequent change of *e- > o-*, whose naturalness he apparently considers demonstrated by the treatment of foreign *e-* in borrowings from Norse and Greek.

8.3.2. The **e-* versus **o-* stage

I will mention three accounts assigned to this reconstructed stage, one relying on segmental conditioning, the others not.

8.3.2.1. Filin

Filin (1962: 195−203), after setting aside some lexemes that supposedly occurred in Common Slavic with inherited **e-* ‖ **o-* doublets (he mentions **jelīxa, *jesenĭ, *jelenĭ*), posits a development of prothesis, including **e- > *je-* in some dialects, and an alternative change of **e- > *o-* (before a syllable containing a front vowel or *ŭ* or *o*) in other dialects. The latter change is supposed to have originated in the east, but spread partly to other areas. Both changes are reflected in the modern East Slavic languages. In addition, the latter change yields alternations which are subject to analogical leveling. Since the two changes overlie an earlier inherited variation, the resulting picture is so opaque that there is no hope of its being correlated with anything observable in the actual attestation.

Note the similarity between Filin's understanding of the two changes as differently oriented sound changes and the remarks at the end of section 2.2. But Filin does not explain why both changes would be reflected in East Slavic, but not elsewhere; he implicitly assumes that the **e- > *o-* change just failed to spread far enough. He does not explain the extraordinary conditioning of the **e- > *o-* change he posits, which cuts across natural phonological classes. Nor does he cite parallel changes from other languages to lend his hypothesis plausibility. His idea that prothesis before CS **e-* developed only after the Second Common Slavic Vowel Shift (CS-II **a* > CS-III **o*) is probably wrong (see sections 1.2 and 5.1.1). But from the fact that the **e-* ‖ **a-* isoglosses do not coincide with the limits of East Slavic he draws the reasonable conclusion that the change of initial CS **e- > *o-* must be assigned chronologically to the very beginning of the disintegration of Common Slavic.

8.3.2.2. Ekblom

Ekblom's account differs from Meillet's (which Ekblom cites from the first [1924] edition of Meillet [1934]) chiefly by supposing a main difference in prothesis between phrase-internal and phrase-initial position and by positing a phonetic change of *e > *ə > *o in the latter environment – with subsequent different generalization patterns and diverse "disturbing influences" (1925: 13) in different Common Slavic dialects. But unlike Meillet, Ekblom assigns these changes to the very beginning of the break-up of Common Slavic.

8.3.2.3. Calleman

Calleman, unlike Filin, presupposes the development of prothesis, but apparently only as an allophonic feature.

> The loss of the prothesis precedes the *(j)e- > o-* change; but it is actually no pre-condition, but rather a concomitant of the tendency to velarization which produced forms like *odin, ozero*. The change occurred regardless of whether the following syllable contained a front vowel. Since the tendency was active in Late Common Slavic, it is not surprising that there are examples of it also in other [i. e., West and South; HA] Slavic languages. But it was strongest in Old Russian, hence this is where we find the most examples of this anlaut change. Old Russian actually seems to have developed initial plosive onsets. (1950: 147)

One can note the detachment of this statement from the data that need to be accounted for. It is in this regard similar to Meillet's and Vaillant's accounts, from which it differs by its chronological perspective, but perhaps not by the author's conviction that the "*e- > *o- change" in essence was a vowel retraction, the labialization of the *o- being of secondary importance (cf. also [1950: 30–31]); this idea seems to be implicit in Meillet's account. The gratuitous "plosive onsets" seem to reflect a notion that plosive onsets are a logical alternative to down-gliding onsets, which is probably not the case (cf. Andersen 1972: 28–31; 1989: 68–69). Perhaps Calleman's "plosive onsets" are an allusion to the discovery that at earlier stages of Indo-European, reconstructed laryngeals were responsible for changes in vowel quality. See also section 8.3.4.

8.3.3. The *e- versus *a- stage

Among the scholars who assign the origin of the LCS *je- ‖ *o- variation to the early Common Slavic period, Stieber expresses the cautious view that the (East Slavic) change of *e* "(maybe with prothesis *i̯e-*)" > *a* > *o* is irregular, that none of the proposed explanations explains everything, but that in any case this was a weakly motivated change, which for some reasons or other did not affect all the words with initial CS **e-* (1979: 31).

Others have espoused more specific hypotheses. I will mention just four.

8.3.3.1. Šaur

Šaur, like Filin, sees the development of prothesis before CS **e-* (in West and South Slavic) and the change of initial CS **e-* > **a-* (in East Slavic) as complementary. His detailed sorting of the lexical material (which was reviewed in section 8.1.2) leaves five items which supposedly allow the investigator to identify the phonological conditioning of the change by inspection. What the lexemes in (8.1 j) have in common is that each contains three syllables with short vowels, none of them lengthened under "metatony"; hence this is the conditioning environment for the CS **e-* > **a-* change. The other relevant lexemes, in which the change does not occur (8.1 g–i), either have a different metrical structure or show evidence of "metatony" or both.

Šaur does not concern himself with the extensive analogical leveling his formula implicitly entails. He ignores the fact that every trisyllabic lexeme with a citation form ending in a short vowel — whatever its inflectional class — has more inflected forms ending in a long vowel than in a short vowel and has some forms with more than three syllables (e. g., CS-II nom.sg. **ezera*, gen.sg. *ezerā*, loc.sg. *ezerē*, dat.sg. *ezerū*, instr.sg. *ezerami* 'lake', or nom.sg. **eseni*, gen.sg. **esenī*, instr.sg. **esenii̯ǫ* 'autumn'). And he does not attempt to explain how or why a word structure with just three short syllables would motivate a change in backness or rounding in just one of the four short vowels of the language — beyond surmising that CS **e* must somehow have been pronounced differently in this environment (1982: 383), which is circular.

The affinity of Šaur's account with the Fortunatov tradition is obvious.

8.3.3.2. Mareš

Mareš's tersely worded theory is quoted below. It does not achieve an explanation, and the machinery with which it attempts one — the transitional *h* — appears completely unmotivated.

> Regarding the Common Slavic prothesis we will note only that *w* probably
> was chosen before high back vowels as a parallel to *j*... In the East Slavic
> words of the type *ozero*, SS *olito*, we agree with the view that there was a
> prothetic, transitional *h* (*ezerǎ* > *hǎzerǎ* > *ǎzerǎ* > *ozero*), which also
> occurs in more recent times, e. g., Sorbian dial. *heleń, heřabc, heřeg*, etc.
> (1969: 70).

Mareš's prothetic *h* is a sort of "notational variant" of Calleman's plosive
onsets (cf. section 8.3.2.2). The Sorbian *h*- Mareš refers to, which is a
completely different phenomenon, and in no way can be regarded a transitional stage from *e*- to *a*-, was discussed in section 5.1.1.

8.3.3.3. Kolomijec'

Kolomijec' assumes, with the majority of scholars, that the (East Slavic)
variants with CS **a*- developed from earlier forms with CS **e*-. She supposes that in Early Common Slavic (roughly equivalent to CS I−II of
section 1.2) a number of lexemes contained initial laryngeals, inherited
from Indo-European, before **e, *ē, *i, *ī*. These laryngeals were palatalized in some dialects, where they eventually yielded initial *j*-, but were
not palatalized in the eastern dialects. As a consequence of the later Common Slavic palatalization of all consonants before front vowels, *e* ceased
to be admitted after plain consonants, and in the eastern dialects, consequently, *e* had to be replaced by its back counterpart *a* after the non-
palatalized laryngeals, "with the exception of specific examples in certain
dialects" (see Kolomijec' [1966: 40−41]).

    Kolomijec' does not cite any evidence for these phantom laryngeals,
nor does she explain why these segments did not occur before back vowels, or why they would not be palatalized before front vowels in pre-East
Slavic. Furthermore, she does not clarify why, if CS **e* and **a* came to
be in complementary distribution in pre-West-Slavic and pre-South-
Slavic, this would produce a replacement of **e* by **a* in pre-East-Slavic,
where **e* occurred both after plain (laryngeal) and palatalized (buccal)
segments. The missing particulars make this account difficult to understand.

8.3.3.4. Georgiev

Georgiev considers the **e*- ‖ **a*- diversity in Slavic and Baltic one single
problem. He points out that the "East Slavic doctrine" has no basis in
the actual geographical distribution of **e*- and **a*- variants, there being
only two Slavic lexemes which have **a*- only in East Slavic, viz. CS **ase-*

tra- and **aseni-*; actually, as we have seen, there are more; cf. table 1.1. Georgiev starts with an etymological analysis, reconstructing not only the Proto-Slavic and Proto-Baltic, but the Proto-Indo-European initials in the relevant set of lexemes, and concludes that the lexemes in (8.6) had initial PS *a-*, PB *a-*, and PIE *a-*.

(8.6)   PS (Georgiev's term) **adinŭ, *ad(ŭ)vā, *alava-* (**alvĭ*), **albedĭ, *albedā, *alĭxā, *amelā, *arbę, *arīlŭ, *ašče, *asenĭ, *aśera, *aśe-trŭ, *ažera-, *elenĭ* (**alni*) (Georgiev's notation)

This finding means that the change that needs to be explained is one of Balto-Slavic **a-* > **e-*. Georgiev hypothesizes that this change was conditioned by a preceding *i*, syllabic or non-syllabic; hence CS **vidimŭ azera* 'we see the lake', but **vidiši-j-äzera* 'you see the lake'. Analogical leveling subsequently produced stems with uniform initials, but with differences from area to area. Georgiev notes that some lexemes occur consistently with **a-*, e. g., LCS **ostrŭ* 'sharp', **ovĭća* 'sheep' (Li. *aštrùs, avìs*), which is difficult to understand on the basis of his account. But he allows as how this may be because the putative change of **a-* > **e-* additionally included some sort of prosodic conditioning which future research will determine.

From a purely phonetic point of view, Georgiev's account is surely weakly plausible, but as a type of explanation, it is like Meillet's (section 8.3.1.4) and Calleman's (section 8.3.2.2) of the crudest grade: it is pretty easy to postulate a sound change with some variable conditioning and a subsequent process of stochastic analogical leveling to take care of its shortcomings.

Note that Georgiev's approach to the Slavic and Baltic data prejudges the important issue whether the developments in these two language groups were indeed comparable; cf. section 9.3.

8.4. The Baltic change

The scholars who have discussed the distribution of *e-* and *a-* doublets in the Baltic languages have not faced the same problems as their Slavist colleagues, for there has never been any Baltic counterpart to the "East Slavic doctrine" (cf. section 8.1.1−8.1.2), and hence no impulse to explain anything away. The Baltic facts are pretty clear (cf. tables 4.1 and 5.4): there is considerable variation in initial *e-* and *a-* reflexes of PB E- among the three languages; Old Prussian in particular shows a greater number of *a-* forms than Latvian, and Latvian a greater number of *a-* forms than Lithuanian – except that in part of the Lithuanian language area (as we first saw in section 2.2) there has been a general merger of initial *e-* and *a-*; cf. Endzelin (1948 [1971]: 31); Stang (1966: 31).

No one, as far as I know, has tried to interpret the geographical distribution of **e-* and **a-* doublets in the three languages; most scholars have been content to state what is plain to see and have spoken simply of a change of *e-* > *a-* (or a tendency for such a change), particularly strongly evidenced by Old Prussian. But an interpretation of the phonological change as such has been proposed. It was put forward by Schmalstieg with reference to Old Prussian and was adopted by Zinkevičius for the Lithuanian change.

Both scholars take their point of departure in the pronunciation of Modern Lithuanian. In Lithuanian, word-internal reflexes of PB E and A came to be in complementary distribution after (i) consonants became palatalized (sharped) before *e* and (ii) OLi. *a* changed to (merged with) *e* after *j*. Assuming that phones in complementary distribution must be allophones of the same phoneme, Schmalstieg interprets the change of initial *e-* > *a-* in Old Prussian as a replacement of one allophone with another (1976: 98); similarly, with reference to Lithuanian, Zinkevičius (1987: 163).

But there are good reasons to doubt both this interpretation and its applicability to earlier stages of Lithuanian and the other Baltic languages. First of all, whereas allophones are by definition in complementary distribution, phones in complementary distribution are not necessarily allophones of the same phoneme. Schmalstieg's assumption that they are is a useful rule of thumb in phonemic analysis, but only if the aim is a description in terms of biunique phonemes. The modern Lithuanian reflexes of PB E and A are certainly sufficiently similar to be allophones of the same phoneme – in fact their realizations are commonly indistinguishable in all but maximally explicit diction (Senn [1957: 70–71] transcribes them [ä], [ä:] and [a], [a:]); the Academy grammar acknowledges their phonetic identity in certain dialects, e. g., Western Upland, but not in the standard language (cf. Ulvydas 1965: 52, 56). But their phonemic identity or distinctness hinges on the way one decides to describe consonantal sharping, as less or as more conditioned. Synchronically, the question of the status of the Modern Lithuanian /e/ : /a/ opposition may very well be moot – provided one ignores the fact that there is still a phonemic distinction between *e-* [æ], [æ:] and *a-* [a], [a:] ın word-ınitial position (see immediately below). The same must be said for Old Prussian, such as it is attested.

In any case, however, the apparent word-internal merger of the reflexes of PB ᴇ and ᴀ in Lithuanian, which may be completed in some dialects, is of such recent date that it certainly has no relevance for the Slavic–Baltic *e-* > *a-* merger. It is definitely later than the qualitative differentiation of long and short vowels, which began, perhaps, in the 1300s (cf. section 2.2), and which followed the **e-* > **a-* merger. It is true that in some parts of the Lithuanian language area, the word-internal merger of *e* and *a* occurred before our earliest attestation in the 1500s. It is documented by Lithuanian writers from the Lowland or Western Upland areas (Mažvydas, Vilentas, Bretkūnas) in the 1500s in such spellings as *kraujes* (for *kraujas* 'blood') and *brolei, broleis* (for *broliai, broliais* 'brothers; nom.pl., instr.pl.'). But these writers represent areas in which the *e-* : *a-* distinction has been maintained in word initial position until the present day (cf. the dialect map, figure 2.1). On the other hand, sixteenth-century writers from central and eastern Lithuania (such as Daukša, Petkevičius, Širvydas) provide no spelling evidence of this supposed vowel merger (cf. Zinkevičius 1987: 163). These writers were natives of areas in which the word-initial *e-* > *a-* merger occurred.

It is difficult to escape the conclusion that the word-initial *e-* > *a-* merger is a different event in the history of Lithuanian from the phonological identification of the reflexes of PB ᴇ and ᴀ in other environments. This conclusion agrees both with the early date of the *e-* > *a-* merger – which occurred prior to the development of prothesis and reflects a typological tendency contrary to prothesis (cf. section 2.2) – and with the fact that it is shared to varying extents with the Baltic dialects represented by Latvian and Old Prussian (cf. table 5.4; but recall that Latvian to some unknown extent may reflect its Northwest Baltic substratum).

Note that whereas the word-internal merger of the PB ᴇ and ᴀ reflexes in Lithuanian occurred only after a complex of syntagmatic phonetic adjustments – of consonants to the tonality of following vowels (the development of sharping), and of vowel allophones to the tonality of preceding and following consonants – the initial *e-* > *a-* merger obviously had a simpler, purely paradigmatic motivation, as pointed out repeatedly above (cf. section 8.3.4).

The temptation to project a phonemic interpretation of the recent, in part still on-going development in Lithuanian into the Common Baltic past where the initial *e-* > *a-* merger was operated should be resisted.

8.5. Conclusion

For over a hundred years the scholarly dialog concerning the Slavic *e-
‖ *a- doublets has moved within the narrow confines of Neogrammarian
sound change theory. The survey in sections 8.1−8.3 has illustrated the
options that were available to the participants in this dialog. They could
posit a more or less narrowly constrained, segmentally or suprasegmen-
tally (or metrically) conditioned sound change, East Slavic or general
Slavic or Balto-Slavic, supplemented with analogical leveling, ranging
from extensive to wholesale, to make up for the unavoidable lack of fit
between the postulated phonological conditioning and the data; additionally, depending on the conditioning hypothesized for the sound change,
there would have to be a preliminary sorting of the data to be accounted
for, through which much of the lexical material attested with LCS *je- ‖
*o- doublets might have to be explained away. We have seen enough
examples both of the hopeless sound laws that have been posited and of
the more or less desperate efforts required to rationalize the elimination
of parts of the data.

In this study, the assumption was made that the actual geographical
distribution of CS *e- and *a- reflexes among the Slavic languages is not
extraneous to the *e- > *a- change, but part of the explanandum.

This entailed a considerable expansion of the data to be examined,
clearly seen in table 7.2.

More importantly, it meant examining these data with methods of
analysis that have never been applied to them before − methods of historical dialectology, both traditional, such as the distributional analysis
in section 3.2, and less traditional, such as the factor analysis in sections
5.3.2−5.3.3; see sections 9.7 and 9.8. And it gave access to patterns of
explanation that are more in tune with twentieth century linguistics (section 1.3.1−1.3.3), and which seem realistic in relation to what is known
about the recent prehistory and earliest history − linguistic and extralin-
guistic − of Slavs and Balts.

But most importantly, this basic assumption opened up for an inquiry
that produced new results both in regard to the Slavic−Baltic *e- > *a-
merger and in regard to the much earlier, much more limited, and much
more enigmatic Rozwadowski's change.

Chapter 9

Perspectives

The following sections explicate some of the theoretical and methodological presuppositions that underlie this investigation and comment on a few questions of terminology that are relevant to the presentation in the preceding chapters.

The first few sections are concerned with notions and terminology relating to the reconstructed stages of Slavic and Baltic and the prehistoric realities these correspond to (sections 9.1–9.4).

Section 9.5 touches on questions of prehistoric phonetics and phonemics.

The last sections discuss several issues of method, such as the central role of assumptions in historical interpretation (section 9.6), the application of the methods of historical dialectology to prehistory (section 9.7), and the exploitation of explananda as evidence (section 9.8).

9.1. Proto-Slavic and Common Slavic

In this work I maintain a terminological distinction between Proto-Slavic and Common Slavic. I use these terms somewhat differently from the scholarly tradition. This makes it desirable to define the terms here and to highlight some of the differences between my usage and that of the tradition.

9.1.1. Proto-Slavic

Proto-Slavic is part of a metalanguage (cf. Hjelmslev 1961: 119–121) devised in order to explicate the development of the Slavic languages from a common source. It can be thought of informally as the earliest stage of Slavic that can be reached by means of the retrospective methods we use in comparative and internal reconstruction.

But Proto-Slavic strictly speaking is not a language state, or even homologous to a language state, for it cannot be correlated with any single point in time. The Proto-Slavic we can reconstruct is a complete linguistic system only in the sense that there is no part of the grammar of the known Slavic languages for which we cannot reconstruct a Proto-Slavic counterpart. But our methods of reconstruction reach different "depth" for different parts of a linguistic system. For instance, Proto-Slavic substantival declension has a more archaic appearance than Proto-Slavic conjugation (with its new periphrastic tenses, its recent imperfect, and renewed imperative). And when we consider the lexicon, where we are often able to demonstrate the relative date of borrowings either by comparison with the source languages or in terms of the relative chronology of Slavic sound changes, it is very obvious that Proto-Slavic includes lexemes of widely different age.

The purpose of the reconstructed Proto-Slavic is to serve as the point of reference without which the chronological development of the attested languages cannot be defined, let alone understood.

9.1.2. Common Slavic

Common Slavic is part of a metalanguage devised in order to explicate the chronological development of Slavic grammar in prehistory from the earliest state that can be reached by our methods of reconstruction. This has traditionally been viewed as a single development from unity to diversity (cf. van Wijk 1956), but in this study two main periods have been recognized – before and after the Slavic Migrations – each with its dialectal diversity. The geographical diversity of Common Slavic *ante migrationes* was largely obliterated by the Migrations, but some of it has been reconstructed here, and more may be uncovered in the future. In Common Slavic *post migrationes*, new geographical diversity developed. This had two sources. First, the Migrations brought dialect features from the earlier period to different parts of the vast new territories. Secondly, the huge dimensions of the new Slavic lands naturally led to a gradual loosening of the bonds of linguistic solidarity among the Slavs, and, as a consequence, the developmental tendencies shared by all parts of the Common Slavic (*post migrationes*) speech area were played out at different rates, with different relative chronologies, and with different outcomes in different regions.

Since our methods of reconstruction reach different depths for different parts of the grammar, reconstructed parts of Common Slavic grammar are more nearly complete and more realistic the closer they are to the attested period and more fragmentary and schematic the farther back in time we go.

Common Slavic *ante migrationes* stretches from the time when the defining features of Slavic first marked the ancestral dialects of Slavic as distinct from other, neighboring Indo-European dialects (see section 9.1.3) until the eve of the Slavic Migrations at the beginning of our era. Common Slavic *post migrationes* is the period from the peak of the Migrations (when the core areas that are Slavic now were in the main settled) until the time when Slavic dialects ceased to develop innovations in conformity with Slavic diachronic tendencies. As far as the vocalism is concerned, which is the focus of attention in this study, the Third Common Slavic Vowel Shift, the so-called Jer Shift, can be taken to define that upper limit (cf. section 1.2; Andersen [1986]). Note that each of these temporal points of reference has to be defined differently for different parts of the Slavic speech area: (i) the Migrations commenced from some areas earlier than from others; (ii) settlement was completed (and, presumably, new regional traditions of speaking were established) earlier in some of the new territories than in others; and (iii) the Third Common Slavic Vowel Shift occurred in the 800s near the center of the Slavic territories and up to several centuries later on the peripheries.

Common Slavic dialects are named according to their location at a given time (e.g., southern Common Slavic *ante migrationes*, or "LCS N-d.", that is, northern dialectal Late Common Slavic) or as precursors of later Slavic languages (e.g., Pre-Slovenian refers to Common Slavic dialects whose linguistic traditions have continued into forms of modern Slovenian).

The Indo-European dialects from which Slavic developed are similarly called Pre-Slavic (cf. Andersen 1986).

9.1.3. Notations for reconstructed forms

The standard notation for reconstructed Proto-Slavic, which is familiar from etymological dictionaries and comparative grammars, represents an extremely shallow level of reconstruction. It employs the vowel symbols of Late Common Slavic (actually of Old Church Slavonic: *i, y, u, ĭ, ŭ, e, o, ě, a, ę, ǫ*) − what is labeled CS-III in section 1.2 − and therefore can only be used to illustrate the most recent phase of Common Slavic. However, this is a period in which Common Slavic had already reached a high degree of dialectal differentiation, which is entirely ignored by the standard notation. For any detailed discussion of the development of Common Slavic, other systems of notation are therefore necessary.

I signal Proto-Slavic reconstructions (in the sense of section 9.1.1) by writing them in small capitals (which makes an asterisk superfluous). The Proto-Slavic phoneme inventory is displayed in table 9.1. The Common Slavic development of the vowel system is summarized in section 1.2. The short high vowels have nonsyllabic variants when they precede a vowel; they are represented by the modern Slavic /v/ and /j/ phonemes. Syllable nuclei are simple or complex. Simple nuclei consist of a single vowel. Complex nuclei consist of a low vowel followed by a short high vowel, or of (any) vowel followed by a nasal or liquid. These are the traditional oral, nasal, and liquid diphthongs. Obstruents and a variety of obstruent clusters occur both as syllable onsets and as syllable codas.

Table 9.1. Proto-Slavic phoneme inventory

Vowels				Sonorants			Obstruents					
I	Ī	U	Ū	M	N		P	B	T	D	K	G
E	Ē	A	Ā		L	R			S	Z	X	

This phoneme inventory presupposes (i) a merger of PIE *a and *o (> PS A) and of *ā and *ō (> PS Ā); Winter's Law and the merger of two Proto-Indo-European stop series (the traditional mediae and mediae aspiratae) in PS B, D, Z, G; (iii) the diphthongization of syllabic sonorants (PIE -R̥- > PS -IR-/-UR-), and (iv) the rise of a RUKI variant of PIE *s (represented by PS X) and the subsequent satəm assibilation and merger of PIE *k̂ with the non-RUKI variant of PIE *s in PS S.

Although several stages of Common Slavic are distinguished in this study (see especially sections 1.2 and 5.1), Late Common Slavic reconstructions are adduced frequently throughout, in part because they tend to be similar to the accustomed shape of the "Proto-Slavic" of the handbooks, in part as a backdrop for highlighting dialect differences within Common Slavic, wherever these are important. The discussion of the word for 'rowan berry' (see section 7.21) can serve as an illustration. The Proto-Slavic forms of this lexeme, PS ĪRB-ĒINĀ- and ĪRB-ĒIKĀ-, are needed to reconcile the attestations Ka. *jerzbina* and Sn. *rbika*. The corresponding forms in early Common Slavic (CS-I) are homologous to the Proto-Slavic forms − CS-I *īrbēinā, *īrbēikā − they are too early to explicate the divergent modern forms. The "standard Proto-Slavic" (LCS) forms *jĭrbina, *jĭrbika belie the marked differences in relative chronology between the two Common Slavic regions these forms evolved in. Thus, LCS *jĭrbina* shows the prothesis, but not the palatal *ŕ* of the Pre-Kashubian form *jĭŕbina* (> Ka. *jerzbina*), whereas LCS *jĭrbika* ignores the monophthongization of the liquid diphthong (CS *-ir- > *-ŕ-) and the consequent lack of prothesis in the Pre-Slovenian *ŕbika*.

In short, the "standard Proto-Slavic" notation can be used to identify forms, but if one needs to give an adequate account of the chronological development of Common Slavic forms, both a more abstract Proto-Slavic and more detailed, accurate dialectal Late Common Slavic representations are needed.

9.2. Proto-Baltic and Common Baltic

A distinction like the one between Proto-Slavic and Common Slavic (see section 9.1) can be made in speaking of Baltic too, but here it is important to note that while it may make sense to speak of Common Baltic innovations and of a Common Baltic period characterized by such shared innovations, there are so many ancient differences among the known Baltic languages that it is unrealistic to speak of a Common Baltic language (or dialects) in reference to any time later than the settlement of (what we know as) the traditional Baltic lands (cf. section 4.4). Baltic scholars who have concerned themselves with this question conclude that one cannot reconstruct a Proto-Baltic. Thus, for instance, Stang wished his "*Urbaltisch*" to be understood as designating not a language, but a dialect area (cf. 1966: 13). This seems very reasonable. But of course one can construct parts of a proto-language if there is practical motivation for it, and in this study, where I need to examine the initial vowels of a few dozen vocabulary items by the Baltic languages, I see no harm in labeling my reconstructions Proto-Baltic. See further section 9.6.

I follow the same practice for Proto-Baltic as for Proto-Slavic and write Proto-Baltic phonemes and forms consistently in small capital letters, without an asterisk. Other reconstructed Baltic forms are written in italics with an asterisk.

9.3. Balto-Slavic versus Slavic−Baltic

In section 4.4 I describe the understanding of the prehistoric relationship among the ancestral dialects of Slavic and Baltic which is assumed in this study. My conception of the modern Slavic and Baltic languages as representing the last surviving fragments of a one-time dialect continuum in Eastern Europe makes it possible to interpret their similarities and differences in conformity with the wave-theory of dialect differentiation, which has been accepted as realistic for generations now and requires no special defense.

Previous scholarship concerned with this question has spoken a great deal about a Balto-Slavic protolanguage, which reflects a different understanding (or different understandings) of these relationships, presupposing a shared origin of Slavic and Baltic in a single, unified community language descended from Proto-Indo-European. As I acknowledge in section 4.4, there is evidence internal to the inherited lexicon of the Slavic and Baltic languages which speaks against this previously hypothesized, more or less distant, unified language stage. And in chapter 6 I mentioned a number of phonological indications that the inherited Indo-European lexical stock of Slavic and Baltic is a composite of several varieties of Indo-European which have been melded together.

All these particulars are strong arguments against the practice, still followed by some investigators and standard in the past, of trying to solve problems in comparative Slavic and Baltic grammar in terms of a reconstructed Proto-Balto-Slavic; among such problems are some referred to in this study, for instance, Kuryłowicz's (1956) examination of the *$iR \parallel$ *uR reflexes of Proto-Indo-European syllabic sonorants (based exclusively on the shared Slavic and Baltic lexicon included in Trautmann [1923]; cf. section 6.4.2) and Georgiev's attempt to reconcile the Slavic and Baltic *$e- \parallel$ *$a-$ doublets (reviewed in section 8.3.3.4).

The fruitfulness of the decision made in this study to reconstruct Proto-Slavic and Proto-Baltic forms independently of one another is apparent in the second-order comparisons between Proto-Slavic and Proto-Baltic forms this decision made possible; cf. sections 5.3.3 and chapter 6. Without an explicit separation of these levels of comparison it would hardly have been possible to identify the ancient isoglosses produced by Rozwadowski's change.

9.4. Extinct languages in Eastern Europe

In this section I wish to touch on two issues relating to the extinct languages spoken in Eastern Europe prior to the Slavic Migrations, one terminological, the other substantive.

First, there is a practical need for a terminology one can use when speaking of the attested and the extinct Baltic languages.

The labels West Baltic and East Baltic have established denotations, which cannot be changed.

I use the term Northwest Baltic for the extinct substratum languages of Latvia and Lithuania (of which we know Curonian, Zemgalian, and Selonian by name); the label Northwest Baltic does not denote any linguistic grouping, but is intended to have only geographical reference.

I use the term Southeast Baltic for the dialects once spoken in present-day Belarus to the south of the areas occupied by Latvians (Latgalians) and Lithuanians before their colonization of the Northwest Baltic areas. These are the extinct dialects spoken by the archaeologists' Dniepr Balts.

By contrast I use Southwest Baltic for the dialects spoken south of what is Old Prussian territory in the Middle Ages, in what is now eastern Poland. In this area we know the tribe of the Jatvingians by name.

It seems reasonable to refer to the Balts in the Pripet basin as Southern.

The real eastern Balts, who occupied the Oka river basin and areas to the east of it, contribute nothing to the issues discussed in this study; of these only the (East) Galindians are known by name (OR *Golädĭ*), who were presumably distinct from the Prussian tribe of the same name, the (West) Galindians (Lat. *Galindia*) whose lands were in the Northeast Polish Lake District.

Nor do the prehistoric Northern Balts, as I call them, shed any light on our issues. These Indo-European settlers spread along the Volga basin to the Kama river and eastward toward the Urals in the second millennium BC (cf. Gimbutas [1963]; Volkaitė-Kulikauskienė [1987: 40–44]) and were gradually absorbed into the West Finnic-speaking populations to the north long before the time we are dealing with here. Among the many Baltic lexemes the West Finnic languages adopted from these early settlers, the only one discussed in this study is PB EKETIĀ- 'harrow' [30]; cf. Thomsen (1889: 267–269).

Secondly, the relationship between Slavic and Baltic and the other components of the prehistoric Slavic–Baltic dialect continuum merits a few words of comment. Traditionally this relationship is discussed as if there was no linguistic diversity in Eastern Europe in prehistory other than what can be extrapolated into the past from the Baltic and Slavic languages we know now. But although we do not know the languages that died out, yielding the field to Slavic in the Middle Ages, we have every reason to suppose that there were languages we do not even know the names of, and that they differed as much from the ancestral dialects of the known Slavic and Baltic languages as these must have differed among themselves then — that is, we can reasonably assume that there were as deep differences in morphology and lexicon among the extinct languages as the ones we observe among the known Baltic languages.

While we have become used to speaking of these extinct languages as Northwest Baltic, Southwest Baltic, and Southeast Baltic, it would be more accurate to restrict the term Baltic to the languages we know and to refer to the lost languages with greater caution and less naivety. The late Warren Cowgill used the term Baltoid (and correspondingly, Slavoid) to refer to these largely unknown linguistic entities. In contexts that call for such caution I speak of Quasi-Baltic and Quasi-Slavic in the same spirit.

9.5. Prehistoric phonemics and phonetics

Section 1.2 describes the sequence of vowel shifts in the Common Slavic period which in this study serves as a practical basis for a division of the Common Slavic (*ante migrationes* and *post migrationes*) phonological development into periods. I first argued for the utility of this periodization in Andersen (1986) (for some theoretical problems relating to questions of periodization see Birnbaum [1987]); this conception is quite similar to that of Gołąb (1991); see also Andersen 1993.

The reconstructed phonological representations used in this study are to be understood as phonemic notation, except that square brackets ([…]) symbolize phonetic representation without regard to phonemic value. Shillings (/…/) are used occasionally to highlight phonemic representations in discussions of phonemic issues and commonly to show the hypothetical phonemic shape of Old Prussian forms.

In synchronic realization rules (or "rewrite rules") the phonemic input is connected to the phonetic output with an arrow (→). Diachronic correspondences, whether between phonetic or phonemic or other entities are marked by ">" (and occasionally "<").

Reinterpretation (abductive innovation) is symbolized by "⇒". For instance, (a) in (9.1)

(9.1) a. /e-/ → [ɛ-] > [i̯ɛ-] ⇒ /je-/ → [i̯ɛ-]

b. (/e-/ → ⌊ɛ-⌋) > (/e/ → ⌊i̯ɛ-⌋)

shows that the pronunciation of initial /e-/ develops a prothetic glide and is reinterpreted as /je-/ with no change in the pronunciation. The first part of this representation (/e-/ → [ɛ-] > [i̯ɛ-]) could alternatively be written as (b), that is, initial /e-/ pronounced without prothesis changes to /e-/ pronounced with prothesis. Representation (a) contains a diachronic correspondence between phonetic realizations; the alternative one, representation (b), expresses a diachronic correspondence between homologous realization rules.

Since there is mostly no need or no basis for claims about the phonetic manifestations of the reconstructed vowels we are dealing with, such symbols as /e/ and /a/ (or *e and *a, ᴇ and ᴀ) should not be read as phonetic symbols, but as phonemic symbols with oppositive values (low front vowel, low back vowel). Shevelov's well-known ad hoc phonetic/phonemic symbols ₑa, ₒa, (1965, 1979) and Gołąb's æ and ɔ (1991) may be adequate for some times and places in Slavic prehistory. But in dealing with four-vowel systems without specific reference to time and place one has to envisage a wide range of phonetic manifestations particularly for the open vowels − as well as contextually, stylistically, and geographically defined variation − minimally of /e/ ranging from [e] over [ɛ] and [æ] to [a] or [ɑ], and of /a/ ranging from [æ] over [a], [ɑ], and [ɒ] to [ɔ] or [o].

The contact interference situation described in the abstract in section 1.3.3 is based on this understanding.

Note that the assumption of a possibly wide range of phonetic vowel manifestations is demonstrably relevant in relation to Late Common Slavic. In the Second Common Slavic Vowel Shift (the qualitative differentiation of long and short vowels) most Slavic dialects developed prothetic *j*- before CS *ā- (which appears to imply that *ā was pronounced [æ:], word-initially [i̯æ:]), while a minority developed prothetic *w*- before CS *ā- (which seems to imply a rounded [ɒ:], [ɔ:], or perhaps [o:], word-initially, say, [u̯ɒ:]), whence such doublets as LCS *jajĭće ‖ *vajĭće 'egg' (PS ᴀ̄IA-); cf. Shevelov (1965: 245). Local differences of this kind, which must have been brought into contact during the period of territorial expansion, may be the source of the widespread, lexically irregular merger of LCS *je- and *ja- discussed in section 5.1.3.

But where there is no evidence for the precise phonetic manifestation of these phonemes, it seems wiser just to represent the phonemic distinctions and make no phonetic claims.

9.6. Dialect geography and migration

The interpretation of the geographical distributions of *e- ‖*a- doublets in chapter 3 and 4 imply a theory of dialect geography − with such basic notions as "center of innovation" and "radial diffusion" − which is assumed familiar. But it is applied here with some notable differences from normal practice.

The interpretation of the two parallel isoglosses in Lithuania (figure 2.1, section 3.7) is standard: the isoglosses are stylized as segments of a circle and the (stylized) curvature of the isoglosses is interpreted as evidence for their distance from the center of innovation. The vermiform northwesterly extension of area 2, which might look like a spearhead on a front, probably adds nothing to the interpretation. It is more directly related to the system of river courses (Nemunas, Nevežys, Dubysa, Venta) which it encompasses. It correlates with the principal corridor of communication between Upland and Lowland Lithuania and is a good illustration of how such avenues of communication may channel innovations through a speech area (cf. Bloomfield [1935: 334]; Andersen [1989]).

This traditional way of interpreting isoglosses has been established on the basis of sociogeographic conditions in Europe since the Middle Ages. When we turn to the much sparser and much less sedentary populations of the period before the Great Migrations, especially in Eastern Europe, and certainly in the distant past, there are no permanently populated areas independent of river basins − the river basins actually define the speech areas through which linguistic features spread. This has to be remembered as a corrective to the way we speak of dialect continua and isogloss configurations in prehistory (as, for instance, in section 4.4). But it is especially relevant to the standard notion of "radial diffusion". When this notion appears relevant in the interpretation of the distant past, it needs to be applied with due attention to the lay of the land; see also the last paragraph of this section.

A second corrective is the following. It is traditionally understood that innovations may spread (or be propagated) throughout a language area by being adopted more and more widely. Often the motivation for a new feature's being adopted is its greater utility or (more narrowly) an association with higher prestige. For a better understanding of the Slavic−Baltic *e- > *a- merger (sections 3.8 and 4.3), however, it is important to recognize that some innovations are diffused principally or solely because they effect a simplification of the grammar. This is probably always the case with phonemic mergers: if a traditional distinction is made by some members of a speech community and regularly neglected by others, new members are more likely to emulate the usage of the latter than the former (cf. Andersen 1988). This is the kind of situation assumed in the scenario in section 1.3.2.

A third corrective is as follows. In the Slavic territorial expansion, linguistic features are not propagated across a language area, but transported to new localities by several waves of settlers coming from different points of origin. The resulting sociolinguistic states of affairs were most likely more chaotic than they were characterized by ordered heterogeneity, and the choice between competing variants might be made, in any individual locality, not on the basis of any established sociolinguistic values (say, age or gender), but merely on the basis of predominance of usage. This is the assumption presented in section 3.3. In the Lithuanian – Latvian expansion into the Baltic northwest, which occurred in a single direction, a somewhat different situation probably obtained: here a development which was internally motivated over a wide area was merely strengthened and accelerated by the influx of new settlers and given greater areal extension; cf. section 4.2.

Sections 3.5 and 3.6 speak of "centrifugal migrations" and "radial routes". The Slavic migration routes illustrate the point about the lay of the land made above, for the ancient road net by which the people traveled probably followed the courses of rivers wherever possible. As a consequence, what we call radial routes of migration may involve a considerable amount of doglegging, as in the Slavic population movement that went south to the Danube river and then up river through the Danube basin to the West Slavic regions, as shown in figure 6.1.

9.7. Reconstructing ante-Migration dialects by projection

This is a comment on the implicational spatial relations that were described in section 3.1 and interpreted in subsequent sections of chapter 3.

I acknowledged in section 3.1 that it is a matter of assumption whether one regards the remarkable implicational relations in the geographical distribution a coincidence without significance, or one decides to interpret them. Here I would like to acknowledge that the decision to interpret them entails further assumptions.

It is standard practice in historical dialectology to interpret a spatial cline in density of attestation, say, of a certain sound change reflex, as evidence of its original direction of spread or of the direction of a secondary retrenchment. This and other standard ways of interpreting diatopic diversity have been established through the study of sedentary language communities. But note that (i) in the *e-* ‖ *a-* attestation we are dealing with data that have been dispersed through migration. Furthermore, (ii) the data are rather scant (from one handful to a few handfuls of lexemes in each region). Finally, (iii) they are somewhat contradictory − the correlation between greater density of attestation and proximal areas in the four West and South Slavic regions appears inverted in East Slavic.

It becomes a matter of assumption then (i) whether it is legitimate to reconstruct the ante-Migration isogloss configuration (sketched in figure 3.1) to which the standard interpretation would apply, (ii) whether the data (displayed in table 3.2) are sufficient to support any interpretation, and (iii) whether the apparent contradiction in the data between East Slavic and West and South Slavic should be explained by a subsidiary hypothesis (as done in section 3.8).

It is my judgement that our knowledge of the external historical context of the linguistic events hypothesized in chapter 3 is sufficient to lend plausibility to the account these assumptions make possible. But it is important and useful to acknowledge that this hypothetical account is based on information that is made available only through the underlying assumptions, and that these assumptions are open to discussion.

As for the initial dilemma − whether to interpret the observed relations or not − that is an issue on a different level, which the practicing historical dialectologist can only resolve in one way: by endeavoring to work out an interpretation. Compare the final remarks in section 6.1.

9.8. Patterns of geographical distribution

The different roles which the geographical distribution of *e-* ‖ *a-* doublets has played in this study deserve comment.

From the time this distribution was first presented in section 1.1 as an ordered tabulation (table 1.1), its evident regularities have been a datum that might be an object of explanation and, in turn, serve as evidence.

Chapter 3 was concerned primarily with explaining the observable regularities in the geographical distribution − the implicational spatial relations which were displayed in table 3.1 and described verbally under example (3.2).

In Chapter 5 another dimension of the pattern came into play, the gradation in geographical attestation among the lexemes involved. This orderly gradation was tacitly turned into evidence. It was used to reveal that each of the several subsets of lexemes with PS E- of different origin − PIE *e- (section 5.3.2), PIE *a, *o-, (section 5.3.3), PS E- from other sources (section 5.3.2) − actually reflects the overall pattern of gradation in a reduced form, and this observation served as basis for the inference that the *e- ‖ *a- doublets in the first set do not reflect qualitative ablaut (*h_1e- ~ *h_1o-), as some investigators have claimed in the past. The gradation was used again in a completely analogous argument in section 8.2.

The reason the several subsets show reduced versions of the overall pattern of gradation is plainly that their members are distributed homogeneously within the set. As far as I can see, there is no necessity for this homogeneity, but it certainly shows that the only source of patternment in the geographical distribution is the process, which was elucidated in sections 3.4−3.6, through which *e- ‖ *a- doublets were transported to the new territories settled during the Slavic expansion. As was pointed out in section 6.1, also the apparently exceptional lexemes with solid *a-attestation in the West Slavic dialects − the southern ante-Migration Common Slavic relic forms with CS* a- that remained unaffected by Rozwadowski's change − were transported by exactly the same routes.

There is nothing really unusual in the fact that one and the same datum − as here the pattern of geographical distribution − enters a historical account in one place as an explanandum and in other places as evidence. But it may be worth drawing attention to as a reminder of the essentially hermeneutic character of historical dialectology − and of comparative linguistics in general.

Chapter 10

Conclusion

The main purposes of this final chapter are to provide a summary of the exposition in the preceding chapters, to restate briefly the results of this investigation, and to offer some concluding remarks. It is divided into sections corresponding to the chapters it summarizes.

This study tries to tackle one of the most intractable sound changes in the prehistory of the Slavic languages. Defined in the 1800s as an "East Slavic change of *je- > *o-", this change is traditionally stated in these terms in textbook accounts and illustrated with a handful of examples, lexemes which occur in some Slavic languages with reflexes of initial LCS *je-, but in East Slavic languages with *o-. The sizeable scholarly literature on the topic, however, has long acknowledged that there may be more than a dozen *je- > *o- doublets with other geographical distributions. A variety of conditioned sound changes have been hypothesized to account for the East Slavic *o- doublets, each one entailing significant amounts of subsequent analogical leveling, and each one forced to explain away more data than the next, in order to avoid dealing with the non-East Slavic *o- doublets.

The account that is put forward in this study differs from preceding ones by taking the actually attested data seriously and undertaking to explain not only their existence, and their different geographical distribution among the Slavic languages, but their striking resemblance to the results of an apparently similar change in the Baltic languages. To do this it adopts a new chronological perspective on the change and views it as a Common Slavic change that occurred before the Slavic Migrations. It explicates the change in terms of a detailed typological parallel and in the end achieves a synthesis of the Slavic and Baltic changes.

10.1. Proto-Slavic E- and A-

Chapter 1 defines one set of Late Common Slavic correspondents for PS A-, and two sets for PS E-, one set of four lexemes with LCS *je- reflexes

(1.1) and another set of twenty lexemes with LCS *je- and *o- reflexes in the modern Slavic languages (1.2) — apparent evidence of a conditioned *je- > *o- change. Traditionally Old Russian borrowings from Old Norse and Greek with OR o- for the initial e- of the donor languages have served to date this putative change as contemporary with (or later than) these approximately ninth-century loan contacts. But here the point is made that these borrowings reflect instead a synchronic phonological constraint in Old Russian (no initial /e/) that resulted from the development of prothetic glides prior to 800; see section 1.1, examples (1.6)–(1.7).

This puts the putative change back in the period before the prothesis, and entails a reformulation of the change in terms of the vocalism of that period, before the qualitative differentiation of Common Slavic long and short vowels, as a partial merger of CS *e- with *a-.

Three scenarios are envisaged for such a change, (i) a phonologically conditioned merger, (ii) interference from a contact language (dialect) lacking a front/back distinction in its low vowels, and (iii) interference from a phonological system with different phonetic realizations of the front/back distinction in its low vowels (section 1.3).

10.2 A typological parallel

The phonological development of Lithuanian offers a well documented, detailed example of an e- > a- merger. Parts of the Lithuanian language area show a development of prothetic glides quite similar to the Common Slavic one; it occurred after the qualitative differentiation of long and short vowels in Lithuanian. But prior to this, initial *e- merged with *a- — in one large area without limitations, but in several contiguous areas with variously constrained outcomes (figure 2.1). The details of these two changes and their interaction afford considerable insight into the nature of both the prothesis and the *e- > *a- merger in Lithuanian.

10.3. The Late Common Slavic *je- ‖ *o- isoglosses

In two areas the outcomes of the Lithuanian changes are similar to the outcome of the Common Slavic *e- > *a- merger. These are areas in which the merger evidently did not occur as a regular change, but where there is a geographical scatter of lexical doublets with *a-* for etymological **e-* (introductory section to chapter 3).

This observation leads to the hypothesis that the geographical distribution of CS **e-* and **a-* doublets in the modern Slavic languages is the composite result of (i) dialect forms from such an area (ii) being transported to all parts of the Slavic territories at the time of the Slavic territorial expansion and (iii) a subsequent process of norm consolidation, in which competing doublets with **e-* and **a-* reflexes gave way to uniform local usage − with **e-* reflexes in some lexemes and **a-* reflexes in others − practically everywhere (section 3.1).

The relevant evidence in support of this hypothesis is (i) observable relations of implication in the modern distribution of **e-* and **a-* doublets (3.2) (displayed in tables 3.1 and 3.2), especially a denser distribution of **a-* doublets in the proximal parts of several of the regions the Slavs settled, and (ii) the (sporadic) textual attestation of competing **e-* and **a-* forms from the Middle Ages to the present (sections 3.2−3.4).

A closer analysis of the modern distribution of **e-* and **a-* doublets suggests that (i) in the area from which they were dispersed they had a relatively orderly distribution, which can be reconstructed by extrapolation (as in figure 3.1); and that (ii) the dispersion resulted in part from the "radial" expansion of the Slavic territories, in part from cross-migrations − what Łowmiański (1963) called mass migrations and group migrations (sections 3.5−3.6).

In the East Slavic languages one expects a greater density of **a-* forms in the proximal Ukrainian area than in the distal Russian areas; but instead there is a denser occurrence of **a-* forms in the Russian Northwest. This is explained as an effect of the Baltic-speaking substratum in Belarus, for the Lithuanian isoglosses in figure 2.1 point to that area as the center of innovation in the Lithuanian **e-* > **a-* merger: as the Baltic-speaking population here adopted Slavic speech in the 400−800s, their native phonological constraint (*e-* → *a-*) weighted the Slavic **e-* ~ **a-* variation in favor of **a-*-initial by-forms, just as other phonological constraints of theirs (e. g., *-Tl-* → *-Kl-*) left their mark on the Russian settler dialects of the northwest (section 3.7).

At the same time, the localization of the center of innovation for the Lithuanian merger makes it possible to identify the area to which the ante-Migration Common Slavic dialects were contiguous and to construct a coherent account of the origin of the Slavic **e-* > **a-* change (section 3.8).

A unified account of the origin and subsequent development of the Slavic **e-* ‖ **a-* doublets is presented as a continuous, chronological narrative in section 3.9.

10.4. The Baltic change of *e- > *a-

Chapter 4 reconstructs Proto-Baltic A- and E- and identifies some two dozen lexemes with different distributions of modern *e-* and *a-* reflexes of PB E- (tables 4.1 and 4.2).

It is seen that the geographical distribution of these reflexes is rather similar to that in Slavic, especially if it is projected back to the period before the colonization of the Northwest Baltic (Curonian, Zemgalian, and Selonian) territories by the Latvians (Latgalians) and Lithuanians. With the aid of this added perspective one can construe the differences in initial vocalism among the modern Baltic languages as a reflection of the northern segment of a circular isogloss system that arose as the Southeast Baltic *e- > *a- merger diffused in all directions. While the southern segment of this isogloss system is reflected in the Slavic languages − severely deformed and greatly fragmented in the Slavic territorial expansion − its western and eastern portions were obliterated by the Slavic colonization of what is now Poland and Russia. The northern section, like the southern one, was in part deformed and in part fragmented by the northwestward movements of Baltic groups that began in the 500s and came to a close only in the 1000−1100s (sections 4.1−4.2).

This fuller account of the Baltic *e- > *a- changes makes it possible to interpret the Slavic and the Baltic word-initial vowel changes in a larger perspective and construe them as a single shared innovation, certainly one of the very last in the prehistory of the Slavic−Baltic dialect continuum that existed in Eastern Europe from the time these Indo-Europeans first established their linguistic traditions here in the second millennium before our era until the eve of the Great Migrations (sections 4.3−4.4).

10.5. Layers of innovation: Slavic, Slavic−Baltic, and Indo-European

Chapter 5 clarifies the relationships between the Slavic−Baltic *e- > *a- merger on one hand and, on the other, several individual word-initial vowel changes which preceded or followed it, and whose effects to varying extents are difficult to distinguish from those of the *e-* > *a-* merger. Only the third part of the chapter (section 5.3) deals with the Indo-European sources of PS, PB E-.

One of the more recent changes is the medieval development of *h*-prothesis in, among other Slavic languages, Lower Sorbian. Here lexical doublets of the type *jeleń* ‖ *heleń* 'deer' have been interpreted by earlier investigators as parallel to the LCS **jelenĭ* ‖ **olenĭ* doublets. This hundred-year-old surmise turns out not to fit the data that have since become available. But the doublets remain interesting, for they suggest that the Slavs who settled Lower Lusatia in the 600s from the south and from the east represented distinct Common Slavic dialects, one still without, the other already with prothetic *j-* before CS **e-*. Since the former group distinguished initial CS **je-* and **e-*, this early diversity was preserved as lexical variation and eventually as dialect differences between doublets with *je-* and *he-* (section 5.1.1).

Another more recent change is the Bulgarian-Macedonian loss of prothesis (a change of *je-* > *e-*), which is reflected already in Old Church Slavonic texts. Although in substance this change is totally unrelated to the Slavic—Baltic *e-* > *a-* merger, its interpretation requires formal phonological considerations similar to those called for in interpreting the development of prothesis (section 5.1.2).

A third change which at one time has been thought related to the putative "East Slavic **je-* > **o-* change" is the widespread, lexically idiosyncratic merger of LCS **je-* > **ja-* which has occurred especially in West Slavic and Western South Slavic dialects at different times during the Middle Ages. The effect of these mergers is to add a certain indeterminacy to part of the modern attestation, but more interestingly they force the historical linguist to consider alternative chronological accounts of the ambiguous data, as is shown in section 5.1.3 (see especially figures 5.2 and 5.3).

An early, genuinely East Slavic change, which may be viewed as a LCS **ju-* > **u-* merger, has traditionally been considered part of, or parallel to, the "**je-* > **o-* change". This change is discussed in an excursus (section 5.1.4), for in reality it is a detail in the development of prothetic glides which is entirely separate from the Slavic—Baltic *e-* > *a-* merger. But it merits discussion in its own right and calls for the same conceptual framework as the changes discussed in the preceding sections of this chapter.

Word-initial liquid diphthongs were metathesized in Common Slavic, and hence it is an interesting question whether words with CS **el-*, **er-*

were affected by the *e- > *a- merger. A few such lexemes are examined individually as part of the corpus of this investigation (chapter 7). They are reviewed in section 5.2, but no generalizations are indicated.

Besides the lexemes with CS *e- ‖ *a- doublets produced by the *e- > *a- merger there are lexemes, in both Slavic and Baltic, with vowel-initial by-forms of other origins, some of which may reflect Indo-European ablaut alternations, including qualitative ablaut. In order to approach the important question whether any of the CS *e- ‖ *a- doublets existed prior to the *e- > *a- merger, it is considered useful to examine a number of different types of word-initial variation, which illustrate the principles of analysis that should be kept in mind when one evaluates the mostly ambiguous attestation (section 5.3.1).

In section 5.3.2 the following inherited Slavic lexemes with possible PIE *h_1e- are examined (bracketed numbers refer to sections of chapter 7): PS EDLI- 'spruce' [4], ELENI- 'deer' [11], ELIKA- 'whitefish' [9], ESENI- 'autumn' [28], ES-MI 'be; 1sg.' [32], EZERA- 'lake' [35], EZIA- 'hedgehog' [37−38]. The geographical distribution of their *e- and *a- reflexes is compared with that of the reflexes of lexemes with PS E- from other sources, which cannot be expected to have qualitative ablaut by-forms: EDEINA- 'one' [1], EDSKE 'still' [2], EDUĀS 'hardly' [3], ELAUA- 'tin; lead' [6], ELEITA- 'gut' [9], ELIXĀ- 'alder' [13], EMELA- 'mistletoe' [18], ESE 'look' [26], EMĒXIA- 'coulter' [44]. There are no differences between the two sets' geographical distributions (see table 5.3), and it can be inferred that qualitative ablaut most likely is not a factor in the *e- ‖ *a- variation.

In section 5.3.3 the inherited Slavic lexemes with PIE *a- (*h_2e-) and *o- (*h_3e-, *h_2o-, *h_3o-) are considered, which cannot show qualitative ablaut: PS ELUKA- 'rancid, bitter' [17], ESERĀ- 'awn; fishbones' [29], ESETI- 'drying rack' [30], and ESETRA- 'sturgeon' [31] with PIE *a-; EPSĀ- 'aspen' [19], ERILA- 'eagle' [22], ERIMBI- 'grouse' [23], and ESENA- 'ash (Fraxinus)' [27] with PIE *o-. These have their PS E- thanks to Rozwadowski's change, an ancient, Pre-Slavic−Baltic change of initial PIE *a-/*o- > *e-. The patterns of geographical distribution of these lexemes are quite similar to the previous sets (table 5.4), a confirmation that the origin of the *e- ‖ *a- variation is the same in all three sets, viz. the *e- > *a- merger and the subsequent dispersion during the Slavic expansion. But four lexemes (two in table 5.3 and two in table 5.4) have similar, atypical distributions. They are interpreted as evidence that Rozwadowski's change left some of the ancestral dialects of Slavic unaffected, creating lexical doublets that existed before the *e- > *a- merger: PS ELAUA- ‖ ALAUA- 'tin; lead' [6], ELIXĀ- ‖ ALIXĀ- 'alder' [13], EPSĀ- ‖ APSĀ- 'aspen' [19], and ERILA- ‖ ARILA- 'eagle' [20].

Section 5.3.4 presents a parallel analysis of the Baltic material with PB E- from PIE *h_1e-, PB E- of uncertain origin, and PB E- from PIE *h_2e-, *h_3e-, etc. It is found that also Baltic has Rozwadowski doublets, besides PB ELUA- ‖ ALUA- 'tin' [6], ELSNI- ‖ ALSNI- 'alder' [13], EPUŠE- ‖ APSĒ- 'ash' [19], also EKETĒ- ‖ AKETĒ- 'icehole; pool' [5] and EŠERIA- ‖ AŠE-RIA- 'perch' [29], and that one pair of doublets distinguishes Baltic from Slavic, PB ELKŪNĒ- ‖ PS ALKUTI- 'elbow' [14].

10.6. PIE *e-, *a-, *o- in Slavic and Baltic

Chapter 6 offers a more thorough discussion of Rozwadowski's change and the questions of when and where it took place.

The fact that Rozwadowski's change gave rise to lexical doublets is significant for its dating. Section 6.1 discusses the striking similarities between Slavic and Baltic E- forms, which suggest that the change preceded the dispersion of their ancestral dialects. This inference is strongly confirmed by the numerous morphological differences exhibited by the doublets, in stem shape and in affixation. An analysis of PB EPUŠĒ- ‖ APSĒ- 'aspen' [19] and of PS ESETI- ‖ PB EKETĒ- 'drying rack; harrow' [30] indicates the conclusion that Rozwadowski's change preceded the stabilization of *Gutturalwechsel* variants. The relations among the E- ‖ A-doublets − Slavic, Baltic, and Slavic versus Baltic − can be mapped as a spatial representation. Projected, *faute de mieux*, against the presumable disposition of Slavs and Balts ca. AD 500 this representation suggests that Rozwadowski's change affected central areas of the Slavic−Baltic dialect continuum more than the northern and southern peripheries, eastern portions more than western.

Section 6.2 shows that Rozwadowski's proposed explanation (1915), which was based on a preliminary screening of the material, is inadequate. There is no apparent basis for formulating the change as a phonological change. It seems worthwhile considering it a result of language contact, either with the non-Indo-European substratum of Eastern Europe (section 6.3) or, more likely, with other Indo-European dialects.

In section 6.4 the Rozwadowski doublets are compared to such well-known Slavic−Baltic phonological irregularities as *Gutturalwechsel* (section 6.4.1), the dual reflexes (-*iR*- ‖ -*uR*-) of Indo-European syllabic sonorants (section 6.4.2), and the deviant reflexes of the Indo-European stop series ascribed to interference from Temematian (section 6.4.3). It is evident that the Rozwadowski doublets can be interpreted in a similar vein (section 6.5). Such an interpretation fits in well with the growing recognition of the composite origin of Baltic and, especially, Slavic and the reasonable understanding that the Indo-European linguistic traditions in Eastern Europe were not established in one fell swoop, but came into being through a lengthy process comprising numerous contact episodes in which different Indo-European traditions were melded together. This interpretation of Rozwadowski's change does not clarify its origin by very much, but at least puts it in a perspective that is realistic.

10.7. The material

Chapter 7 surveys the material on which this investigation is based lexeme by lexeme. The introductory remarks compare this corpus to the corpora of the recent investigations by Šaur (1982) and Popowska-Taborska (1984) (tables 7.1 and 7.2) and explains the manner of presentation in the forty-four sections of which the rest of the chapter is composed. Each section makes explicit what bearing Rozwadowski's change and the Slavic–Baltic *e- > *a- merger have (or may have) on the etymological explication of the given lexeme. In the process, a great many details are clarified and some new ideas are contributed. Particularly worthy of note are some particulars relating to the areal diversity of the defunct Slavic–Baltic dialect continuum, which can be gleaned from the data; see, for instance, PS ELIXĀ- 'alder' [13], ERIMBI- 'grouse; rowan' [20–21].

10.8. Alternative approaches

Chapter 8 gives the long scholarly tradition devoted to the Slavic *je- > *o- change its due and discusses the contributions on the corresponding Baltic change.

The Slavic scholarly tradition is examined from three points of view, (i) the question whether the Slavic *je- ‖ *o- diversity is due to a specifically East Slavic change (section 8.1), (ii) the diverse ways the material has been categorized in efforts to explain away the data that would not fit the proposed explanations (section 8.2), and (iii) the sorts of sound change that have been envisaged (section 8.3). The main purpose is to show to what extent this hundred-year long discussion has been hampered by dogma (the "East Slavic doctrine"), by a reluctance to confront the data, and by a limited understanding of sound change.

By contrast the Baltic *e- > *a- change has been explicated in modern terms, but in a chronological perspective which has made the change appear to be a recent allophonic change, rather than the old phonemic merger it must have been, and without attention to the diatopic diversity of the change in Baltic.

10.9. Perspectives

Chapter 9 makes explicit some of the conceptual apparatus presupposed in the preceding chapters, clarifies some of the terminology, and touches on some questions of method that are more conveniently raised apart from the presentation. It contains sections on Proto-Slavic and Common Slavic (section 9.1), Proto-Baltic and Common Baltic (section 9.2), the question of a Proto-Balto-Slavic (section 9.3), the character of the extinct languages in Eastern Europe (section 9.4), questions of reconstructed phonemics and phonetics (section 9.5), dialect geography in relation to the Migrations (section 9.6), the problem of reconstructing pre-migration dialects on the basis of the post-migration dialect differences (section 9.7), and the exploitation of patterns of geographical distribution as evidence (section 9.7).

10.10. Conclusion

This chapter has provided a summary of the presentation in the preceding chapters and has restated the main results of this investigation, chapter by chapter, with references to the relevant parts of the preceding exposition.

Very briefly, this investigation has examined the Proto-Slavic and Proto-Baltic lexical material reconstructible with initial E- using the methods of comparative and historical dialectology. Both language groups have lexemes with E- of uncertain origin, E- from PIE *h_1e-, and E- from PIE *h_2e-, h_3e-, and *h_xo-. Lexemes in the last mentioned set have their initial E- due to a Pre-Slavic−Baltic change of PIE *a-/*o- > *e-, which left discernible areal differences in the Slavic−Baltic dialect continuum, probably at a distant time.

Slavic and Baltic E- has undergone additional change, yielding both *e- and *a- reflexes in Common Slavic and in Common Baltic without any identifiable conditioning. It is argued here that the irregular reflexes of PS, PB E- result from a merger of *e- > *a- in a central part of the Slavic−Baltic dialect continuum. The change diffused lexically into the ancestral dialects of Slavic in the south and of Baltic in the north and west. Subsequently both these language areas were deformed and fragmented by the Slavic expansion and the East Baltic colonization of the Baltic Northwest. But there remains sufficient evidence in the geographical distribution of *e- and *a- reflexes in both language groups to point to this reconstructed sequence of events.

References

Andersen, Henning
 1968 "IE *s after *i, u, r, k* in Baltic and Slavic", *Acta Linguistica Hafnien-sia* 11: 171–190.
 1972 "Diphthongization", *Language* 48: 11–50.
 1986 "Protoslavic and Common Slavic: Questions of periodization and terminology", in: M. S. Flier–D. S. Worth (eds.), *Slavic Linguistics, Poetics, Cultural History. In Honor of Henrik Birnbaum on his Sixtieth Birthday, 13 December 1985.* (*International Journal of Slavic Linguistics and Poetics* XXXI / XXXII.) Ohio: Slavica, 67–82.
 1988 "Center and periphery: Adoption, diffusion, and spread", in: J. Fisiak (ed.), *Historical dialectology, regional and social.* (*Trends in Linguistics: Studies and Monographs* 37.) Berlin: Mouton de Gruyter, 39–84.
 1989 "Understanding linguistic innovations", in: L. E. Breivik – E. H. Jahr (eds.), *Language change. Contributions to the study of its causes.* (*Trends in Linguistics: Studies and Monographs* 43.) Berlin: Mouton de Gruyter, 5–28.
 1993 "Capitolo 14: Lingue slaviche", in: A. Giacalone Ramat – P. Ramat (eds.), *Le lingue indoeuropee.* Bologna: Il Mulino, 441–480.
 In press "A glimpse of the homeland of the Slavs: ecological and cultural change", *Journal of Indo-European Studies* 24.
Anttila, Raimo
 1969 *Proto-Indo-European Schwebeablaut.* (*University of California Publications in Linguistics* 58.) Berkeley – Los Angeles: University of California Press.
Arumaa, Peeter
 1964 *Urslavische Grammatik, I: Einleitung: Lautlehre.* Heidelberg: Carl Winter Universitätsverlag.
Avanesov, Ruben Ivanovič – K. K. Krapiva – Ju. F. Mackevič
 1963 *Dyjalektalahičny atlas belaruskaj movy* [Belarussian dialect atlas]. Minsk: Vydavnictvo Akademii navuk.
Baran, Vladymyr Danylovyč – Denys Nykodymovyč Kozak – Rostyslav Vsevolodovyč Terpylovs'kyj
 1991 *Poxodžennja slov'jan* [The origin of the Slavs]. Kyjiv: Naukova Dumka.
Beekes, Robert S. P.
 1969 *The Development of the Proto-Indo-European laryngeals in Greek.* The Hague: Mouton.
Bernštejn, Samuil Borisovič
 1961 *Očerk sravnitel'noj grammatiki slavjanskix jazykov* [An outline of Slavic comparative grammar]. Moskva: Izdatel'stvo Akademii Nauk.

Bezzenberger, Adalbert
1897   Review of Erich Berneker. *Die preussische Sprache. Texte, Grammatik, etymologisches Wörterbuch. Beiträge zur Kunde der indogermanischen Sprachen* 23: 285–320.

Bezlaj, France
1977   *Etimologiški slovar slovenskega jezika, I. A–J.* [An etymological dictionary of Slovenian, I. A–J]. Ljubljana: Slovenska akademija znanosti i umetnosti – Mladinska knjiga.

Birnbaum, Henrik
1987   "Some terminological and substantive issues in Slavic historical linguistics. (Reflections on the periodization of the Slavic ancestral language and the labeling of its chronological divisions)", *International Journal of Slavic Linguistics and Poetics* 35/36: 299–332.
1992   "Von ethnologischer Einheit zur Vielfalt: Die Slaven im Zuge der Landnahme auf der Balkanhalbinsel", *Südost-Forschungen* 51: 1–19.
1993   "On the ethnogenesis and protohome of the Slavs: The linguistic evidence", *Journal of Slavic Linguistics* 1: 352–374.

Bloomfield, Leonard
1935   *Language.* London: Allen & Unwin.

Borkovskij, Petr Savvič – Viktor Ivanovič Kuznecov
1965   *Istoričeskaja grammatika russkogo jazyka* [A historical grammar of Russian]. (2nd edition.) Moskva: Izdatel'stvo Akademii Nauk.

Boryś, Wiesław
1984   "Słowiańskie relikty indoeuropejskiej nazwy brony (wschsłow. *osetĭ*, pol. *jesieć* a ide. **oketā*" [Slavic relics of the Indo-European word for 'harrow' (East Slavic *osetĭ*, Polish *jesieć*, and PIE **oketā*)], *Acta Baltico-Slavica* 16: 57–63.

Brejdak, A. B.
1988   "Zapadnaja granica latgal'skogo i selonskogo plemen po dannym jazyka v XIII–XIV v." [Linguistic evidence for the western limits of the Latgalian and Selonian tribes in the thirteenth to fourteenth centuries], in: V. V. Ivanov (ed.), *Balto-slavjanskie issledovanija 1986,* Moskva: Nauka, 219–228.

Būga, Kazimieras
1924   *Lietuvio kalbos žodynas* [Lithuanian dictionary]. Kaunas: Valstybės spaustuvė.
[1961] [Reprinted in: Z. Zinkevičius (ed.), *Rinktiniai raštai, III* [Collected writings, III]. Vilnius: Valstybinė politinės ir mokslinės literatūros leidykla, 9–483.]

Bulaxovskij, Leonid Arsen'evič
1958   *Istoričeskij kommentarij k russkomu literaturnomu jazyku* [A historical commentary on Standard Russian]. (5th edition.) Kyjiv: Radjans'ka škola.

Calleman, Birger
1950   *Zu den Haupttendenzen der urslavischen und altrussischen Lautent-
        wicklung. (Publications de l'Institut Slave d'Upsal* 3.) Uppsala: Alm-
        qvist & Wiksell.
Cowgill, Warren
1965   "Evidence in Greek", in: W. Winter (ed.), *Evidence for laryngeals.*
        (*Janua Linguarum*, Series maior XI.) The Hague: Mouton, 142–180.
Dejna, Karol
1981   *Atlas polskich innowacji dialektalnych* [An atlas of Polish dialect in-
        novations]. Warszawa – Łódź: Państwowe Wydawnictwo Naukowe.
Diels, Paul
1963   *Die slavischen Völker.* Wiesbaden: Otto Harrassowitz.
Durnovo, Nikolaj
1924–1925 "Spornye voprosy o.-sl. fonetiki. I. Načal'noe *e* v o.-sl. jaz." [Con-
        troversial issues in Common Slavic phonetics. I. Initial *e* in Slavic],
        Slavia 3: 225–271.
1924   *Očerk istorii russkogo jazyka* [An outline of the history of Russian].
        Moskva – Leningrad: Gosudarstvennoe izdatel'stvo.
[1962] [Reprinted in: *Slavistic Printings and Reprintings* XXII. s'-Gra-
        venhage: Mouton.]
Dybo, Vladimir Antonovič
1975   "Zakon Vasil'eva-Dolobko v drevnerusskom (na materiale Čudov-
        skogo Novogo Zaveta)" [Vasil'ev and Dolobko's law in Old Russian
        (evidence from the Čudovo New Testament)], *International Journal
        of Slavic Linguistics and Poetics* 17: 7–81.
1981   *Slavjanskaja akcentologija. Opyt rekonstrukcii sistemy akcentnyx par-
        adigm v praslavjanskom* [Slavic accentology. Attempt at a reconstruc-
        tion of the accentual paradigms of Proto-Slavic]. Moskva: Nauka.
Ekblom, Richard
1925   *Der Wechsel* (j)e- ~ o- *im Slavischen.* (*Skrifter utgivna av Kungliga
        Humanistiska Vetenskaps-Samfundet i Uppsala* 22: 4.) Uppsala:
        Almqvist & Wiksell.
Endzelin, Jan
1923   *Lettische Grammatik.* Heidelberg: Carl Winters Universitätsbuch-
        handlung.
1948   *Baltu valodu skaņas un formas* [The sounds and forms of the Baltic
        languages]. Riga: Latvijas valsts izdevnieceba.
[1971] [*Jānis Endzelīns' Comparative phonology and morphology of the Baltic
        languages.* Translated by W. R. Schmalstieg – B. Jēgers. The Hague:
        Mouton.]
Filin, Fedot Petrovič
1962   *Obrazovanie jazyka vostočnyx slavjan* [The genesis of the language of
        the Eastern Slavs]. Moskva – Leningrad: Izdatel'stvo Akademii
        nauk SSSR.

Fortunatov, Filipp Fedorovič
1890   "Phonetische Bemerkungen zu Miklosich's *Etymologisches Wörter-buch der slavischen Sprachen*", *Archiv für slavische Philologie* 12: 95–103.
1919   *Lekcii po fonetike staroslavjanskago (cerkovnoslavjanskago) jazyka* [Lectures on the phonetics of Old (Church) Slavonic]. Petrograd: Tipografija Rossijskoj Akademii Nauk.
[1972]   [Reprinted Berlin: Zentralantiquariat der Deutschen Demokratischen Republik.]
Fraenkel, Ernst
1962–1965 *Litauisches etymologisches Wörterbuch, 1–2.* Heidelberg: Carl Winter Universitätsverlag – Göttingen: Vandenhoeck & Ruprecht.
Friedrich, Paul
1970   *Proto-Indo-European trees. The arboreal system of a prehistoric people.* Chicago–London: University of Chicago Press.
Galton, Herbert
1973   "Zwei urrussische Lautstudien", *Zeitschrift für Slavische Philologie* 37: 55–62.
Gamkrelidze, Tamaz Valerianovič – Vjačeslav Vsevolodovič Ivanov
1984   *Indoevropejskij jazyk i indoevropejcy. Rekonstrukcija i istoriko-tipologičeskij analiz prajazyka i protokul'tury, I–II* [Indo-European and the Indo-Europeans. A reconstruction and a historico-typological analysis of a proto-language and a proto-culture, I–II]. Tbilisi: Izdatel'stvo tbilisskogo universiteta.
Georgiev, Vladimir Ivanov
1957   "Koncepcija ob indoevropejskix guttural'nyx soglasnyx i ee otraženie na ètimologii slavanskix jazykov" [An interpretation of the Indo-European velar consonants and its reflection in Slavic etymology], in: K. Taranovski (ed.), *Beogradski Međunarodni slavistični sastanak.* Beograd: Naučno delo, 511–517.
1963   "Praslavjanski *je > o* ili *a > ja > je*?" [Proto-Slavic *je > o* or *a > ja > ja*?], *Slavistični studii. Sbornik po slučaj V Meždunaroden Slavistićen Kongres v Sofija*: 9–15. Sofia: Nauka i izkustvo.
Gimbutas, Marija
1963   *The Balts.* London: Thames & Hudson.
1971   *The Slavs.* London: Thames & Hudson.
Gołąb, Zbigniew
1972   " 'Kentum' elements in Slavic", *Lingua Posnaniensis* 16: 53–82.
1981   "Kiedy nastąpiło rozszczepienie językowe Bałtów i Słowian?" [When did the linguistic differentiation of Balts and Slavs occur?], *Acta Baltico-Slavica* 14: 121–133.
1987   "Etnogeneza słowian w świetle językoznawstwa" [The ethnogenesis of the Slavs in the light of linguistics], in: G. Labuda – S. Tabaczyński (eds.), 71–79.

1992   *The origins of the Slavs. A linguist's view.* Ohio: Slavica Publishers.

Handke, Kwiryna

1972   "Kaszubsko-słowińskie protetyczne *v-* przed nagłosowym *j-* oraz *i-*" [Kashubian-Slovincian prothetic *v-* before initial *j-* and *i-*], *Studia z filologii polskiej i słowiańskiej* 11: 95−99. Warszawa: Państwowe Wydawnictwo Naukowe.

Hjelmslev, Louis

1961   *Prolegomena to a theory of language.* Translated by Francis J. Whitfield. Madison − Milwaukee − London: University of Wisconsin Press. Revised English edition of *Omkring sprogteoriens grundlæggelse* (1943), København: Ejnar Munksgaard.

Holzer, Georg

1989   *Entlehnungen aus einer bisher unbekannten indogermanischen Sprache im Urslavischen und Urbaltischen.* (Österreichische Akademie der Wissenschaften. Philosophisch-historische Klasse. Sitzungsberichte 521.) Wien: Verlag der österreichischen Akademie der Wissenschaften.

Horálek, Karel

1962   *Úvod do studia slovanských jazyků* [Introduction to the study of the Slavic languages]. Praha: Nakladatelství Československé Akademie Věd.

Huld, Martin E.

1990   "The linguistic typology of the Old European substrata in North Central Europe", *Journal of Indo-European Studies* 18: 389−424.

In press "Tin and lead in Ancient Central Europe", *General Linguistics.*

Il'inskij, Grigorij Andreevič

1923   "K voprosu o čeredovanii glasnyx rjada *o, e* v načale slov v slavjanskix jazykax" [On the question of the variation of word-initial *o, e* in the Slavic languages], *Slavia* 2: 232−276.

1925   "Ešče raz o slavjanskix dubletax tipa *jelenĭ : olenĭ*" [The Slavic doublets of the type *jelenĭ : olenĭ* one more time], *Slavia* 4: 387−394.

Ivanov, Vjačeslav Vsevolodovič − Vladimir Nikolaevič Toporov

1961   "K postanovke voprosa drevnejšix otnošenijax baltijskix i slavjanskix jazykov" [On the problem of the earliest relations between Baltic and Slavic], in: V. V. Vinogradov et al. (eds.), *Issledovanija po slavjanskomu jazykoznaniju* [Studies in Slavic Linguistics]. Moskva: Izdatel'stvo Akademii Nauk, 273−305.

1980   "O drevnix slavjanskix ètnonimax (osnovnye problemy i perspektivy)" [On the ancient Slavic ethnonyms (basic problems and perspectives)], in: V. D. Koroljuk (ed.), *Slavjanskie drevnosti − ètnogenez: Material'naja kul'tura Drevnej Rusi* [Slavic antiquities − ethnogenesis: the material culture of ancient Russia]. Kyjiv: Naukova dumka, 11−45.

Jakobson, Roman
1929   *Remarques sur l'évolution du russe comparée à celle des autres langues slaves* (*Travaux du Cercle Linguistique de Prague*, 2).
[1962]   [Reprinted in his *Selected writings, I: Phonological studies*. The Hague: Mouton, 7–116.]
1963   "Opyt fonologičeskogo podxoda k istoričeskim voprosam slavjanskoj akcentologii. Pozdnij period slavjanskoj jazykovoj praistorii" [Attempt at a phonological approach to the diachronic problems of Slavic accentology. The recent period of Slavic linguistic prehistory], in: *American contributions to the Fifth International Congress of Slavists, Vol. I: Linguistic contributions.* The Hague: Mouton.
[1971]   [Reprinted in his *Selected writings, I: Phonological studies*, 664–689, The Hague: Mouton.

Jakubinskij, Lev Petrovič
1953   *Istorija drevnerusskogo jazyka* [A history of Old Russian]. Moskva: Gosudarstvennoe učebno-pedagogičeskoe izdatel'stvo.

Kazlauskas, Jonas
1968   *Lietuvių kalbos istorinė gramatika (Kirčiavimas, daiktavardis, veiksmažodis)* [A historical grammar of Lithuanian. Accentuation, the noun, the verb]. Vilnius: Mintis.

Kiviniemi, Eero
1982   *Rakkaan lapsen monet nimet. Suomalaisten etunimet ja nimenvalinta* [A well-loved child has many names. Finnish given names and name choice]. Helsinki: Weilin & Göös.

Klemensiewicz, Zenon
1974   *Historia języka polskiego, I* [A history of Polish, I]. Warszawa: Państwowe Wydawnictwo Naukowe.

Koivulehto, Jorma
1991   *Uralische Evidenz für die Laryngaltheorie* (Österreichische Akademie der Wissenschaften. Philosophisch-historische Klasse. Sitzungsberichte 566.) Wien. Verlag der österreichischen Akademie der Wissenschaften.

Kolomijec', Vera Titovna
1966   "Rozdil II. Fonetyka" [Chapter 2: Phonetics], in: O. S. Mel'nyčuk (ed.), *Vstup do porivnjal'no-istoryčnoho vyvčennja slov'jans'kyx mov* [Introduction to the comparative study of the Slavic languages]. Kyjiv: Naukova Dumka, 22–111.

Kott, F. St.
1910   *Dodátky k Bartošovu slovniku moravskému* [Addenda to Bartoš's Moravian dictionary]. Praha.

Krajčovič, Rudolf
1975   *A historical phonology of the Slovak language.* Heidelberg: Carl Winter Universitätsverlag.

Kropilak, Miroslav
1977—1978   *Vlastivedný slovník obci na Slovensku* [Geographical index of towns and villages in Slovakia], I—III. Bratislava: Veda.

Kuryłowicz, Jerzy
1956   *L'apophonie en indo-européen.* Wrocław: Ossolineum.

Kuznecova, Ol'ga Danilovna
1974a   "O slovax s protezoj *j* (na materialax južnorusskix govorov)" [On words with prothetic *j* (evidence from South Russian dialects)], in: F. P. Filin — F. P. Sorokoletov (eds.), *Dialektnaja leksika 1974.* Leningrad: Nauka, 70—81.
1974b   "Slova s protetičeskim *j* na severe" [Words with prothetic *j* in the north), in: F. P. Filin — F. P. Sorokoletov (eds.), *Dialektnaja leksika 1974.* Leningrad: Nauka, 82—98.

Labuda, Gerard — Stanisław Tabaczyński
1987   *Studia nad etnogenezą Słowian i kulturą Europy wczesnośredniowiecznej, I* [Studies in the ethnogenesis of the Slavs and in European culture in the Early Middle Ages, I]. Wrocław: Ossolineum.

Lamprecht, Arnošt
1987   *Praslovanština* [Proto-Slavic]. Brno: Univerzita J. E. Purkyně.

Laučjute, Jurate Aloizovna
1982   *Slovar' baltizmov v slavjanskix jazykax* [A dictionary of Balticisms in the Slavic languages]. Leningrad: Nauka.

Levin, Jules
1974   *The Slavic element in the Old Prussian Elbing Vocabulary.* (*University of California Publications in Linguistics* 77.) Berkeley — Los Angeles — London: University of California Press.

Łowmiański, Henryk
1963   *Początki Polski. Z dziejów Słowian w I tysiącleciu n.e., II* [The origins of Poland. On the history of the Slavs in the first millennium of our era, II]. Warszawa: Państwowe Wydawnictwo Naukowe.

Lukina, Galina Nikolaevna
1968   "Staroslavjanskie i drevnerusskie varianty s načal'nym *a—ja, ju—u, e—o* v jazyke drevnerusskix pamjatnikov XI—XIV vekov" [Church Slavic and Old Russian variants with initial *a—ja, ju—u, e—o* in Old Russian texts of the eleventh to fourteenth centuries], in: S. G. Barxudarov (ed.), Moskva: Nauka, 104—114.

Majtán, Milan
1972   *Názvy obcí na Slovensku za ostatných dvesto rokov* [Place names in Slovakia during the last two hundred years]. Bratislava: Vydavateľstvo Slovenskej Akademie Vied.

Malingoudis, Phaedon
1981   *Studien zu den slavischen Ortsnamen Griechenlands, I: Slavische Flurnamen aus der messenischen Mani.* (Akademie der Wissenschaften

und der Literatur, Mainz. Abhandlungen der geistes- und sozialwis-senschaftlichen Klasse 1981, 3.) Wiesbaden: Franz Steiner Verlag.

Mareš, František

1969   *Diachronische Phonologie des Ur- und Frühslavischen.* München: Wilhelm Fink Verlag.

Martynov, Viktor Vladimirovič

1977   "Semantičeskie arxaizmy na južnoslavjanskoj jazykovoj periferii" [Semantic archaisms on the South Slavic linguistic periphery], in: M. A. Borodina (ed.), *Areal'nye issledovanija v jazykoznanii i ètnografii* [Areal studies in linguistics and ethnography]. Leningrad: Nauka, 180−185.

1981   "Baltijskij leksičeskij ingredient praslavjanskogo jazyka" [The Baltic lexical component in Proto-Slavic], *Acta Baltico-Slavica* 14: 175−187.

1983   *Jazyk v prostranstve i vremeni. K probleme glottogeneza slavjan* [Language in space and time. On the glottogenesis of the Slavs.] Moskva: Nauka.

1985   "Glottogenez slavjan" [The glottogenesis of the Slavs]. *Voprosy jazykoznanija* 6: 43−54.

Mažiulis, Vytautas

1988   *Prūsų kalbos etimologijos žodynas, I. A−H* [An etymological dictionary of Old Prussian, Vol. I: A−H]. Vilnius: Mokslas.

Meillet, Antoine

1934   *Le slave commun.* (2nd edition.) (*Collection de manuels publiées par l'Institut d'études slaves* 2.) Paris: Librairie Honoré Champion.

Moszyński, Leszek

1989   *Wstęp do filologii słowiańskiej* [An introduction to Slavic philology]. Warszawa: Państwowe Wydawnictwo Naukowe.

Nepokupnyj, Anatolij Pavlovič

1989   *Obščaja leksika germanskix i balto-slavjanskix jazykov* [The shared lexicon of the Germanic and Balto-Slavic languages]. Kyjiv: Naukova dumka.

Nikolaev, Sergej L'vovič

1989   "Sledy osobennostej vostočnoslavjanskix dialektov v sovremennyx velikorusskix govorax. 1. Kriviči (okončanie)" [Traces of East Slavic dialect features in contemporary Russian dialects. 1. The Kriviches (conclusion)], in: V. V. Ivanov (ed.), *Balto-slavjanskie issledovanija 1987.* Moskva: Nauka, 187−224.

Nissilä, Viljo

1975   *Suomen Karjalan nimistö* [Finnish Karelian name usage]. Joensuu: Karjalaisen kultuurin edistämissäätiö.

Otrębski, Jan

1965   *Gramatyka języka litewskiego, II. Nauka o budowie wyrazów* [A grammar of Lithuanian, Vol. II: Word formation]. Warszawa: Państwowe Wydawnictwo Naukowe.

Pauliny, Eugen
1963   *Fonologický vývin slovenčiny* [The phonological development of Slovak]. Bratislava: Vydavateľstvo Slovenskej Akadémie Vied.
Pokorny, Julius
1959—1969 *Indogermanisches etymologisches Wörterbuch*, I—II. Bern — München: Francke Verlag.
Popowska-Taborska, Hanna
1984   *Z dawnych podziałów Słowiańszczyzny. Słowiańska alternacja* (j)e- : o- [An Old Slavic dialect boundary. The Slavic variation *(j)e- : o-*]. (*Prace Slawistyczne* 37.) Wrocław: Wydawnictwo Polskiej Akademii Nauk.
Ramovš, Fran
1936   *Kratka zgodovina slovenskega jezika, I* [A brief history of Slovenian, I]. Ljubljana: Akademska Založba.
Rasmussen, Jens Elmegård
1989   *Studien zur Morphophonemik der indogermanischen Grundsprache* (*Innsbrucker Beiträge zur Sprachwissenschaft* 55). Innsbruck: Institut für Sprachwissenschaft der Universität Innsbruck.
Rozwadowski, Jan
1915   "Przyczynki do historycznej fonetyki języków słowiańskich" [Contributions to Slavic historical phonetics], *Rocznik Slawistyczny* 7: 9—21.
[1961]   [Reprinted in his *Wybór pism, II, Językoznawstwo indoeuropejskie* [Selected writings, II: Indo-European linguistics]. Warszawa: Państwowe Wydawnictwo Naukowe, 331—340.]
Schmalstieg, William R.
1976   *Studies in Old Prussian. A critical review of the relevant literature in the field since 1945.* University Park — London: Pennsylvania State University Press.
Schrijver, Peter
1991   *The reflexes of the Proto-Indo-European laryngeals in Latin.* Amsterdam — Atlanta, Ga.: Rodopi.
Schuster-Šewc, Heinz
1987   "Zu den ethnischen und linguistischen Grundlagen der westslavischen Stammesgruppe der Sorben/Serben", in: G. Labuda — S. Tabaczyński (eds.), 153—160.
1993   "Zur Problematik der Entstehung des Niedersorbischen", *Die Welt der Slaven* 37: 344—358.
Sedov, Valentin Vasiľevič
1981   "Načaľnyj ètap slavjanskogo rasselenija v oblasti dneprovskix baltov" [The initial phase of Slavic settlement in the territory of the Dniepr Balts], *Balto-slavjanskie issledovanija 1980*: 45—52. Moskva: Nauka.
1982   *Vostočnye slavjane v VI—XIII vv. (Arxeologija SSSR s drevnejšix vremen do srednevekov'ja v 20 tomax)* [The Eastern Slavs in the sixth

to thirteenth centuries (The archaeology of the U.S.S.R. from the earliest times until the Middle Ages in 20 volumes)]. Moskva: Nauka.

1987   "Origine de la branche du nord des Slaves Orientaux", in: G. Labuda − S. Tabaczyński (eds.), 161−166.

Senn, Alfred
    1957   *Handbuch der litauischen Sprache, I: Grammatik.* Heidelberg: Carl Winter Universitätsverlag.

Serebrennikov, Boris Aleksandrovič
    1957   "O nekotoryx sledax isčeznuvšego indoevropejskogo jazyka v centre Evropejskoj časti SSSR, blizkogo k baltijskim jazykam" [On certain traces of a lost Indo-European language, closely related to Baltic, spoken in the central part of the USSR], *Trudy Akademii nauk Litovskogo SSR,* serija A, I: 69−74.

Shevelov, George Y.
    1965   *A prehistory of Slavic. The historical phonology of Common Slavic.* New York: Columbia University Press.

    1979   *A historical phonology of Ukrainian.* Heidelberg: Carl Winter. Universitätsverlag.

Skok, Petar
    1971   *Etimologijski rječnik hrvatskoga ili srpskoga jezika, I: A−J* [Etymological dictionary of the Croatian or Serbian language, Vol. I: A−J]. Zagreb: Jugoslavenska akademija znanosti i umjetnosti.

Sławski, Franciszek
    1974   *Słownik prasłowiański I: A−B* [Common Slavic dictionary, Vol. I: A−B]. Wrocław − Warszawa − Kraków − Gdańsk: Ossolineum.

    1991   *Słownik prasłowiański, VI: E−Ę−Ě* [Common Slavic dictionary, Vol. VI: E−Ę−Ě]. Wrocław − Warszawa − Kraków − Gdańsk: Ossolineum.

Smoczyński, Wojciech
    1981   "Indoeuropejskie podstawy słownictwa bałtyckiego" [The Indo-European foundations of the Baltic lexicon], *Acta Baltico-Slavica* 14: 211−240.

    1986   "Uwagi o słowniku bałtycko-słowiańskim" [Some observations on the Balto-Slavic lexicon], in: J. Majowa (ed.), *Język i jego odmiany w aspekcie porównawczym* [Language variation in a comparative perspective]. (*Prace Slawistyczne* 53.) Wrocław: Państwowe Wydawnictwo Naukowe, 17−45.

Sobolevskij, Aleksej Ivanovič
    1907   *Lekcii po istorii russkogo jazyka* [Lectures on the history of Russian]. (4th edition.) Moskva: Universitetskaja tipografija.

    1962   [Reprinted in: *Slavistic Printings and Reprintings* XXXVII. s'-Gravenhage: Mouton.]

Stang, Christian S.
    1966   *Vergleichende Grammatik der baltischen Sprachen.* Oslo − Bergen − Tromsö: Universitetsforlaget.

1971   *Lexikalische Sonderübereinstimmungen zwischen dem Slavischen, Bal-
           tischen und Germanıschen.* (Skrıfter utgıtt av det Norske Videnskaps-
           Akademi i Oslo, II: Hist.-Filol. Klasse, Ny Serie 11.) Oslo — Bergen
           — Tromsö: Universitetsforlaget.
Stanislav, Ján
1958   *Dejiny slovenského jazyka, I. Úvod a hláskoslovie* [The history of Slo-
           vak, Vol. I: Introduction and phonology]. (2nd edition.) Bratislava:
           Vydavateľstvo Slovenskej Akadémie Vied.
Stieber, Ždźisław
1979   *Zarys gramatyki porównawczej języków słowiańskich* [An outline of
           Slavic comparative grammar]. Warszawa: Państwowe Wydawnictwo
           Naukowe.
Šaur, Vladimír
1986   "Původ *o*- ve východoslovanském typu *olen'*, *ozero*" [The origin of
           o- in the East Slavic type *olen'*, *ozero*], *Slavia* 55: 378 – 383.
Šaxmatov, Aleksej Aleksandrovič
1915   *Očerk drevnejšego perioda istorii russkogo jazyka* [A sketch of the
           earliest period in the history of Russian]. (*Ènciklopedija slavjanskoj
           filologii* 11,1.)
[1967]   [Reprinted in *Russian Reprint Series*, LXI. The Hague: Europe Print-
           ing.]
Taszycki, Witold
1961   "Z dawnych podziałów dialektycznych języka polskiego, II. Przejście
           ja > *je*" [Some ancient dialect boundaries in Polish, II. The change *ja*
           > *je*], in: M. Karaś (ed.), *Rozprawy i studia polonistyczne, II* [Polonist
           treatises and studies]. Wrocław: Ossolineum, 71 – 148.
Thomsen, Vilhelm
1889   *Berøringer mellem de finske og baltiske (litauisk-lettiske) Sprog (Vi-
           denskabernes Selskab. Sproglig-filosofiske Klasse).* København: Gyl-
           dendalske Boghandel.
[1921]   Translated as "Berührungen zwischen den finnischen und den bal-
           tischen (litauisch-lettischen) Sprachen. Eine sprachgeschichtliche Un-
           tersuchung" in his *Samlede Afhandlinger, IV* [Collected Writings, IV].
           København: Gyldendalske Boghandel — Nordisk Forlag.
Toporov, Vladimir Nikolaevič
1975   *Prusskij jazyk. Slovar'* [Old Prussian. Vocabulary]. *A – D* Moskva:
           Nauka.
1979   *Prusskij jazyk. Slovar'* [Old Prussian. Vocabulary]. *E – H* Moskva:
           Nauka.
1980   *Prusskij jazyk. Slovar'* [Old Prussian. Vocabulary]. *I – K* Moskva:
           Nauka.
1990   *Prusskij jazyk. Slovar'* [Old Prussian. Vocabulary]. *L (laydis – *lut-* &
           *mod-). Moskva: Nauka.

Toporov, Vladimir Nikolaevič — Oleg Nikolaevič Trubačev
1962   *Lingvističeskij analiz gidronimov verxnego Podneprov'ja* [A linguistic
         analysis of the hydronyms of the Upper Dniepr Basin]. Moskva: Iz-
         datel'stvo Akademii Nauk.
Trautmann, Reinhold
1923   *Baltisch—Slavisches Wörterbuch.* Göttingen: Vandenhoeck & Ru-
         precht.
Trubačev, Oleg Nikolaevič
1963   "O praslavjanskix leksičeskix dialektizmov serbo-lužickix jazykov"
         [Some Proto-Slavic lexical dialectisms in the Sorbian languages], in:
         L. E. Kalnyn' (ed.), *Serbo-lužickij lingvističeskij sbornik* [Studies in
         Sorbian linguistics]. Moskva: Izdatel'stvo Akademii Nauk, 154—172.
1967   "Iz slavjano-iranskix leksičeskix otnošenij" [On some Slavic—Iranian
         lexical relations], *Ètimologija 1965*: 3—81.
1968a   *Nazvanija rek pravoberežnoj Ukrainy. Slovoobrazovanie. Ètimologija.
         Ètničeskaja interpretacija* [River names in Ukraine west of the
         Dniepr. Morphology. Etymology. Ethnic interpretation]. Moskva:
         Nauka.
1968b   "O sostave praslavjanskogo slovarja (problemy i resul'taty)" [On the
         composition of the Proto-Slavic lexicon (problems and results)], in:
         V. V. Vinogradov et al. (eds.), *Slavjanskoe jazykoznanie. VI meždu-
         narodnyj s"ezd slavistov. Doklady sovetskoj delegacii* [Slavic linguis-
         tics. Sixth international congress of Slavists. Contributions of the
         Soviet delegation]. Moskva: Nauka, 366—378.
1974   *Ètimologičeskij slovar' slavjanskix jazykov. Praslavjanskij leksičeskij
         fond* [An etymological dictionary of the Slavic languages. The Proto-
         Slavic lexical stock], 1 (**a—*besědĭlivŭ*). Moskva: Nauka.
1979   *Ètimologičeskij slovar' slavjanskix jazykov. Praslavjanskij leksičeskij
         fond* [An etymological dictionary of the Slavic languages. The Proto-
         Slavic lexical stock], 6 (**e—*golva*). Moskva: Nauka.
1981   *Ètimologičeskij slovar' slavjanskix jazykov. Praslavjanskij leksičeskij
         fond* [An etymological dictionary of the Slavic languages. The Proto-
         Slavic lexical stock], 8 (**xa—*jĭvolga*). Moskva: Nauka.
1987   *Ètimologičeskij slovar' slavjanskix jazykov. Praslavjanskij leksičeskij
         fond* [An etymological dictionary of the Slavic languages. The Proto-
         Slavic lexical stock], 14 (**labati—*lěteplŭjĭ*). Moskva: Nauka.
1991   *Ètnogenez i kultura drevnejšix slavjan. Lingvističeskie issledovanija*
         [The ethnogenesis and culture of the Ancient Slavs. Linguistic inves-
         tigations]. Moskva: Nauka.
Udolph, Jürgen
1979   *Studien zu slavischen Gewässernamen und Gewässerbezeichnungen.
         Ein Beitrag zur Frage nach der Urheimat der Slaven.* (*Beiträge zur
         Namenforschung*, Neue Folge 17.) Heidelberg: Carl Winter Univer-
         sitätsverlag.

Ulvydas, K. (ed.)
1965   *Lietuvių kalbos gramatika, I tomas. Fonetika ir morfologija* [Lithuanian grammar, Vol. I: Phonetics and morphology]. Vilnius: Mintis.
Vaillant, André
1950   *Grammaire comparée des langues slaves, I: Phonétique.* Lyon − Paris: Éditions IAC.
1958   *Grammaire comparée des langues slaves, II. Morphologie.* Lyon − Paris: Éditions IAC.
1974   *Grammaire comparée des langues slaves, IV. La formation des noms.* Paris: Klincksieck.
Varbot, Žanna Žanovna
1984   *Praslavjanskaja morfonologija. Slovoobrazovanie i ètimologija* [Proto-Slavic morphophonemics. Word formation and etymology]. Moskva: Nauka.
Vasmer, Max
1941   *Die Slaven in Griechenland.* (*Abhandlungen der preussischen Akademie der Wissenschaften*, Philosophisch-historische Klasse 12.) Berlin: Walter de Gruyter.
Volkaitė-Kulikauskienė, Regina (ed.)
1987   *Lietuvių etnogenezė* [The ethnogenesis of the Lithuanians]. Vilnius: Mokslas.
van Wijk, Nicolaas
1956   *Les langues slaves. De l'unité à la pluralité.* (*Janua Linguarum.* Series minor 2.) s'-Gravenhage: Mouton.
Winter, Werner
1978   "The distribution of short and long vowels in stems of the type Lith. *ěsti: vèsti: mèsti* and OCS *jasti: vesti: mesti* in Baltic and Slavic languages", in: J. Fisiak (ed.), *Recent developments in historical phonology.* The Hague: Mouton, 431−446.
Xaburgaev, Georgij Aleksandrovič
1976   "Ešče raz o vostočnoslavjanskom (i russkom) načal'nom *o-* (: *je-*)" [The East Slavic (and Russian) initial *o-* (: *je-*) one more time], in: K. V. Gorškova (ed.), *Voprosy russkogo jazykoznanija, I.* Moskva: Moskovskij Gosudarstvennyj Universitet, 205−218.
1980   *Stanovlenie russkogo jazyka (posobie po istoričeskoj grammatike)* [The emergence of Russian (a handbook in historical grammar]. Moskva: Vysšaja škola.
Zinkevičius, Zigmas
1966   *Lietuvių dialektologija. Lyginamoji tarmių fonetika ir morfologija* [Lithuanian dialectology. Comparative dialect phonology and morphology]. Vilnius: Mintis.
1987   *Lietuvių kalbos istorija, II. Iki pirmųjų raštų* [The history of Lithuanian, II. Up to the first texts]. Vilnius, Mokslas.

Zubatý, Josef
    1903   "Zu den slavischen Femininbildungen auf -*yńi*", *Archiv für slavische*
              Philologie 25: 355−365.
Žuravlev, V. K.
    1965   "Genezis protezov v slavjanskix jazykax" [The rise of prothetic con-
              sonants in Slavic], *Voprosy jazykoznanija* 4: 31−43.

Index of Authors

Index of Languages and Peoples

The Baltic, Indo-European, and Slavic metalanguages (e. g., Common Slavic, Quasi-Slavic, Proto-Slavic, Tememation) are included in the Index of Subjects.

Index of Subjects

Index of Words

1. Armenian

ezr 150
ełn 127, 131
haçi 143
orjik' 141
oskr 105
ozni 86, 150

2. Baltic

2.1. Curonian

Alxnewadt 128, 129
Alxwalke 128, 129
Amelen, Amulle 134
Aserowischen 149
Eezeryne 149
Egel, Eglinen 119
Esser Semmen 149

2.2. Latvian[1]

abi 54
abols 134
acešas (d.) *145–166*
acs 54
adata 54, 119
akacis 120
akots 56
àlga 56
Alksna 128, 129
Alksnene 128, 129
àlksnis *128–130*
alkt 56
Alnace 131
âlnis *131–132*
Alsvanga 129
alus 56, 133
alva *120–121*
āmuļi *133–135*
anksteri 56
Apsa 135
apse *135–136*
ar 57
aȓkls 57

asara 57
asaris 145
ass 57
Asva 148
Aža 150
Ažẹ̄ni 150
Ažẹ̄ns 150
balanda 122
cȩ̀rmauksis 106
ecēšas 55, *145–146*
Egle 119
egle *119*
Ẹgluoņa 119
Ẹlkune 131
ȩ̀lkonis *130–131*
Elnẹ̄ni 131
elvede *132*
elvete *132*
ẽrce *140*
èrglis *139–140*
ẽrkšķis *140–141*
èrzelis *141*
es *148–149*
esmu *147–148*
ezers *149–150*
ezis *150–151*
eža *150*
grumêt 108
gùlbis 124
gumstât 108
ie 57
iȓbe *136–138*
irbene (d.) *138–139*
jauja *154–155*
kvitêt 106
lemesis 156
òdze 56
ògle 56
ôlekts *130–131*
òsa 56
ôsis *142–143*

---

[1] Italicized page references are to the relevant portions of chapter 7. Additional page references for all the Baltic languages are gathered in the word index for Proto-Baltic (2.5) below.

---

[2] Italicized page references are to the relevant portions of chapter 7. Additional page references for all the Baltic languages are gathered in the word index for Proto-Baltic (2.5) below.

[3] Italicized page references are to the relevant portions of chapter 7. Additional page references for all the Baltic languages are gathered in the word index for Proto-Baltic (2.5) below.

2.5. Proto-Baltic[4]

---

[4] Italicized page references are to the relevant portions of chapter 7.

3. Celtic
3.1. Breton

3.2. Gaulish

3.3. Irish

3.4. Welsh

4. Germanic
4.1. English

[5] Italicized page references are to the relevant portions of chapter 7. Additional page references for all the Slavic languages are gathered in the word index for Proto-Slavic (10.9) below.

10.10. Proto-Slavic[6]

---

11. Proto-Indo-European

11. Finnic
11.1. Estonian

11.2. Finnish